Feminism in the News

Representations of the Women's Movement since the 1960s

Kaitlynn Mendes
De Montfort University, UK

First published 2011 by
PALGRAVE MACMILLAN

Palgrave Macmillan in the UK is an imprint of Macmillan Publishers Limited, registered in England, company number 785998, of Houndmills, Basingstoke, Hampshire RG21 6XS.

Palgrave Macmillan in the US is a division of St Martin's Press LLC, 175 Fifth Avenue, New York, NY 10010.

Palgrave Macmillan is the global academic imprint of the above companies and has companies and representatives throughout the world.

Palgrave® and Macmillan® are registered trademarks in the United States, the United Kingdom, Europe and other countries.

ISBN: 978–0–230–27445–7

This book is printed on paper suitable for recycling and made from fully managed and sustained forest sources. Logging, pulping and manufacturing processes are expected to conform to the environmental regulations of the country of origin.

A catalogue record for this book is available from the British Library.

Library of Congress Cataloging-in-Publication Data

Mendes, Kaitlynn, 1983–
    Feminism in the news : representations of the women's movement since the 1960s / Kaitlynn Mendes.
        p. cm.
    Includes index.
    Summary: "An exploration of the representations of the women's movement, its members, and their goals between 1968 and 2008 in the British and American press. Examining over 1100 news articles, the book analyses the nuanced ways feminism has historically been supported, marginalized and debated in the mainstream press" – Provided by publisher.
    ISBN 978–0–230–27445–7 (hardback)
    1. Feminism and mass media. I. Title.
P96.F46M46 2011
070.82—dc23   2011018674

Printed and bound in Great Britain by
CPI Antony Rowe, Chippenham and Eastbourne

For my family, Helder, Lynn, Matthew, Justin, Ben and Layla

Contents

List of Illustrations   viii

List of Abbreviations   ix

Acknowledgements   x

Introduction   1

1 Contextualizing the Issues   12

2 Reporting the Women's Movement, 1968–82   48

3 Reporting Equal Rights, 1968–82   90

4 Reporting Feminism in 2008   131

Conclusion   161

Notes   166

Bibliography   173

Index   197

Illustrations

Tables

2.1 Genre by newspaper, 1968–82   53
2.2 Causes and solutions to women's
    inequality/oppression, 1968–82   62
3.1 Journalist gender by genre, 1968–82   97
4.1 Issues associated with feminism, 2008   141

Figures

2.1 News articles on feminism by publication, 1968–82   51
2.2 Total news pegs, 1968–82   55
2.3 'It's wrong to be equal' *Daily Mirror*   81
2.4 'Why Adrienne doesn't want to be a man' *Daily Mirror*   82
3.1 News articles on equal rights by publication, 1968–82   92
3.2 'All women's liberationists hate men and
    children' *Chicago Tribune*   104
4.1 News articles on feminism by publication, 2008   133

Abbreviations

CDA	Critical Discourse Analysis
EEOC	Equal Employment Opportunity Commission
EOC	Equal Opportunity Commission
ERA	Equal Rights Amendment
LGIM	Legitimate goal, illegitimate movement discourse
MP	Member of Parliament
NBFO	National Black Feminist Organization
NOW	National Organization for Women
NWPC	National Women's Political Caucus
TUC	Trades Union Congress
WINP	Women's inequality? No problem discourse

Acknowledgements

I would like to thank everyone who has helped me in writing this book, particularly Barbara Freeman who inspired me to pursue this topic in the first place, and Cynthia Carter who provided endless hours of guidance and discussion. I am grateful to all of my colleagues at De Montfort University, particularly Stuart Price for his friendship, Helen Wood who took the time to read my manuscript, and Tim O'Sullivan who believed in me in the first place. Finally, I would like to thank my entire family, who have always supported me.

Introduction

> Feminism is blamed, completely erroneously, for everything –
> spiralling property prices (working couples), unemployment
> (women stealing men's jobs), teenage delinquency (feminists
> driving men to abandon their sons), reality television (the
> 'feminization' of the culture) and increasing sexual violence
> (now that women don't defer to them, men have suffered a
> violent 'identity crisis'). (Orr 2003, p. 15)

Forty years after the Second Wave feminist movement took the western world by storm, this excerpt from the UK daily newspaper *The
Independent*, embodies common perceptions of feminism's legacy. Rather
than being celebrated like other social movements of the twentieth century (Civil Rights, gay liberation, the environmental movement), feminism has been turned into a 'dirty word' – a euphemism for the old,
unattractive, unfeminine and unkempt, which, unsurprisingly, many
avidly disavow. Yet, at the same time, it is common to support feminist goals such as equal rights, through the phrase 'I'm not a feminist,
but ...'. As a young woman growing up in this supposedly 'post' feminist
era – a time when feminism is considered unnecessary or dead – such
constructions raise questions not only about why feminism is held in
such contempt, but whether this has always been the case. Has there
ever been a time when feminists were celebrated in the news, and, if so,
what ideologies were used in such accounts? Finally, to what extent are
discourses of feminism localized, or do they transcend national boundaries in areas experiencing feminism in similar 'waves'?

My work enters into a debate about how to make sense of public
constructions of feminism, and what this tells us about the changing nature of gender (and thus power) in Britain and the US between

1

1968, when feminist activism increased in both countries, and 2008, 40 years on. While questions about the extent to which the media influence audiences are highly contested, it is generally agreed that the news acts as most people's main source of information on the world (Barker-Plummer 2000; Gitlin 2003; Rhode 1995; van Zoonen 1992). Furthermore, as an arena of feminist inquiry, the media are one of the most important sites for exploring patriarchy because their images of women teach society the required rules of femininity (Bordo 1993). Consequently, the media's potential for sparking (or preventing) social change is enormous and thus merits closer inspection.

Drawing upon (socialist) feminist theory, this research provides an opportunity to de-construct how a group of select American and British newspapers have historically contributed to the (re)production of hierarchical, gendered ideologies. Implicit in these hierarchies are further distinctions such as race, class, ethnicity and sexuality, which never function in isolation, and both oppress and privilege women in different degrees. While this book is certainly not the first to examine news of feminism, it builds upon previous work through its longitudinal and cross-national focus, dissecting how constructions of feminism have evolved over time, and how patriarchy functions along with capitalism, racism and heterosexism in the western world. Using both content and critical discourse analysis of over 1100 news articles in four British (*The Times, The Guardian,* the *Daily Mirror,* and the *Daily Mail*), and four American newspapers (*The New York Times, The Washington Post, The Washington Times,* and the *Chicago Tribune*), this study can also be seen as part of a larger feminist project aimed at 'reclaiming the F-word' (Redfern & Aune, 2010). While this is by no means an easy task, it is assisted through an exploration into what it has historically meant to be a feminist, and, in doing so, investigates the ideologies used to both support and slander feminism. Furthermore, it seeks to identify a range of contemporary discourses in the news which highlights why feminist activism is urgent today. It also contributes in part to an historic understanding of women's place in the world, and an account of their battles, both won and lost, which can inform future feminist strategies by keeping 'feminists from having to reinvent the wheel every fifty years or so' (Baumgardner & Richards 2000, p. 68). As a result, this book aims not only to trace the development of discourses of feminism but to provide feminists, academics and scholars tools for combating the range of anti-feminist discourses that permeate both the news media, and popular culture more widely.

While what is now often referred to as 'Second Wave' and 'Third Wave' feminism greatly interests me, this is not an investigation of the history of feminist activism, but rather a study examining media *representations* of it. As such, it does not attempt to determine what *really* happened during various waves of feminist activism but instead seeks to 'interrogate what is quietly assumed to be true, and to expose the manifestations of power intrinsic to any one representation of an event or moment in history' (Hemmings 2005; Hesford 2005, p. 230). That said, the comparatively small sample size means this research should be read more as a case study than as a definitive account of mediated feminism in the west – and while this book contributes to the 'storying' of feminism, much more work is needed, from a variety of perspectives, places and publications, before we can claim to have a full understanding of the movement and its mediations (see also Hemmings 2005). Although this book will not provide a detailed history of the women's movements, the trajectories of feminist 'waves' in Britain and the US are worth noting.

Women's liberation

> There is no 'beginning' of feminism in the sense that there is no beginning to defiance in women…. Female resistance has taken several historical shapes (Rowbotham 1972, p. 16).

When thinking about the history of women's quest for greater rights, it is clear that the struggle has been a long one. There is ample evidence that 'feminist' ideas, have existed since the medieval times, long predating modern women's movements (Bryson 2003). Despite the long-standing presence of feminist ideas and agitation in society, epitomized in publications such as Mary Wollenstonecraft's (1792) *A Vindication of the Rights of Woman,* an organized feminist movement as such did not emerge until the mid-1800s in both Britain and the US. While often referred to as the 'First' feminist movement, it in fact comprised several fractured movements, which fought for greater legal and economic rights for women, child custody, access to education and protection against physical and sexual abuse (Bryson 2003; LeGates 2001; Sanders 2006). Similar to the women who would take up the feminist cause in post-war society, First Wave feminists disagreed over philosophies and tactics to achieve their goals, and it is impossible to define in one sentence what women wanted (Bouchier 1983; Bryson 2003; Tickner 1988). In part, their differing tactics and approaches were direct results of how they entered First Wave feminism. Many joined as part of the temperance movement, understanding that women married to drunks should have both legal protections and a way out of the violence and humiliation it often brought. Others campaigned for women's rights after their involvement with the anti-slavery campaigns, recognizing that as wives, white women were just as much their husband's property as the slaves they were trying to free (Bryson 2003).[1] From an historical standpoint, despite the plurality of feminist positions and campaigns, woman's suffrage became (historically constituted as) the dominant issue of this First Wave by the nineteenth century and was achieved in 1920 for women in the US and in 1928 for UK women.[2]

The Second Wave

While it would be unfair to claim that women stopped agitating for social change after winning the vote, a more accurate statement is that feminist activism was in 'abeyance' until the late 1960s, when the Second Wave of large-scale feminist activism began (Davis 1991; Taylor 1989). Emerging first in the US, spurred on, in part, by Betty Friedan's book *The Feminine Mystique* (1963) which discussed (mainly white, middle-class) women's unhappiness with their limited gender roles and sense of isolation in the suburban nuclear family, the movement quickly spread to other western nations. Many Second Wave feminists in the US had been actively involved in the Civil Rights and student New Left movements and quickly realized the hypocrisy in promising freedom to black people, while withholding it from women (Bryson 1992, p. 182). Not long after, British women, inspired by a combination of demands for equal pay and better educational and employment opportunities, began to organize and campaign. Through their involvement in the Campaign for Nuclear Disarmament (CND), anti-Vietnam movement and trade unions, they began to question and challenge the sexism they experienced on a daily basis. While it is tempting to posit that this movement was an offshoot of American feminism, it was in fact a home-grown response to British sexual politics (Fairbairns 2003). As Bouchier (1983) explained, 'American society is sufficiently like the British to be immediately understandable, but sufficiently different to produce a distinct feminist response' (p. 3).

One worthwhile difference between the movements was the varying ideological positions that not only impacted the development of feminist political theory but also led to the establishment of varying political goals, organizational structures and tactics. The US movement, shaped predominantly by liberal feminism, became primarily defined around two issues: abortion and the proposed Equal Rights Amendment (ERA), which sought to guarantee equality under the law, regardless of gender. Based on liberal theory, liberal feminism had much stronger roots in the US than in the UK. In the US, assumptions about people's 'natural' rights, which governments may not intrude upon, formed the ideological basis of documents such as the US Declaration of Independence (1776) (Donovan 1985). Following from this then, liberal feminism states that women, like men, are rational beings and are therefore entitled to basic human rights and equal opportunities (Bryson 2003). Consequently, liberal feminists do not aim to revolutionize society by challenging the economic, judicial, educational or social systems in place, but instead often seek redistribution of existing social and economic rewards along more egalitarian lines (Bouchier 1983).

While liberal feminism certainly dominated the US feminist scene, radical feminism also became a popular conceptual and political framework, developing out of the New Left student movement (Bouchier 1983). In the UK, radical feminism's popularity and visibility rapidly grew in the late 1970s, when groups such as Revolutionary Feminists emerged, targeting men as the enemy and campaigning publicly against sexual violence, rape and pornography (Collective 1981). Because radical feminist theory developed in tandem with the Second Wave, evolving with the movement, it is extremely difficult to discuss a singular radical feminist theory. Nevertheless, all branches of radical feminism view women's oppression as *the* fundamental political oppression, and the root of all other forms of oppression (Mitchell 1971), which remains more or less constant over time and place (Reid & Stratta 1989, p. 21). 'Patriarchy' is the key term for radicals. It describes men's power over women – an imbalance that exists in all known societies and functions by organizing sexual differences ideologically (by stating that masculinity and femininity are 'natural'), and hierarchically (where masculinity is constructed as dominant and femininity as subordinate) (Millett 1971). Despite its grassroots popularity, the radical movement is said to have been 'half-hidden', shying away from and mainstream media attention and the large organizational bodies that liberal feminists produced (Bouchier 1983).

Where liberal and radical feminist theories were prominent in the American movement, radical and socialist theory inspired her British sisters. Where radical feminist theory argues that patriarchy is the key site of women's oppression, socialist feminists, inspired by Marxist thought, argued that class was also central to this debate (Bryson 2003; Whelehan 1995). Although Marxist thought had long been incorporated into mainstream political discourse in Europe, it was comparatively absent in the US, accounting for the differing ideological stances between the two countries (Bryson 2003, p. 222). However, despite their differing political traditions, both the British and American movements campaigned for similar issues, including access to abortion, 24-hour child care and an end to physical and sexual violence against women. Importantly for this project, by 1969 equal rights were high on the agenda in both nations, and are the focus of Chapter 3. Another worthwhile difference between the movements is their relationships with the news media. While many American feminists had a sophisticated understanding of journalistic routines and conventions, frequently targeting news outlets with press releases and notices of events (Fox 2010), the UK movement was rarely as concerned with creating a viable mainstream public image, nor did it initially comprise many women with specific media skills (though many developed these throughout the movement with the creation of alternative feminist publications). Consequently, the US movement produced several 'media stars', who acted as spokespeople (and reliable sources for journalists), whereas the UK movement tended to oppose this type hierarchical organization, preferring instead to use a collective political structure (with no clear, reliable source to whom journalists could routinely turn for information). Additionally, the UK movement formed with little or no formal structure of effective communication tools outside of London, limiting its ability to connect with other groups, organizing large events and attract media attention (Bouchier 1983). These factors ensured that women's liberation was not predominantly featured on UK newsstands, though there was an incredible amount of feminist publishing taking place in alternative publications (Bouchier 1983).

The end point of the Second Wave feminist period is a topic of much contention. Despite their declaration to the contrary, media commentators have spoken of the 'death' of feminism since the 1970s, and particularly in the 1980s (for an overview, see Genz & Brabon 2009, p. 41). According to some, feminism died because it achieved its goals and was no longer needed (McRobbie 2007, 2009). For others, its death was linked to its loss of appeal for women, or their recognition of the newfound 'problems' it brought (Faludi 1992). Whatever the case, there is ample evidence that in both countries feminist activism indeed did not die out in the 1980s but was largely ignored by the mainstream news media. Furthermore, claims of its death were part of an overall 'backlash' used to discredit the movement and reinforce patriarchal ideologies (Baumgardner & Richards 2000; Faludi 1992; Henry 2004). However, despite the formation of new feminist organizations since the 1980s, such as The Feminist Majority, or the Third Wave Foundation in the US, or Object in the UK, it has become 'common sense' to understand the movement as both having 'died' in the 1980s and having been 'reborn' in the 1990s (Henry 2004).

Third-Wave feminism

While the First and Second Wave feminist movements have clear identities and spokespeople in the western world, the same cannot be said for the Third Wave. In part, it is because many Second Wave feminists are still actively campaigning for the same issues (therefore, this 'new' wave is in fact, not new at all), and in part there is disagreement over what the term itself means. Henry (2004) argues that Third Wave feminism can be understood in three ways. First, and perhaps the most common definition is of a generational shift, referring to feminist born during or after the Second Wave (see also Dean 2009). As self-proclaimed Third Wave feminists, Baumgardner and Richards (2000) write: 'We're not doing feminism the same way that the seventies feminists did it; being liberated doesn't mean copying what came before but finding one's own way – a way that is genuine to one's own generation' (p. 130). In this sense, while Third Wave feminists are often interested in similar issues as their Second Wave sisters, they go about challenging them in different ways. For example, while many Second Wave Feminists resisted being labelled 'girls', and rejected traditionally feminine activities such as knitting, baking, and wearing makeup, these are all elements of modern life that some Third Wavers have reclaimed (Baumgardner & Richards 2000).

Second, Third Wave feminism can be understood as an ideological shift, incorporating queer, postmodern postcolonial and black feminist theory. If understood in this way, Third Wave feminism can be said to have been initially developed by women of colour in the early 1980s, building upon perceived inadequacies of Second Wave feminist political theory (Dean 2009; Mann & Huffman 2005). For example, many criticized white, middle-class feminist theories for claiming to 'speak' for all women's experiences, when they really only applied to a select (privileged) group (Barrett & McIntosh 2005 [1985]); Bryson 2003; hooks 1982). Furthermore, rather than treating multiple forms of oppression (e.g., race, class, gender, sexuality and ability) as separate or distinct, Third Wavers examined how these identities interlocked with one another to produce new forms of oppression.[3] This meants that rather than treating oppression in a hierarchical manner, which labelled some categories more oppressive than others (e.g., gender was more oppressive than race), Third Wave feminists corrected these oversights by arguing that oppression exists in many connected forms, paving the way for previously ignored categories such as age, physical ability, and sexual orientation to be scrutinized (Mann & Huffman 2005). Though it took time to filter its way in, feminists have since re-thought various political theories to incorporate these criticisms (see Barrett & McIntosh 2005 [1985]). As a result, there is ample evidence that current feminist political thinkers (including that from the socialist camp), conduct their work with these new insights in mind (see Gillis et al. 2004; Holmstrom 2002).

A final way that Third Wave Feminism can be conceptualized is as a particular historical moment, indicating that feminist ideology has adapted to the current cultural climate. As a result, it articulates 'a particular ideological stance in relation to contemporary social and political realities' (Henry 2004, p. 35). In other words, it understands that the world has changed since the Second Wave and argues that feminist ideology, too, must adapt with the times. In part, this understanding of Third Wave feminism can be seen as a rebellion from the Second Wave. As Baumgardner and Richards note: 'The difference between the First, Second and Third Waves is our cultural DNA. Each generation has a drive to create something new, to find that distinctive spark' (2000, p. 129).

While these are three different understandings of the Third Wave, this book is not committed to adopting one particular paradigm, but is instead interested in how news media represent feminist activism over time and space. Furthermore, it should be noted that while some call themselves the Third Wave, others have used the term 'postfeminist' to indicate their feminist identity. This term is wrought with much confusion (see Genz & Brabon 2009), but it is important to note that 'postfeminist' can be applied to both those who avidly disavow feminism, arguing that it is unnecessary or redundant, while simultaneously being adopted by those who embrace the feminist identity but want to separate themselves from the Second Wave.

Book outline

Chapter 1 begins with a contextualization of relevant literature, which serves as the theoretical foundation for the book. It begins by borrowing from sociology the understanding that journalists *make* or manufacture, and do not simply act as mirrors reflecting 'reality' through the news. It then moves on to discuss the constructed nature of news to concepts of ideology, hegemony and representation, focusing specifically how previous feminist scholars have used these concepts to elucidate women's roles both in popular culture and the news media. Next, the chapter turns to theories around framing, news and gender, social movements and news, and the women's movement and the news. The chapter concludes with a discussion about the project's methods (content and critical discourse analysis). Here I also elaborate on my choice of format, publications, search terms and time-frame.

Chapter 2 marks the first of three chapters detailing the empirical analysis. Focusing on the height of the Second Wave, 1968 to 1982, in four publications, *The Times*, the *Daily Mirror*, the *Chicago Tribune*, and *The New York Times*, this chapter examines how the news media constructed news of Second Wave feminists by asking questions about the ideologies embedded in the text, and what they tell us about British and American society at the time. The chapter also examines how feminism has been discursively constructed, contested and negotiated over time and space. What possible consequences have these discourses had for the feminist movement? Who gets to 'speak' on behalf of the movement and frame its concerns? Whose voices are omitted or marginalized? Through the use of content analysis and critical discourse analysis, I argue that, overall, coverage was fragmented and contradictory, not only between publications and nations but often within the same newspaper or article itself. This provides insight into the extent to which an ideological battle over how to define women's role was being waged. Despite the nuances in coverage, one of the most surprising findings was that feminism had significantly more support throughout the height of the Second Wave than previous scholars have suggested. In fact, just over half of all articles in this sample could be said to carry supportive frames, constructing the movement as necessary, liberating, and as having worthy goals. Yet, while feminism was supported throughout the time period, it was clear that a shift was taking place. For example, as the movement developed, it became increasingly defined as 'radical' by opponents in an effort to de-legitimise it. In response, many (liberal) feminists began to demarcate between their 'legitimate', largely reformist agenda, and their 'illegitimate' sisters, who sought revolution and dramatic changes in traditional gender roles.[4] While many journalists and feminists were undoubtedly trying to construct the movement in a positive light, it has had the lasting legacy of creating tension between acceptable (reformist), and unacceptable (revolutionary) forms of feminism. Consequently, I argue that support for feminism is not enough on its own to be celebrated if it means marginalizing radical feminist views.

Chapter 3 details the representations of equal rights in the news between 1968 and 1982 in *The Times*, the *Daily Mirror*, the *Chicago Tribune*, and *The New York Times*, arguing that they, too, were constructed in a nuanced manner, with differences being particularly evident between the two nations. These results are often the product of differing socio-political contexts, the ways equal rights were sought after, and the format, readership and political leanings of the publications in which they appeared. While I argue that discourses supporting equal rights attained hegemony, the liberal framework through which they were constructed failed to challenge gender roles, thus preventing a radical restructuring of society, and, thus, true liberation for women. Additionally, this chapter provides evidence of an emerging neoliberal discourse, which blames individual women, rather than wider social structures and systemic inequalities when women failed to achieve 'equality'. A key element of this chapter is its focus on the disassociation between equal rights and feminism, thus constructing the latter as largely redundant. I argue that such discourses can be labelled postfeminist, and emerged in the mid-1970s, much earlier than previously thought.

Chapter 4 examines the results from 443 news articles on feminism published in 2008 in the original four publications, plus four new ones (*Daily Mail, The Guardian, The Washington Post* and *The Washington Times*). One of the most noticeable findings from this period was that, despite its negative connotations, feminism was once again frequently supported. What is noticeable about this support however, is that it was often launched from a defensive position, for example, arguing how feminism *had not* harmed society, or was *still needed*. Clearly, then, the persistence of negative representations indicates the success of oppositional groups, who worked hard to frame feminists as lesbians, man-haters, aggressive deviants and unfeminine women who were out of touch with what most (middle-class, white) women wanted. While women have made many gains in society, it is clear from the articles that those who challenge patriarchal authority continue to be seen as a threat, are socially marginalized and are often labelled a 'feminist' as a result.

One major focus of this chapter is the noticeable shift towards the 'lifestyling' of feminism. Here, feminism's focus shifted from an ideology aimed at improving women's lives, to a shallow expression of one's identity. As a result, a series of articles emerged discussing the compatibility of beauty and feminism, or if patriarchal regimes such as wearing makeup, altering the body and engaging in domestic work could be considered 'feminist' because women, with their newfound equality, freely choose to engage in such activities. Consequently, while many news articles 'celebrate' these new found freedoms, they (re)separate the personal from the political, and discourage (large-scale) investment in social change. What is interrogated here is whether consumer choices can really be seen to 'liberate' women, and furthermore, (how) these consumer choices can address issues such as sexual discrimination, differences in pay and the persistence of violence against women. Chapter 5 begins by summarizing and discussing the findings from Chapters 2 through 4. It concludes by taking an overall look at the ways that feminism and its goals of equal rights have been constructed over a 40-year time period, and makes statements about the current climate in both the US and the UK. It also argues that a serious interrogation is needed in order to re-claim feminism and challenge the prevailing 'postfeminist sensibility' that characterizes gender representations in the US and UK (Gill 2007). Furthermore, the chapter raises questions about the future of the feminist agenda and offers strategies for feminist activists and journalists interested in social change, providing suggestions on how they might avoid the de-legitimizing coverage and stereotypes present in much of the mainstream media. With this, it is hoped that they are brave enough to conceptualize a new form of journalism, inspired by feminist thought and consideration.

1
Contextualizing the Issues

This chapter aims to establish a theoretical grounding for the study through exploring how concepts of ideology, hegemony and representation have been used in the past by feminist scholars to elucidate women's roles in popular culture. Furthermore, the chapter analyses the constructed nature of news, using the concept of framing to discuss how gender, social movements and the women's movement have been represented in the press. The chapter will then go on to explain how the research was carried out with the use of both content and critical discourse analysis.

Ideology, hegemony and representation

Ideology, as we understand it today, comes from a Marxist tradition of examining class and power relations, and refers to a system of beliefs, which are partial, misguided and distorted and conceal real imbalances of power in society (Williams 2003).[1] Karl Marx used ideology to examine why the working class did not rebel against dominant classes and contended that ideology was the expression of a class position, where those owning the means of production controlled the means of mental production as well. Consequently, he concluded that the ruling class were responsible for maintaining and (re)producing ideologies that favoured the dominant class by representing certain social inequalities as 'normal' and 'natural'. As Marx (1976, p. 59) famously stated, 'The ideas of the ruling class are in every epoch the ruling ideas. The class which is the ruling material force of society is at the same time its ruling intellectual force'.

While Marx was important for identifying how ideology is used to construct class distinctions as natural, other scholars have since advanced his theory to incorporate other forms of (interlocking) oppression such as gender, age, race, ethnicity and sexuality (Barrett & McIntosh 2005; Davis 1990; Elshtain 1981; Hartmann 1997). Another important development was Italian theorist Antonio Gramsci's (1971) rejection of Marx's view that oppressed groups were simply 'brainwashed' by the dominant classes. Instead he developed the concept of hegemony, where ideological dominance is not simply *imposed* by the ruling class but is a process of *negotiation*, whereby dominant groups work to convince society that they are best equipped to fulfil their needs and desires. Furthermore, ruling groups never get complete consent, because, as Gramsci notes, it is not always easily given and is a 'complex mental state which varies from person to person because some are more socialised than others' (as cited in Lears 1985, p. 570). However, if ruling groups want to maintain hegemony, they must find views appealing to a wide range of society, and at times selectively accommodate views from subordinate or marginalized groups (Lears 1985). This means that dominant ideologies shift over time and even incorporate some (less radical) aspects of counter-ideologies in their attempts to remain dominant. For example, patriarchy has made several concessions regarding women's status in society, giving them the right to vote and participate in the public sphere while keeping gendered hierarchies intact. The way dominant ideologies negotiate counter-ideologies will be a key theme of my analysis, particularly regarding gender roles, the division of labour, and issues regarding race, class and sexuality, to why people do not revolt against their oppression.

While ideology and hegemony are important concepts in themselves, they also form the base for understanding representation, which Hall (1997) states is the production of meanings through language of the concepts in our minds. Studies of representation seek to explore hidden structures and uncover ideologies embedded in texts – ideologies which contribute to systems of power in society. Studies of gender representation therefore seek to analyse how power flows through binaries such as masculinity/femininity and the private/public spheres. The comparative and longitudinal aspect of this research will be particularly useful, examining whether or how these ideologies have changed over time and space, thus tracing women's (lack of) progress since the 1960s.

Gender roles and the public/private sphere

During the Second Wave, an important distinction was made between sex and gender, which forms an integral part of socialist feminist theory. Where sex is understood as *biological* differences between men and women, gender refers to socially imposed *cultural* differences such as masculinity and femininity. Gender dictates how to dress, act and behave as a man or a woman, and is maintained through the presence of underlying ideologies (patriarchy, capitalism and race/ethnicity) – ideologies that position masculinity and femininity as binaries. For example, where (white, heterosexual, middle class) men are seen to be strong, aggressive, sexual, intelligent and interested in public affairs, (white, heterosexual, middle class) women are constructed as weak, passive, asexual, irrational and interested in private affairs (Friedan 1963; Gallagher 1981).[2] Feminists challenged these binaries throughout the Second Wave, which ranked masculine attributes more highly than feminine ones and provided a rationale for keeping (middle class) women in the private sphere. Consequently, gender has been described as 'a socially imposed division of the sexes' (Rubin 1997, p. 40) largely based around its organization of labour (Rakow & Kranich 1991). Gender, therefore, should not be thought of as universally homogenous or static but as something that changes over time (Carter & Steiner 2004).[3]

Like masculinity and femininity, the private and public spheres constitute another ideologically imposed binary, where the former includes (mostly unpaid) work performed in the home, such as domestic labour and childcare, the latter constitutes most activities that take place outside the home, including paid employment and politics (Jaggar 1983). While it is easy to believe that the public/private binary has existed since the beginning of time, scholars demonstrate it only began to develop in the late eighteenth century, alongside a growing industrial revolution, particularly advanced in the UK but also occurring in the US and other Western nations. During this period, most men's, and some women's, employment increasingly took place in the public sphere rather than in the fields or within the home. As bourgeois and working-class men's power increased, the public world became associated with that power, and the home became associated with moral values and support (Macdonald 1995). It was during this time that the family wage ideology also developed and played a vital role in shaping the labour market, largely classifying women as unskilled or semiskilled workers, who were sectioned off into lower-paying jobs (Cirksena & Cuklanz 1992; Coote & Campbell 1982; Rakow 1992).

While more women participate in the paid workforce than ever before, and as traditional gender roles have shifted, the public/private and masculine/binaries remain complex arenas where patriarchy and capitalism continue to exist – albeit in new forms. Studies show that women continue to perform most domestic labour and have failed to penetrate higher echelons at work (Equality and Human Rights Commission 2008 cited in Walter 2010, p. 209). Furthermore, reasons for these imbalances are often attributed to the notion of 'free choice' and 'natural gender roles' – the former used to indicate that women choose not to go for more senior posts (or *choose* to prioritize family over work), and the latter used to (re)construct many domestic tasks (particularly child rearing) as 'women's work' (Walter 2010). While discussions of free choice and 'natural' gender roles will be addressed in depth in the analysis, it is first important to get a brief overview of how women have been represented in the non-news media.

Representation of women in popular culture

When examining representations of women in popular culture, a mixture of qualitative and quantitative analysis has been used to uncover and expose ideologies and stereotypes underlying media texts, in hope of changing media content and social structure (Meyers 1999, p. 11). Most of this research shows that the media do not represent the actual number of women in the world (51 per cent), or their contributions to the labour force, implying that women are less important than men (Global Media Monitoring Project 2005, 2010; Pingree & Hawkins 1978; van Zoonen 1994). Because scholars recognized that this was a one-dimensional side of representation, and that counting men and women only scratches the surface of the realities of media (de Bruin 2000), they are now conducting more complex analysis concerned with nuances and subtleties that are carried in various meanings. Meyers (1999) suggests that the diversity in approaches has allowed for the possibility of many interpretations of the fractured nature of gendered images – a very different outcome from Tuchman et al.'s book *Hearth and Home* (1978), which was among the first to systematically analyse women's representation in mediated popular culture. The book concludes that the media were strong enough to 'symbolically annihilate' women, who were unevenly represented in the media (p. 3). Thirty years later, much has changed. Meyers (1999, p. 12) contends that Tuchman's finding of symbolic annihilation is no longer an appropriate blanket term for media portrayal of women, but rather, 'current images are fractured, inconsistent, contradictory, torn between misogynistic notions about women and their roles, and feminist ideals of equality' – a finding corroborated by other academics as well (Meyerowitz 1993; Projansky 2007).

While representations invariably overlap between different media forms, it is still worthwhile to examine each individually, beginning with women's magazines, television and film and advertising.

Women's magazines

Magazines were one of the first media to be examined in depth by feminist scholars and have undergone several conceptual shifts since the 1960s. Since then, there is sustained evidence of changes both in *how* women are represented and *what* messages are (re)produced. Gill (2007, p. 184) identified five discernable shifts in magazine content in the past 20 years alone. These include an increased focus on celebrity; the sexualization of the body, which increasingly becomes the key site of expressing one's femininity; the adoption of feminist rhetoric and messages used to promote personal empowerment (often through consumption); an increased focus on work in and outside the home; and an increased emphasis on heterosexual sex and messages about how to please men.

The way women's magazines have been conceptualized and analysed has also shifted dramatically since the 1960s. Initial studies viewed women's magazines as problematic because they *distorted* the realities of women's lives by constructing domestic activities as the road to self-fulfilment, ignoring women's ambitions for a life outside the hearth and home (Friedan 1963; Tuchman 1978b). As a result, magazines were not seen as a site of innocent pleasure but an arena that undermined women's 'real' identities. These studies therefore called for more 'positive' images of women, which was seen as a first step towards their emancipation. Excluded from these studies, however, was an analysis of the ideological foundations on which these images were based.

Later studies, influenced by concepts of ideology and hegemony, moved away from analysing *images* of women and began examining *representations*, noting how magazines naturalized a limited range of femininities and behaviour, and sought to challenge these with feminist critiques (Ballaster et al. 1991; Glazer 1980; Gough-Yates 2003; Macdonald 1995; McRobbie 1989, 1996). In her examination of women's magazines, Marjorie Ferguson (1983, p. 2) explains that the ideologies presented in magazines 'tell women what to think and do about themselves, their lovers, husbands, parents, children, colleagues, neighbours or bosses. It is this, the scope of their normative direction, rather than the fact of its existence, which is truly remarkable'. While Ferguson went on to discuss how women's magazines created a 'cult of femininity', which 'provides charters or codes that legitimize attitudes, beliefs, behaviour and institutions within the female world', (p. 39), others have noted shifts in these femininities over time, arguing there is not presently one single template for femininity, but many versions presented in various magazines (Gill 2007).

Particularly noteworthy is that where femininity was once articulated through discourses of love and romance, it is increasingly constructed through one's (hetero)sexuality (Currie 1999; Durham 1996; Gill 2007; Gough-Yates 2003; Machin & Thornborow 2003; McRobbie 1996; Mooney 2008). Such shifts are particularly apparent in teen magazines, where femininity is increasingly presented as a body characteristic in need of constant work and monitoring (Currie 1999; McRobbie 1991; Wolf 1991). Such monitoring requires consumption of various beauty products, which are presented as integral components in one's achievement of independence, self-fulfilment, empowerment and success with boys (Budgeon & Currie 1995; Gill 2007; van Zoonen 1995; Wolf 1991). The increased link between femininity and consumption is a widely identified postfeminist theme that can also be found in a variety of other media, targeting both men and women (Durham 2003; Dyer 1987; Gauntlett 2002; Gill 2003; Macdonald 2004; Negra 2009; Ogersby 2001; Springer 2007; Taft 2004; Tasker & Negra 2007; Thornham & Pengpeng 2010; Walter 2010). While the link between consumption and happiness has always played a role in women's magazines, Wolf's study (1991) details how this message, which she terms 'the beauty myth', erodes many of the women's movement's achievements because it redirects their attention from political gains, to purchasing products to maintain appropriate levels of femininity. Gill also argues that although experimenting with hair, fashion and make-up can be pleasurable activities for girls, discourses promoting these behaviours displace the 'extent to which feminine appearances are normatively expected of girls and women', and that 'opting out' of femininity for girls is difficult for them and comes with significant costs (p. 188). These discourses are therefore part of a wider neoliberal ideology where power comes from individual, rather than collective action, thus reducing the insistence on a unified struggle to resist oppression (McRobbie 2009; Zazlow 2009).

While such conclusions certainly are depressing, they overshadow some of the more positive shifts in women's magazines, including the rise of feminist publications that challenge patriarchal discourses through which women understand their lives.[4] Furthermore, others have noted an increased tendency to present equal partnerships between men and women in (sexual) relationships (McRobbie 1996, p. 192) – a change that has largely been credited with the feminist movement (Gill 2007), and one that has led to the inclusion of more confident, modern, independent and sexually assertive women (Gough-Yates 2003). Others however note that there is little diversity in women's/teen magazines regarding class, sexuality and ethnicity, arguing that white, middle-class heterosexual women continue to be presented as the norm (Durham 1996; Projansky 2007), although others have noted instances where lesbian identities are acknowledged (McRobbie 1996).

While it is easy for scholars analysing women's magazines to argue that they are 'bad' for women, Third Wave feminists and feminist cultural scholars have sought to reclaim women's magazines and other cultural texts as legitimate arenas of pleasure. In particular, those influenced by Gramsci's notion of hegemony allow people to view media texts as an arena of political contest, not just ideological manipulation (Currie 1999; Gough-Yates 2003; Hebron 1983; Hermes 1995; Projansky 2007; Winship 1987). The Gramscian framework made magazines a site where women's oppression became debated and negotiated, rather than simply reinforced (Gough-Yates 2003, p. 10). Additionally, researchers have found that while messages tend to promote notions of traditional womanhood and femininity, they can still be a source of pleasure for women (even feminists). Women's magazines are consequently polysemic, unstable and subject to subversive interpretations, even if they are incapable of urging women to change wider social structures (Ballaster et al. 1991; Currie 1999; Durham 1996; Hermes 1995; McCracken 1995; Meyerowitz 1993; Winship 1987). As Grimshaw (1999 cited in Gill 2007, p. 196) argued, 'It is perfectly possible to agree in one's head that certain images of women might be reactionary or damaging or oppressive, while remaining committed to them in emotion and desire'. While I agree that these studies are useful for easing the guilt many women felt for enjoying such texts, the ideological messages embedded within them still merit scrutiny, as do questions of why such ideologies persisted in the first place.

Television and film

While women's magazines have been a very popular focus of feminist study, television and film have also been thoroughly analysed (for overviews see: Baehr & Dyer 1987; Byerly & Ross 2006; Carter & Steiner 2004; Gauntlett 2002; Gill 2007; Meyers 1999; Negra 2009; Tasker & Negra 2007; Tuchman et al. 1978). Specific genres have received particular attention, including soap operas (Ang 1985; Brunsdon 1997, 2000; Geraghty 1991; Jackson 2006), talk shows (Engel Manga 2003; Grindstaff 2002; Shuttac 1997; Wilson 2003; Wood 2009), film noir (Hanson 2007;

Kaplan 1983), horror (Weaver & Carter 2003; Creed 1993; Jancovich 2002), romantic comedies (McRobbie 2007; Negra 2008, 2009; Thoma 2009) and drama (Akass & McCabe 2004; D'Acci 1994; McCabe & Akass 2006; Moseley & Read 2002; Richardson 2006). An historic examination of research demonstrates that in the 1970s, women were still more likely to be shown within, rather that outside, family settings, particularly in situation comedies, and that men continue to dominate women (Lemon 1978). However, throughout the Second Wave movement, into the 1980s, a more diverse range of characters is evident. While traditional images of femininity are present, shows such as *Cagney and Lacey, Murphy Brown* and *Kate and Allie* celebrated women's careers and achievements, depicting them as having lives outside the domestic sphere. Not only did police detectives Christine Cagney and Mary-Beth Lacey solve crimes, but they dealt with issues such as rape, breast cancer, abortion, balancing a family and being career women. While changes to the show were made to keep it 'feminine', including replacing the original Cagney because it was thought she was too 'aggressive', the show was groundbreaking in its representations of the lives women could lead (D'Acci 1994). These shows, influenced by the women's movement, raised important issues from sexual equality to the cultural political agenda, which became more prominent throughout the 1980s and onwards (Arthurs 2004).

Similar 'progressive' representations of women became apparent in film, as feminist messages were increasingly incorporated. However, as the backlash towards feminism became more pronounced in the 1980s and early 1990s, a new string of postfeminist films emerged, addressing the 'problems' feminism produced, while providing traditional, family-orientated 'solutions' such as retreating from the world of work to the home, where 'real' happiness is often found (see Negra 2009 for a full discussion). Other films incorporated 'girl power' rhetoric, while ignoring many of the barriers or discriminatory practices that have historically oppressed women (Levine 2008). Many feminist scholars are critical of such (anti)feminist narratives, which they argue undo feminism, while 'simultaneously appearing to be engaging in a well-informed and even well-intended response to feminism' (McRobbie 2004, p. 255). Consequently, the postfeminist narratives presented in many Hollywood films both de-politicize and undermine feminism and its potential for collective action.

A review of the research indicates that although the vast majority of media culture (and research) focuses on white, middle class, heterosexual women (Levine 2008), some have taken an interest in minority women. In August 1977, for example, the US Commission on Civil Rights released a report on women and minorities' employment with local broadcasters and television stations. The report found that minorities and women were under-represented on both network dramas and news programmes, noting that when included, it was in either token or stereotypical roles. A range of other studies found that African-American and Latina women were used to reinforce traditional racial and gender-based hierarchies, being depicted as faithful companions to white women and, sometimes, men (Gillespie 1999). Minority women are also frequently shown as maids, prostitutes, concubines, Jezebels, divas, sexually emasculating bitches, hostile, aggressive and bitter women (Anderson 1997; Freydberg 2004; Gray 1995; Marciniak 2008; Springer 2007).

Recent research has focused on the complicated relationship between black women and the home, arguing that when black characters 'make it' to the middle class, they lose their authenticity as a black person. Furthermore, rather than ushering middle-class black women back to the home, several Hollywood films urge women to remain in racially prescribed jobs, such as in beauty shops or in soul food restaurants (Springer 2007, p. 269). This is because while home is a place where white women find themselves, it is a place where black women lose their connection to being black (p. 272). These studies highlight the fact that minority women in popular culture are not only un- or misrepresented, but that they obtain meaning only through relationships with others or their environment. Gillespie concludes that these stereotypes serve to validate the economic subjugation of black women who are forced to find servile jobs (1999, p. 90). While the above research demonstrates that studies on minority women do exist, a more thorough examination is needed of how 'race' ties in with other forms of identity, such as age, sexuality and religion.

While women in television and film have undergone vast changes, the final media worth examining are advertising and art.

Advertising and art

Advertisements have been a particularly strong focus for feminist scholars because they are viewed as potentially debilitating, demeaning and inaccurate (Lazier & Kendrick 1993, p. 200). In addition, gender ideologies have traditionally been advertisers' biggest resource and are used to market products to specific audiences (Jhally 1987). Initial feminist analyses of advertisements have tended to examine women's sex roles, and document countless images of submissive wives and mothers, located within domestic settings (Goffman 1979). Others examined power imbalances between men and women, demonstrating how advertisements depicted a parent-child relationship between them, where women symbolized the child, had less power and were shown as smaller than men and more submissive (Goffman 1979). One early study, conducted by Belkaoui and Belkaoui (1976), tested whether feminist complaints about women's stereotyped roles in advertisements were true. Within previous studies, there was never an attempt to place findings within a historical context, and in order to correct this oversight, they examined eight general periodicals for one week in January 1958, 1970 and 1972 (*Life, Look, Newsweek, The New Yorker, Reader's Digest, Saturday Review, Time, U.S. News,* and the *World Report*). The authors identified a shift in representations over time, from women in family roles to more decorative roles, which portrayed them as non-active adults, included merely for aesthetic display (p. 171). They therefore concluded that advertisements had not kept up with advances in women's lives and continued to portray them in a limited variety of roles (p. 172).

Later studies demonstrated contradictory representation of women in advertisements. While some advertisers in the 1980s were keen to use feminist ideas to sell products for the 'independent' woman, others completely ignored such messages and instead reproduced images of good wives and mothers (Macdonald 1995, pp. 88–89). Still, scholars have observed improvements in advertisements in recent years. Lazier and Kendrick (1993), for example, contend that the 1990s has witnessed the emergence of non-stereotypical, pro-female advertisements (p. 207). This is perhaps unsurprising, as women continue to find themselves in centralized roles in an ever-increasing commodity culture (Negra 2009; Wolf 1991).

Though perhaps advertisements are becoming 'pro-female', this has occurred in tandem with one of the largest shifts in the media in general – from women as *passive* sexual objects to *active* sexual subjects (Gill 2007). This increased *sexualization* of the media presents a new theoretical development from discussion of *objectification* and is more difficult to criticize because women actively place themselves in sexual roles. This shift has been perpetuated by the emergence of ideologies equating femininity – which was once primarily associated with psychological characteristics such as passivity – with *physical* attributes such as sexuality. Gill (2007, p. 81) argued that all representations of women are now being 'refracted through sexually objectifying imagery: in the boardroom and in the bedroom, in the kitchen and in the car, the wife and mother or executive or pre-teenager, women are being presented as alluring sexual beings'. What is also worthwhile noting is that while all women might be sexual beings, the hegemonic sexuality presented is one of heterosexuality (Gough-Yates 2003), although images of (attractive, white) lesbian women have also been used in advertising for men's pleasure (Gill 2007, p. 200).

While advertisements have been the focus of many studies, others examine different forms of popular culture, such as John Berger's *Ways of Seeing* (1972). This analysed representation of women through art, arguing that women are depicted quite differently from men, not because of innate differences between masculinity and femininity but because 'the 'ideal' spectator is always assumed to be male and the image of the woman is designed to flatter him' (p. 64). Berger contends that women in Western cultures are trained to look at themselves from a masculine perspective and are represented through symbols (see also Mulvey 1975).

Regarding minority women in advertising, several studies demonstrate an overall absence of such bodies (Hooks 2000; Lachover & Brandes 2009). This is becoming increasingly true with the rise of globalization, where non-Western countries increasingly use advertisements exported from the US (Steeves 1993, p. 41). When non-Western women are shown, however, they are often depicted as exotic or as the 'other', and represent 'soul', 'authenticity', or 'sexual availability' (Gill 2007, p. 88). Other studies indicate that racial difference is commoditized in our current postfeminist climate and can be purchased through such means as ethnic clothing, food and bronzer (to keep darker skin all year-round) (Springer 2007).

Though the studies presented above are by no means an exhaustive list, they do provide a sense of the type of research conducted on women in the media. It is clear, then, that representations of women have changed over time, reflecting a shift in the socio-political landscape in the Western world. However, what begs to be answered is: if these shifts necessarily represent an improvement, as many are steeped within neo-liberal, postfeminist and post-colonial values, which reinforce patriarchy, racism, capitalism and other oppressive ideologies. So, how do these observations about women change when applied to representation of women in the news media, where women were active participants, openly demanding less-restrictive representations of themselves? In order to answer this question, we must first examine literature pertaining to the social production of news, news framing and gendered aspects of the news, social movements' relationship with news, and finally news of feminism.

The manufacturing of news

While this study could have focused on films, music or many other media, I selected newspapers because their daily publication and wide circulation give them potential for quickly disseminating timely information about the women's movement to millions each day. Newspapers also present a forum for many types of styles – news, features, editorials, comment, letters to the editor, advertisements and cartoons – all in the same publication, facilitating the opportunity for diverse discussion about the movement. As media scholar Claire Wardle (2004, p. 7) writes, newspapers do not just include the voice of the reporter:

> They also they include voices of the authorities, voices of those most closely involved with the events, and voices of readers who want to share their views via the letters pages. Newspapers therefore reflect the available discourses [...] from those directly involved to the reaction of wider society.

Tracking the news over time and space allows us to map changing ideologies and journalistic practices that could otherwise be thought of as permanent, unchanged or unchangeable (Sparks 2000). Additionally, Schudson (1989) suggests that comparative work is important in making visible journalistic patterns and conventions that researchers and journalists take for granted, particularly when the practices from one country have become the focus of most research, such as with the US (Wardle 2004, p. 13).

This project also understands that journalists *make* or manufacture, and not simply act as mirrors reflecting 'reality' through the news. It is widely accepted that the news media are not neutral unselective recorders of events (Oliver & Maney 2000, p. 464) but 'construct' reality. As sociologist Gaye Tuchman (1976, p. 97) stated: 'to say that a news report is a story, no more, but no less, is not to demean the news, not to accuse it of being fictitious. Rather, it alerts us that news, like all public documents, is a constructed reality possessing its own internal validity'. Ericson et al. (1987, p. 15) further argued that news discourse is important to examine because it is 'one of the important means by which society comes to know itself', and that studying 'the ways in which journalists make sense of the world is a significant way to understand society'. Consequently, this study will not seek to examine whether mediated representations of feminists are 'fair', 'balanced', or 'accurate', but instead aims to examine the discourses – and thus the ideology and power structures – used to publicly construct this social movement, its members and their goals over a 40 year time period. Hall (1996, p. 201) defines discourse as 'a group of statements which provide a language for talking about – i.e., a way of representing – a particular kind of knowledge about a topic'. Discourse in this study will be used to analyse how masculinity and femininity are constructed, and what role, if any, oppressive ideologies such as capitalism, racism and patriarchy play in these constructions. While the underlying ideologies might remain constant, the specific rhetoric is likely to change, depending on the newspaper format and target audience. As a result, it is important to examine what consequences these might have in my analysis.

Newspaper format and target audiences

When discussing newspapers, it is important to note a variety of cross-national differences between the US and UK, which were important for the selection of publications for analysis. To begin, newspapers in each country have different emphases – with a national focus in the UK and a metropolitan focus in the US (Wardle 2004, p. 25).[5] Another important consideration was political leanings. Where British newspapers are well known to be openly partisan, American newspapers remain, in theory, more independent. Consequently, in both countries it was crucial to use publications at varying ends of the political spectrum. Finally, while publications come in three main formats, 'broadsheets', 'mid-market' and 'tabloid', there are differences in how some of these terms are understood.[6] In the US for example, it is important to note that 'tabloids' report on important social, political and economic issues, and the word is used to describe the newspaper size, shape and circulation figures (Luce 2010). 'Supermarket tabloids', on the other hand, mean something very different, and refer to weekly publications focusing exclusively on entertainment, celebrity, gossip, human interest and scandal (Bird 1992; Conboy 2006). While supermarket tabloids have been known to report important hard news stories (Conboy 2006), their weekly production schedule and general aversion to 'serious' news render them an inappropriate choice for this study. Although the term 'tabloid' also refers to the size and shape of British newspapers, it is a term more closely associated with crime, scandal, entertainment and celebrity news. While these papers report on politics, the economy and society, this is done from a more colloquial, emotive and often sensational point of view and can be seen in publications such as *The Sun* and the *Daily Mirror* (Conboy 2006; Sparks 2000; Wardle 2004).[7] The alleged focus on entertainment and human interest stories does not mean that UK tabloids will shy away from issues I am interested in, but rather that they might address them in different ways. As Wardle (2004) contends, UK tabloids are as valuable, if not more so, to study than broadsheets because of their large circulation and openly populist mission to 'give a voice' to the majority. Other academics have argued that tabloids are seen to be closer to the lives and concerns of audiences and therefore can be quicker to identify significant new social trends or public issues (Sparks 2000).

Similar to tabloids, mid-market publications also differ in their meanings in the US and UK. In the latter, mid-market newspapers fall somewhere in between broadsheets and tabloids in terms of content – they do not carry enough 'serious' or hard news to be considered broadsheets, yet they are not as overly sensational to be labelled tabloids, though they share their shape and size. The *Daily Mail* is one example of a British mid-market paper (Conboy 2006; Halloran et al. 1970; Harcup and O'Neil 2001). In the US, however, 'mid-market' is not a commonly used term, as newspapers are either defined by their shape and size (i.e., tabloid or broadsheet) or by circulation figures (Luce 2010).

While tabloid and mid-market papers differ in the US and UK, the term 'broadsheet' faces no such barrier. In both nations, broadsheets are meant to 'facilitate political involvement and democratic participation' in society (Sparks 2000, p. 27), and scholars have identified *The New York Times*, the *Chicago Tribune*, the *Washington Post*, *The L.A. Times*, *The Times*, the *Daily Telegraph* and *The Guardian* as current examples (Halloran et al. 1970; Harcup and O'Neil 2001; Wardle, 2004). Although there are historical differences between newspaper formats in Britain, scholars have recently begun to challenge such categorical distinctions, arguing that tabloids often use as much information as broadsheets, which, in turn, are increasingly including more entertainment-based stories (Franklin 1997; Harcup & O'Neil 2001; Sparks & Tulloch 2000). Franklin even argues that, 'The history of the British press, since the emergence of popular journalism, has been a history of newspapers increasing shifting its editorial emphasis towards entertainment' (1997, p. 72). However, while there might be some blurring of content, there are still noticeable differences in the way news is presented. Tabloids for example, act as dramatic storytellers and rely heavily on the use of 'personal' stories over social or institutional ones (Conboy 2006; Macdonald 2000). They are also known to frequently use humour, ridicule, metaphors, slang and puns in storytelling (Allan 2005; Conboy 2006), whereas such findings have not been reported in regards to broadsheets.

Hard vs. soft news

In the late 1970s, Tuchman et al. (1978) wrote, 'The ability to define events as news is raw political power' (p. 186). However, not all news is equally valued, and the ability to classify the news into 'hard' vs. 'soft' is a testament to this. 'Hard' news is a term encapsulating stories about politics, the economy, social change or other events that take place in the 'public' world, traditionally comprising mostly men. 'Soft' news, on the other hand, includes stories set in or affecting the private sphere and connotes non-pressing, light or unimportant events or issues. It often includes articles about cooking, fashion and furniture and homemaking. Soft news has also traditionally included news stories that were seen to affect women, whether these issues occurred within or outside the home. Tuchman (1978a) states that one main difference between the two types of news is the urgency to publish the information: where 'hard' news typically represents news that cannot be delayed, 'soft' news does not need immediate publication. Notions of hard and soft news are integral to the tabloidization debate, as many media scholars criticize the increasing presence of soft news in all areas of the paper, particularly the front pages (Franklin 1997; Thussu 2007). Studies also indicate that women are more likely to report on and appear as sources in soft news, whereas the same holds true for men regarding hard news (Lachover 2005; Global Media Monitoring Project 2005, 2010; Ross 2007; Rhode 1995; Tuchman et al. 1978; Women in Journalism 1998). Consequently, such findings point to the gendered nature of news, which has become a focus for academics.

Gender and news

While scholars have long examined representations of women in the non-news media, much contemporary research explores the gendered nature of news, with particular attention paid to how gender relations shape and influence news practices, forms, institutions and audiences (Carter et al. 1998; Freeman 2001; North 2009; Ross 2001, 2007). Common questions include: Has the increase of female journalists changed the news? Do journalists commonly employ feminist perspectives when doing the news? Is there a gender divide in use of sources? What types of stories do men and women typically cover, and where in the newspaper will they appear? Many of these questions are difficult to answer because, until recently, research ignored gender when analysing journalistic professional values, norms and conventions (Lavie & Lehman-Wilzig 2003). However, some scholars contend that the women's movement had a major impact on how reporters and editors thought, defined, selected and edited news (Mills 1990, 1997), and that the increased presence of female journalists had *expanded* the conception of what news was, casting a wider net on issues and events that could be considered newsworthy (Marzolf 1993). This included more human interest stories, greater attention to audience needs and desires, emotional investment in stories, and sensationalism (van Zoonen 1998, p. 41).

Despite these advances, however, many scholars continue to argue that both the newsroom, and the news itself, remain gendered (Byerly & Ross 2006; Freeman 2001; North 2009; Ross 2005) and that such practices are difficult to challenge because workplace routines and norms force reporters to conform to dominant (patriarchal) values (Creedon 1993a). These include the dominance of a 'macho news culture' the sex-segregation of tasks, valuing 'hard' over 'soft' news, and reinforcing detached objectivity (which is seen as masculine) over empathetic subjectivity (which is seen as feminine). Following from this then, although there has been an increase in female journalists, sources and women's issues in the news, scholars argue that certain news practices should be thoroughly interrogated, and in some cases discarded (Rakow & Kranich 1991). For example, in what ways does the inclusion of personalizing information such as age, appearance and marital status benefit the story? Does it serve any purpose aside from localizing women within (or outside) appropriate feminine parameters? Why is objective, detached reporting always seen as the preferable way to share information, and why are 'soft' news stories valued less than their 'hard' news counterparts? Though Eisenstein (1981) optimistically claimed that such patriarchal structures could not help but change as more women participate in the media and ask for support, others disagree, noting that the newsroom culture has remained masculine because few women challenge the patriarchal ideologies underling journalism practices (North 2009; Ross 2005; van Zoonen 1998). Furthermore, studies of Canada, the US, Europe and Australia (North 2009; Robinson 2005) highlight the persistence of gender discrimination and sexual harassment in newsrooms, arguing they are important mechanisms used to maintain male superiority.

Is there a 'womanview?'

While the news itself is certainly masculine, feminist academics have also pondered whether there is something innate about women that would cause them to 'do' the news differently than men. Several scholars have argued that women possess a 'womanview', which arises from their different position in society. This perspective then makes them more interested in audiences, story background and context, and makes them more likely to interview other women (De Bruin 2000; Mills 1997; Ross 2007; van Zoonen 1998).[8] Kahn and Goldenberg (1991b) supported some of these theories when examining press coverage of female candidates for the US Senate in 1984 and 1986. They explained that female reporters were more likely than men to cover electoral races with female candidates, and that in their stories, female journalists discuss 'female' issues more than their male colleagues (1991b, p. 193).[9] More recent studies on women in politics have also confirmed such trends (Falk 2010). On the other hand, small- (Ross 2001) and large-scale studies in the US (Weaver & Wilhoit 1996) and the UK (Henningham & Delano 1998) demonstrate that gender is an unreliable predictor of professional values and journalistic practices, and argue that socio-economic differences and political values are better predictors of journalists' attitudes and values. In the mid-1970s, Doris A. Graber (1978) interviewed over 1500 men and women to see whether their news agendas differed, and found them to be neither large nor consistent, making it difficult to attribute them to the factor of sex itself (pp. 18, 28, 34). van Zoonen (1994, 1998) agreed, and among others (Bleske 1997; Delano 2003; Schudson 2003; Sebba 1994; Zoch & Turk 1998), argued that standardized news organization practices meat that individual news actors will operate in much the same way, regardless of gender, with the only exception being women's tendency to interview a larger number of female spokespeople. This means that it should not be surprising if female journalists in my sample are more likely to include female sources, and vice versa for male journalists and male sources.

Furthermore, when asked whether journalists (male or female) utilized a feminist perspective in their work, only a limited number of journalists affirmed this (Byerly & Warren 1996; North 2009; Ross 2001), suggesting that support for the movement or more radical critiques of patriarchy, capitalism or other forms of interlocking oppression (such as race or sexuality) will likely be rare though should not be completely absent. As Strutt (1994) argued, unlike other social movements, the Second Wave had media workers within its ranks who organized and agitated for change through their coverage of the women's movement and other feminist issues (pp. 60–61).

Source selection and gender

How journalists select their sources is a topic that has been debated and analysed in past years. Zoch and Turk (1998) tell us that stories are shaped by journalists' choice of sources, which tend to be people who are like themselves – educated, male, white, middle class – or those with political or economic power (p. 764; see also Ross 2007). Reporters, however, tend to blame intense deadlines and lack of minorities/women in positions of power as the reason for lack of diverse sources (Global Media Monitoring Project 2010; McCarthy et al. 1996; Zoch & Turk 1998). Scholars such as Hall et al. (1978) and Becker (1967) maintain that it is the powerful whose high status and top positions privilege them to become 'primary definers' of topics, giving them the power to 'set the limit for all subsequent discussion by framing what the problem is' (Hall et al. 1978, p. 59). Additionally, the fact that these people and organizations have power renders them newsworthy alone, assigning them legitimacy needed to comment on a vast array of events and issues (Hall et al. 1978). If such theories are true, then the disproportionate use of male sources leaves little room for the inclusion of other voices, notably women, minorities and others who seek to challenge the status quo (Manning 2001; Rhode 2001; Ross 2007, p. 454). Rather than accepting this, scholars claim that the sociology of journalism needs to be re-evaluated through a feminist lens, examining how men and women of differing ethnicities and classes negotiate their roles in a white, masculine news culture (Rhode 2001, pp. 51–52).

As a result, scholars have since critiqued the masculine news culture for ignoring the everyday politics and happenings in news organizations, for being atemporal and for overlooking how marginalized and minority groups at times are able to define events (Schlessinger & Tumber 1999 [1994] cited in Atton & Wickenden 2005, p. 348; Manning 2001). While considering these criticisms, it is also useful to acknowledge that since the majority of powerful people are men, it is therefore reasonable to assume that most newspaper sources will be male. This leads to the question of how women and men are used as sources. Research consistently demonstrates that women are under-represented in national, international and global news media (Frohlich 2007; Geertsema 2009; Global Media Monitoring Project 2000, 2005, 2010; Steeves 1997) and is a consequence of a lack of female reporters and a general sense of gender inequality in newsrooms (Frohlich 2007; Zoch & Turk 1998, p. 764). While research demonstrates that women are more likely to interview other women, men are still disproportionately used as sources for information (Ross 2005; Zoch & Turk 1998), particularly in international news (Global Media Monitoring Project 2000, 2005, 2010). Furthermore, while women are more likely to be included as members of the public, men are more likely used as 'experts' (Global Media

Monitoring Project 2010; Ross 2007). For example, older studies show that men comprise 85 per cent of newspaper quotes or sources, 75 per cent of television interviewees and 90 per cent of the most used pundits (Bridge 1993). More recent research indicates that improvements have been made, but women continue to comprise only 24 per cent of all news sources globally (Global Media Monitoring Project 2010). When women are included as news sources, they are defined vis-à-vis the principal (mainly male) news actor (Carter et al. 1998; Ross 2007; Zoch & Turk 1998), are quoted as victims (Global Media Monitoring Project 2005, 2010) and are portrayed as wives, mothers, sex objects, glamour girls, virgins, whores, passive, dependent and indecisive (Gallagher 1981). The prognosis is worse for women of colour, who are rarely, if ever, used as sources, and often have men speaking on their behalf (Rakow & Kranich 1991; Ross 2007). As a result, it is worthwhile to interrogate how much agency feminists are awarded, and the extent to which the characterizations mentioned above hold true.

Genre and story placement

Another important aspect of framing is article placement – regarding both stories about women and by women. When the National Organization for Women (NOW) analysed the *Washington Post* newspaper in the 1970s, it found that almost all news writers were male and that hard news about women did not appear in the appropriate news sections but were relegated to the women's pages (NOW 1973 as quoted in Pingree & Hawkins 1978). More recent research (Global Media Monitoring Project 2010; Ross 2005) also indicates that female journalists are often assigned to 'softer' or more marginal areas of journalism (human interest news, consumer news, culture, education and social policy). One question this research will pose, then, is whether feminism was considered to be a 'hard' or 'soft' news story. This will be achieved through analysing both story genre and page placement. The closer the story is to the front of the newspaper, and the genre it occupies, will indicate how important news editors felt feminism was.

Framing, social movements and news

The way a story constructs – or frames – an event is a widely used concept for academics in a variety of fields (linguistics, sociology, communication, media studies, political science, policy studies and psychology) and is an important concept for this project as well. Goffman (1974) first introduced the term 'framing' in the mid-1970s and used it to refer to a system of classifications allowing us to 'locate, perceive, identify and label' the diverse phenomenon we encounter (p. 21). Since then, however, different framing theories – or paradigms – have emerged.[10] One paradigm defines it as an analytical concept for the study of news, understanding that any representation of reality involves 'framing' (Kitzinger 2007) or selecting 'some aspects of a perceived reality to make them more salient in a communicating text in such a way as to promote a particular problem definition, causal interpretation, moral evaluation, and/or treatment of recommendations' (Entman 1993, p. 52). Frames are therefore understood as unavoidable (Gitlin 2003), and when analysed they give 'meaning to a vast array of symbols, while helping to organize the world for journalists and readers' (Gamson & Wolfsfeld 1993, p. 384). Frames also contain particular ideologies, which are presented to readers as 'truths' (Philo 1999), and it is 'precisely this masking of artifice by passing it off as apparent "reality" which makes journalism more art than craft ... and which gives the practice of journalism its dangerous power' (Ross (2007, p. 451).

Secondly, framing can be understood as a process (conscious or not) used by journalists, which allows them to select 'relevant' facts, assign them meaning, and order them in an 'appropriate' way (Benford & Snow 2000; Kitzinger 2007, p. 134; Reese 2001). Journalists are 'framers' of reality when deciding whom to interview, what to ask, what angle to take and how the story will be ordered (Kitzinger 2007, p. 137). Frames are useful for journalists because they enable them to process lots of information quickly and routinely, recognize events as important, assign them to familiar categories and package it effectively for its audiences. As a result, frame analysis has been particularly useful for scholars examining social movements, as it helps to explain how movements mobilize people and resources, and how they define and identify events, issues, causes, problems, solutions and key players. For this project, questions will be asked, such as: Were feminists constructed as 'ordinary' or 'deviants'? Did the movement apply to middle-class or working-class women? Was the movement revolutionary or reformist? What problems and solutions to women's inequality/oppression were posed? Such questions will help to determine how feminism has been constructed.

News of social movements

For new social movements, the media are seen to play an important role in understanding social change, shaping public consciousness and policy (Barker-Plummer 2010; Rhode 1995) and determining whether social movements are constructed in a 'positive' or 'negative' light (Baylor 1996). Gamson and Wolfsfeld (1993) write that when the powerful want change, they do not rely on the media, because they often have resources to lobby in private. It is therefore the powerless, including most new social movements, who often need media coverage the most but have the least access to it and, as a result, are not able to spread their message. The news media is given heightened importance because it is most people's only source of information on social movements (Barker-Plummer 2000; Gitlin 2003; Rhode 1995; van Zoonen 1992) and therefore not only defines what is significant but provides a framework for how to interpret these events (Hall et al. 1978). In this sense, the news media act as a form of 'deviance-defining elite', and provide an 'ongoing articulation of the proper bounds to behaviour in all organized spheres of life' (Ericson et al. 1987, p. 3). Scholars claim that journalists are central to reproducing social order, are quick to identify abnormal behaviour (which is often viewed as inherently newsworthy), and suggest appropriate responses to deviance (Ericson et al. 1987; Wardle 2004). Regarding feminism, I should therefore expect newspapers, at least initially, to identify feminists as deviants for their attempts to enter (and expand notions of) the public sphere, challenge traditional notions that (white, middle-class) women are passive, asexual, heterosexual, maternal, unskilled, and irrational. Because the news media cannot ignore social movements forever (Gitlin 2003), they can report on reformist, rather than revolutionary goals (Morris 1973b), give it frivolous coverage, or hope it goes away (Rhode 1995).

Consequently, it is important for movements to control their mediated representations as much as possible, and according to Gamson and Wolfseld (1993), the greater the resources, organizations, professionalism, coordination and planning within a movement, the greater its media standing and likelihood that their chosen frames will be used. However, knowing how to attract (the right kind of) media attention is not easy, and those individuals or groups with an understanding of the rhythms, values and conventions of news organizations are most likely to succeed (Manning 2001, p. 67). This is a disadvantage for female-based movements, because women have historically lacked social and economic resources and power. This was particularly true for the largely grass-roots British women's movement, which lacked larger organizational structures and was less interested and skilled in creating a viable mainstream public image. Many American feminists, on the other hand, had a sophisticated understanding of journalistic conventions and often worked within the media industry. For example, a founding member of the US organization NOW was PR specialist Muriel Fox, who understood, and was successful in attracting media attention through generating press releases and news stories (Fox, Personal Interview 2010). Furthermore, the US movement produced several 'media stars', who acted as spokespeople for the movement (and reliable sources for journalists), while the UK movement tended to oppose this type of hierarchical organization, preferring instead to use a collective political structure (with no clear, reliable sources to whom journalists could routinely turn for information). The UK movement was also hampered by its lack of formal structure and effective communication tools outside of London (Bouchier 1983, p. 95), limiting its ability to connect with other groups, organizing large events and attract media attention. These factors ensured that women's liberation was not predominantly featured on UK newsstands (1983, p. 103), although there was an incredible amount of feminist publishing taking place in alternative publications, from newspapers to journals to books.

While movement members struggle to put forward their preferred frames, journalists must keep in mind an assumed audience, and tend to place stories in familiar frames that maintain a 'common-sense' stock of knowledge (Hall et al. 1978) and are therefore more likely to resonate if drawn from existing cultural values, beliefs and narratives (Benford & Snow 2000). Consequently, social movements often try to amplify these values. However, in the case of the women's movement, it was precisely these common-sense ideologies (i.e. gender roles and division between the private and public spheres) that much feminist rhetoric challenged.

The media also have a variety of tactics for de-legitimizing social groups or their goals. These include using misrepresented or distorted images (Gitlin 2003; Martindale 1989), ignoring them altogether (Gitlin 2003; Morris 1973a; Shoemaker & Reese 1991), focusing on 'fringe' sections and associating the movement with extremist views or tactics (Rhode 1995), dividing the movement into 'legitimate' and 'illegitimate' sections (Gitlin 2003; van Zoonen 1994) and de-contextualizing events from issues causing them (Kerner 1968; Martindale 1989). A variety of these tactics have been used in news of various women's movements, which will be discussed next.

News of feminism

When it comes to women's issues, scholars note that they are underrepresented in mainstream media (Kahn & Goldenberg 1991a). Rhode

(1995) reasoned that because the media have long ignored women's issues, it was therefore unsurprising that little attention was paid to women's liberation. While there have been numerous studies examining media coverage of the American Second Wave movement, I have come across only one piece of research examining the same topic in the UK (see Morris 1973a).[11] Additionally, only one study (to my knowledge) focuses exclusively on women's rights (Butler & Paisley 1978), though none specifically on equal rights.[12] In Britain, there have also been several studies examining specific political issues, such as the anti-nuclear, women-only protest at Greenham Common (Couldry 1999; Cresswell 2006; Roseneil 1995; Young 1990).

When asked about how she feels feminism or the women's movement is represented in the news today, former NOW publicist Muriel Fox responded: 'Frankly, I don't think they [the media] recognize how important the story still is', adding that 'Some people think it's all been done, and it's all happened. The revolution has taken place. Most of us who were in the Second Wave still say we are still in the Second Wave, not the Third Wave, because the major issues haven't been resolved' (Fox, Personal Interview 2010). While several feminists, such as Fox, lament the absence of feminism in the news, it is also apparent that little academic research has examined feminist activism in the news since the 1980s. (For exceptions, see Ashley & Olson 1998; Dean 2010; Hollows & Moseley 2006; Lind & Salo 2002; Redfern & Aune 2010; Whelehan 2000; Walter 2010.) Instead, research has focused on the presence of (post)feminist sentiments or discourses in popular culture more widely (see Gerhard 2005; Gill 2007; Jamal 2004; Levy 2005; McRobbie 2009; Negra 2009; Tasker & Negra 2007; Thoma 2009; Varvus 2002, 2007; Whelehan 2005). Consequently, the lack of research into contemporary representations of feminism, particularly in areas outside the US, is a gap this research fills.

Deviant feminists

Because few women have historically held positions of power in the public sphere, academics have noticed that they usually only receive media coverage when 'acting out', or breaking away from traditional gender roles (Pingree & Hawkins 1978, p. 122). While this included demonstrations and protests, it also encompassed any actions that went against traditional expectations of women (such as public speaking, participating in the public sphere for causes other than philanthropy or religion). As a result, those involved in the movement were seldom viewed in a positive light (Bradley 2003; Freeman 2001). In fact, when reading the literature, one is left with a pervasive sense of negative media images and representations. The news media often focused on conflict between feminists and frequently cast debates among women as 'catfights' (Douglas 1994) – a tool used to de-politicize their views. Furthermore, academics have contended that the media labelled any women who were too outspoken or forthright as 'feminist,' usually of the 'militant' or 'radical' variety', regardless of how they identified themselves (Bradley 2003; Freeman 2001, p. 75; Goddu 1999). Such sentiments are echoed in personal memoirs of the women's movement in Britain. Feminist activist Sue O'Sullivan (n.d.) recalled: 'Almost from the beginning the media misconstrued and belittled feminists and their concerns, creating the mocked and mythical persona of the humourless, sour, man-hating women's libber'. Similarly, in the US, Susan Douglas (1994, p. 163) argued that the media were responsible for feminism's negative connotation:

> There is no doubt that the news media of the early 1970s played an absolutely central role in turning feminism into a dirty word and stereotyping the feminist as a hairy-legged, karate-chopping commando with a chip on her shoulder the size of China.

One study of the US women's movement between 1966 and 1986 shows that the news media presented feminists as less important, less legitimate and more deviant than anti-feminist (Ashley & Olson 1998), while 20 years later, another study contended that feminist portrayals had not improved (Lind & Salo 2002). This later study concluded that the media frequently demonized feminists, portraying them as 'crazy, ill-tempered, ugly, man-hating, family-wrecking, hairy-legged, bra-burning radical lesbians' (p. 218). van Zoonen (1992) also focused on how the media labelled anyone a 'feminist' whose activities they disapproved of. Such findings confirm Strutt's assertion that the media employ negative narratives in an attempt to marginalize those whose views run contrary to the general consensus (pp. 261–62). Such was the case with the Dutch movement, where the media framed consciousness-raising groups as 'feminist', and 'deviant', because they excluded men (van Zoonen 1992, pp. 467–88). These studies demonstrate how hegemony operates, as the discourse seeks to marginalize and de-legitimize those who challenged capitalist and patriarchal binaries such as masculinity/femininity and the public/private sphere. Instead, traditional gender roles are constructed as both 'natural' and as the foundation of a strong, healthy, happy society.

Another common method of maintaining patriarchal hegemony was through the image of the feminist bra-burner, which became an icon for the women's movement, after *New York Post* reporter Lindsey van Gelder jokingly used it as a metaphor for women's defiance of traditional gender roles at the 1968 Miss Universe pageant. Although no bras were actually burnt that night, the media's constant reference to feminists as bra-burners not only trivialized their cause but refused them status as legitimate political subjects (Hinds & Stacey 2001; Rhode 1995).

At other times, the media trivialized feminists by focusing on their appearances and behaviours over the issues they were campaigning for, thus leaving readers knowing more about the speaker's speaking style than the speech itself (Freeman 2001; Goddu 1999; Lind & Salo 2002; Rhode 1995). One commonly cited example is news coverage of the 1970 Women's Strike for Equality rally, organized by Betty Friedan, and NOW, where 50,000 women marched down New York's 5th Avenue. While *The New York Times* reported the demonstration, it put almost as much focus on Friedan's trip to the hairdresser that day as it did to the strike itself (Bradley 2003). Additionally, many news stories' first reference to female speakers usually included information about marital status and motherhood rather than professional credentials (Lind & Salo 2002). Though it could be argued that describing personal details is a common news convention, particularly in feature stories, it is worthwhile to note that these conventions are gendered and tend to be used exclusively with women (Rhode 1995; Global Media Monitoring Project 2005, 2010) and are consequently problematic.

Feminist support

While most movement scholars have focused on the vast amount of negative media coverage, others have indicated that representations were more complex than previously thought. Sheriden et al. (2007) contend that media constructions of feminism in Australian press varied over time, depending on the issue – a finding confirmed by other scholars as well (Dean 2010; Freeman 2001; van Zoonen 1992). Even NOW co-founder Muriel Fox recalls many examples of supportive coverage of the movement, particularly in its early days (Fox, Personal Interview 2010). In some cases, feminist goals of equal rights were legitimized, while feminism itself was de-legitimized (Sheridan et al. 2007; van Zoonen 1992). There is also evidence that being labelled a feminist could be beneficial, as 'feminists' were frequently afforded more agency than 'women' (Lind & Salo 2002, p. 221). Furthermore, many argue that the Second Wave's was instrumental in raising the media's interest and awareness of feminist issues, such as rape, domestic violence, abortion and sexual harassment, thus helping to reframe many 'personal' issues as 'political' ones (Benedict 1992; Carter 1998; Kitzinger 2004; North 2009; Rohlinger 2002; Worthington 2008).

Representing postfeminism

As previously mentioned, since the 1980s, there have been countless studies examining the emergence of postfeminist discourses in popular culture (Arthurs 2003; Levy 2005; McRobbie 2009; Negra 2009; Tasker & Negra 2007; Whelehan 2005), yet few studies have attempted to document the construction of postfeminism or Third Wave feminism in the news. One exception is research conducted by Susan Faludi, who famously examined the news media's delight in reporting not only the downfall of the Second Wave women's movement, but also a string of 'problems' it created for women in its aftermath, including a rise in female criminals, a 'man shortage', and increased infertility. Others discussed trends such as the 'mommy track', which traced a growing number of women opting out of their high-paid careers to be stay-at-home mothers (Faludi 1992; Gill 2007; Negra 2009; Valenti 2007; Varvus 2007). While these studies discuss (post)feminist discourses, they are not explicitly interested in representations of (post)feminism itself, thus begging the question, how is it represented contemporarily? Is there a clear distinction between current and past feminisms, or even feminist waves? What issues are associated with (post)feminism?

Although few studies since the turn of the century systematically examine representations of (post)feminists in the news (for an exception, see Dean 2010), several scholars have asked young women how they understand feminism, and whether it is a term they embrace. The results here are contradictory, with some studies indicating feminism is a thing of the past (Bulbeck & Harris 2007; Jowett 2004), while others suggest most young women today hold (liberal) feminist beliefs, even if they do not necessarily call themselves feminists (Zazlow 2009). Jowett's (2004) interviews with British women argues that many young women reject feminism, not because of old media stereotypes but because it is assumed that women are equal, and it is therefore irrelevant (p. 99), thus reproducing postfeminist rhetoric found in popular culture (McRobbie 2007). Such findings suggest that public constructions of feminism have shifted over time, and increasingly incorporate neoliberal themes of individual agency, empowerment and freedom, which are found more widely in popular culture. It is therefore likely that I, too, will encounter such themes when examining contemporary constructions of (post)feminism or the Third Wave.

Beyond the 'positive' and negative

While most studies examining news of feminism invariably discuss whether accounts were 'positive' or 'negative', there were many other aspects of coverage that were also analysed. This includes intervention on behalf of specific journalists, movement access to media and utilization of movement spokespeople. These elements reveal different aspects of coverage that will be useful to keep in mind when analysing my data. For example, because news of feminism appears to be overwhelmingly negative, it is worthwhile asking who was responsible for constructing these stories, and what, if any, feminist interventions were made (or attempted). In several cases, female journalists or editors are credited for ensuring that the women's movement received coverage. Barker-Plummer (2000), Bradley (2003), Freeman (2001a) and Tuchman (1978c) praised a range of female journalists who supported and wrote about the movement. On the other spectrum, some journalists consciously avoided covering the movement, or reported unsympathetic accounts for professional reasons (Mills 1997).

Eileen Shanahan of *The New York Times* frequently reported on the Equal Rights Amendment (ERA) and wanted to propose a women's liberation beat. However, she changed her mind on this point because she said she knew she would only be considered a 'professional' as long as she continued to cover topics such as tax legislation, the Federal Reserve, and the budget (cited in Mills 1997, p. 50). Had she admitted wanting to cover the women's movement full time, she felt she would be seen as 'crazy Shanahan who's always screaming and shouting and wanting to cover some silly-assed women's story' (cited in Mills 1990, pp. 60–61). US feminist Gloria Steinem recalled a *New York Magazine* colleague warning her from writing about feminism: 'You've worked so hard to be taken seriously, Gloria. You must not get involved with those crazy women' (cited in Thom 1993, p. 223). Barker-Plummer interviewed *Newsday* reporter Marilyn Goldstein, who described how an unsympathetic editor made supporting and accurately reporting the women's movement difficult:

> I wrote a series on women's rights and he told me, 'Get out there and find an authority who'll say this is all a crock of shit.' I'm quoting to you. I wrote of how the women's movement parallels the black movement, and he pulled that all out. So when people say, 'A good

series, Marilyn,' I say, 'If you really want to learn about the women's rights movement, look in my waste basket' (cited in Barker-Plummer 2000, p. 132).

While individual journalists undoubtedly played an important role in dictating story tone, not all negative coverage can be blamed on news workers. Rakow (1992), for example, argues that the news is a masculinist discourse that will always marginalize sentiments that threaten its hegemony, while Tuchman proposed that the news structure is to blame: 'Newspapers' very emphasis upon established institutions and those with institutionalized power may account in part for their denigration of women and the women's movement' (1978b, p. 28). Others blamed (mostly male) editors. Molotch (1978) wrote that the news media struggled to treat women's liberation seriously because it did not interest men, who comprise the majority of newsmakers and newsreaders. He added that when it was initially covered, reporters disproportionately focused on bra-burning, a refusal to conform to gender norms (e.g., no make-up, fancy clothes) and refraining from sexual activity with men (p. 182), thus de-politicizing their aims and turning it into a fringe movement.

Movement access to media

While it is important to examine how journalists publicly construct social movements, it is also important to examine movements' access to the media. This is particularly worthy of attention given that the many US (liberal) feminists were already well-placed within media organizations and thus had more opportunities for access (both because they had journalistic training and were aware of news conventions). While groups like NOW were successful in attracting media attention and focusing it on the ERA, not all women believed these mainstream organizations were the best outlet for disseminating information on feminist issues. Radical and socialist feminists in both nations were often ideologically positioned to reject the (mostly) male-dominated mainstream media, which they viewed as part of the problem, rather than a solution to social change. Instead, these feminists produced their own alternative publications, giving them control over their representations (Barker-Plummer 2010; Hole & Levine 1971; Steiner 2005). In several instances, radical groups rejected the mainstream media because it always sought out a leader who would speak on everyone's behalf. Not only did many radicals reject the hierarchical nature of such relationships, preferring instead to speak as a collective, but many feared that once a spokesperson was chosen, the movement would then be defined by that individual, 'discrediting her personal life rather than dealing with her politics' (*off our backs* 1970 as quoted in Bradley 2003, p. 75). Such was the case with US feminist Kate Millett, who was lambasted after a *Times* magazine article outed her as a lesbian.

Many radicals also refused to deal with any males in the media, which presented a challenge because female reporters were far fewer in number in those days. This often meant that some stories were excluded because of reporters' inability to find an 'authoritative' source, while in other instances it provided the media with an opportunity and an excuse to ridicule the movement and their 'unnatural' aversion to men. Because radical feminist networks during this period consisted of loosely based groups, often organizing events independently of one another, they did not necessarily seek out the mass media in the same ways as liberal feminist groups. Consequently, I expect that the news media will report on liberal feminist groups more often than their radical or socialist counterparts. While some feminist scholars have criticized such an insular approach (McLaughlin 1993), others contend that certain publications are better suited for presenting counter-hegemonic ideologies than others, and therefore choosing which media to speak can therefore be seen as a justified strategy (Steiner 2005, p. 314).

Framing feminism

In line with many other studies on media coverage of social movements, several researchers analysed how feminism has been framed. Others have investigated how feminists have attempted to frame themselves through press releases, noting their frequent success (Barnett 2005; Rohlinger 2002). When analysing the news media coverage, a common theme among scholars is their tendency to employ liberal analyses to the causes and solutions of women's inequality, which largely ignored issues of race, class and other structural inequalities (Rhode 1995; van Zoonen 1992). This is perhaps no surprise given that liberal feminist groups were more inclined than radical or socialist groups to seek media coverage. Such coverage encouraged individual action, rather than cooperative behaviour, as a way to bring about change (Bradley 2003; Sheriden et al. 2007). For example, one common storyline emphasized the need for individual, rather than social, transformation when the workplace was not in line with women's needs (Rhode 1995), therefore suggesting that women either need to adopt more masculine qualities (without becoming too manly) or retreat back to the private sphere where they can transform into a more 'authentic' self. Other studies confirm the maintenance of gender ideologies and the public/private binary, noting how frames of work and family were often pitted against one another, as the media constantly struggled to define women's place in society (Costain et al. 1997; Dean 2010). Consequently, as the battle for ideological dominance was waged, I should expect to find an array of contradictory articles regarding gender roles and women's place in the public and private spheres.

While most of the focus thus far has been on news coverage of feminism, Butler and Paisley's study (1978) of mainstream popular magazines analysed coverage of the ERA and considered subtle ways in which news reports had framed stories by emphasizing one of two positions: (i) the ERA would strengthen women's legal protections, or (ii) the ERA would weaken women's protections. They argued that ERA articles regarding economic and legal issues used the first frame, while stories on marriage and family issues tended to use the second. Although not explicitly stated, it would be my guess that articles supporting the first frame were written in a more positive light and perhaps had a more diverse range of representations for women than the second, which likely cast women in rigid roles relating them to the family and femininity.

While it is unfortunate that few studies examined news of equal rights or the British women's movement, this gap only reinforces and highlights the importance of international, cross-cultural research. Because few people have conducted cross-national research of representation, it is therefore important to discuss methodological issues at stake.

Methodology

While this project could have been approached from a variety of perspectives, I consciously chose a (socialist) feminist stance in order to contribute to the field of feminist media studies. As Sue Curry Jansen (2002) declared, gender shapes much of our life experience and should be a major consideration, not a variable, if we are to understand 'the multiple and multifaceted ways that gendered patterns of communication and gendered distribution of power are variously constructed and replicated by different social institutions and structures of knowledge' (p. 37). The socialist feminist position, like others, is important because it understands various interlocking forms of women's oppression (e.g., race, class, gender, ethnicity, age) and treats them as a collective, rather than an individual problem (Bryson 2003). While radical feminists were the first to recognize and develop a concept of patriarchy, their position has been critiqued for its overtly deterministic view towards biological sex (Bryson 2003) and their omission of the role capitalism plays in women's oppression. Socialist feminists believe that men oppress women, not because of biological maleness, but because of structural social and economic relations with women (Coote & Campbell 1982). A socialist feminist perspective is therefore preferred in this analysis for its ability to focus specifically on patriarchal, capitalist, racist and heterosexist ideologies. While the choice to use a socialist feminist framework was rather straightforward, other decisions regarding this project were more complex.

Timeline

This study examines news coverage during two different timelines. The first is during what I define as the most politically active period of the Second Wave women's movement, 1968–1982. Though feminist activism began earlier in the US than in the UK, I identified 1968 as a starting year because this is when several equal rights events in both countries began to occur.[13] I chose 1982 as the end year because this was when the American ERA – a piece of legislation that stipulated women's equality in all spheres of life and was heavily supported by the feminist movement – was defeated, and many considered the movement dead as a result. In Britain, 1982 was around the time when the women's movement transferred their energy to other types of activism, most notably the peace protests at Greenham Common airfield.[14] Although it would be incorrect to state that feminist activism 'died' in 1982, there is compelling evidence that within the UK, feminism was shifting more towards single-issue campaigns, such as the peace movement, whereas in the US, the rise of conservatism quelled, but did not eradicate, (public discussion of) the movement's activities.

The second period under investigation is 2008, and of how (post)feminism or the Third Wave was reported from 1 January to 31 December. This year was selected because I was interested in dipping into contemporary discourses surrounding feminism in the news media, and at the time of my investigation, this was the most recent year with data available. Incidentally, 2008 is also 40 years on from my initial investigation and thus provides a nicely capped timeline.[15] While unremarkable in many ways, 2008 proved an interesting year to examine because it witnessed a US presidential election where two prominent female candidates ran for office. Senators Hillary Clinton and Barack Obama competed with one another for the Democratic Party ticket, while Governor Sarah Palin was chosen as Republican John McCain's running mate.

While the election took place in the US, it was also widely reported on in the British media. Because of its shorter length, the analysis of data from 2008 is meant to provide a snapshot of how feminism was constructed and should be viewed as a case study, in which more research on the topic would be fruitful.

Newspaper choice

Because of cross-national variations in geography, classification and political leaning of newspapers in the US and the UK, and because newspapers die, change hands and re-invent themselves, selecting an appropriate range of newspapers was one of the most important and challenging tasks of this project. While eight publications were selected in total, only four were examined during the height of the women's movement – *The Times, The Daily Mirror, The New York Times,* and the *Chicago Tribune,* with another four added for analysis in 2008 – *The Guardian, Daily Mail, The Washington Post,* and *The Washington Times.* The decision to broaden the number of newspapers contemporarily was taken because the original four publications produced only around 200 articles, and I felt that the analysis would be stronger with a larger dataset.[16]

All eight of my publications were chosen for a number of reasons. To begin, I was interested in selecting a range of conservative and liberal publications, which would reflect the diverse opinions in circulation. While this was more easily identified in the UK, where publications are openly partisan regarding political parties and many social issues, such distinctions are more subtle in the US, though arguably still identifiable. The following publications were selected for their more conservative political positions and an assumed opposition to feminist activism, feminists and their goals: *The Times, The Chicago Tribune, The Washington Times,* and *Daily Mail* (Dean 2010; Decter 2002; Edwards 2002; Jenkins 1985; Wendt 1979). Conversely, I selected the *New York Times, The Washington Post, Daily Mirror,* and *The Guardian* for their more liberal stance, reputed commitment to social justice (Dean 2010; Edwards 2002; Sutter 2001; Taylor 1993) and assumed support for feminism. Secondly, I wanted newspapers ranging from the more populist, such as the *Daily Mirror* and *Daily Mail,* to those aimed at the more elite markets such as *The New York Times, The Times, Chicago Tribune, The Washington Times,* and *The Washington Post* (Conboy 2006; Hagerty 2003; Jenkins 1985; Wendt 1979). The inclusion of newspapers catering to a broad range of people and social classes was important because it provided the opportunity to dip into the varying discourses and styles that a large portion of newspaper readers consumed daily. Thirdly, I chose my US newspapers based on geographical location. In addition to selecting cities identified as media hotspots, such as New York, and Washington (Sigal 1973, p. 111), I also selected areas with active feminist movements. While three of my four US publications are based in New York and Washington, DC, I also decided to include a Chicago-based paper, as Illinois was the target for a nationwide campaign to ratify the ERA, and was also home to Phyllis Schlafly – a prominent anti-feminist who publicly opposed the ERA and many other feminist issues.

Because I only examined eight newspapers, I am aware that my findings are limited only to the newspapers under examination, and I will use these findings to identify trends and patterns of coverage rather than making broad conclusions about all press coverage during this period.

Search terms

Identifying appropriate search terms was more challenging than anticipated. We take it for granted today that the women's movement was always called the 'women's movement' or 'Second Wave feminism', and that feminists were always called 'feminists', or 'women's libbers'. I discovered, after reading many articles, and through trial-and-error with the search terms in online databases, that the vocabulary during my time period was still being developed and differed not only by country but among newspapers as well. Where 'women's lib' was commonly used in British tabloids such as the *Daily Mirror*, newspapers such as *The New York Times* referred to it as the 'women's movement' or the 'feminist movement'.

Between 1968 and 1982, my original set of search terms regarding the movement and its members included: 'women's liberation', 'women's liberation movement', 'women's movement', 'Second Wave feminism', 'women's lib', 'women's libber', 'libber', 'liberated women', 'feminism' and 'feminist'. While this brought up an enormous amount of articles in *The New York Times*, and the *Chicago Tribune,* the results were far more limited in the UK (particularly in *The Times*). Consequently, I eventually had to broaden my search term to 'women', which brought in relevant articles that were subsequently filtered.[17] In 2008, I used the terms 'feminism', 'feminist', and variations of 'women's liberation'.

Regarding equal rights stories between 1968 and 1982, my search terms varied slightly in each country, as the specific legislative tools or campaigns differed. In the US, my search terms included 'equal rights and women', 'Equal Rights Amendment', 'equal opportunity', 'sex discrimination', 'equal employment opportunity commission' and 'EEOC.'[18] In the UK, my search terms originally included 'equal rights and women', 'equal rights', 'sex discrimination act', 'discrimination', 'equal pay act', 'equal pay', 'equal opportunity', 'equal opportunity commission' and 'EOC.'[19] However, these terms brought forth too few articles in comparison with the US and therefore limited my ability to claim comparability, resulting once again in a broadening of my search terms to include 'liberation', which proved to be fruitful.

While historical research on the Second Wave indicates that equal rights and opportunities were one of its main goals, it is less clear what issues feminism is most associated with today. Various feminist websites and books reveal a diverse range of issues, from reproductive freedom, to domestic and sexual violence, sexual freedom, sexual objectification, lesbian rights, equal pay, rights and opportunities, and more (Fawcett Society 2009; NOW 2010; Object 2010; Redfern & Aune 2010; Valenti 2007). Consequently, I decided it would be better just to collect all articles on feminism and see which issues were discussed rather than to search out the issues in hopes that individual feminists or feminist groups were also mentioned in the articles.[20]

Methods

As some feminists have encouraged, this project used a combination of quantitative and qualitative methods. Multiple methods increase the likelihood of understanding issues in women's lives by adding layers of information and by validating and reinforcing each other (Reinharz 1992, p. 201). In this case, a combination of quantitative content analysis and qualitative critical discourse analysis (CDA) were used. Simply speaking, quantitative analysis is a way of measuring things and often assigns numerical values to variables and constructs models and equations to interpret their importance. As a popular quantitative tool, content analysis is useful for analysing large amounts of data, its meanings, symbolic qualities and content (Deacon et al. 1999; Krippendorff 2004). Furthermore, it is capable of revealing patterns of news content, making evident previously unarticulated assumptions about how the news is structured and presented (Ericson et al. 1991). More importantly, some scholars note that content analysis can be used to disclose international or cross-national differences in communication (Krippendorff 2004, p. 45), making it a particularly useful tool for this project. Though not claiming to be objective, content analysis is methical, where all material is submitted to the same set of categories that have been explicitly identified. This ensures a degree of reliability in establishing media patterns or representation (Deacon et al. 1999, p. 133). Content analysis also establishes a procedure to find what is relatively constant and what might change over time. Having a method capable of identifying these patterns is useful for my project, whose timeline spans 40 years.

However, despite these benefits, content analysis is a descriptive tool and does not critique constructions of women within representational systems such as newspapers (Brown 1997, p. 402). This is where CDA comes in. This method is specifically interested in the relationships among language, social practice, ideology and power. CDA is also strictly political, and unapologetic for this stance, making it a good fit for a feminist project that seeks to identify, challenge and, hopefully, change oppressive practices in society. Both content analysis and critical discourse analysis have also been used successfully in the past for research on news, gender and representation (Ashley & Olson 1998; Carter 1998; Huddy 1996; Richardson 2007; Tuchman et al. 1978; van Dijk 1991; van Zoonen 1992, 1994).

Conducting the analysis

When analysing the data, I began by reading through each article twice – once to familiarize myself with it, and once to focus on the content and critical discourse analysis. When conducting the content analysis, key questions asked included date, page placement, story length, genre, news peg, sources used, source gender, overall tone of the article and problems and solutions regarding women's inequality. The last two I felt were particularly important because the media have often been accused of presenting individual solutions or explanations to complex problems (Cottle 1993). While most of the coding process was straightforward, there were a few challenges. For example, in several articles there was more than one 'answer' to the questions posed. Such was the case regarding source identity, where those quoted could have been categorized in several ways (e.g., wife and feminist). In such cases, I coded the identity that was most prominent, and if all things were equal, the first label mentioned.

Although I tended to conduct the quantitative analysis first, I also took notes on each article of themes, quotations, narratives, metaphors, rhetoric or positions that seemed salient or ideologically rich. After closely reading each article, I attempted to assess which ideologies were prioritized, whom the discourse served, what it revealed about the society in which it was produced and how it helped/hindered the movement and their goals. I made notes about both the extraordinary and ordinary aspects of coverage, often pulling sections out to use in my analysis. Because I analysed my publications separately and organized my articles in chronological order, I was able to anecdotally trace the emergence of discourses over time within each publication and article. Additionally, when I noticed certain patterns emerging, I would make note of it, and came back to several of these themes when writing up the data. While I accurately predicted some patterns of discourse, there were others identified through a frequency analysis of the content that I would not have noticed without the statistical evidence. Consequently, a combination of the two methods was beneficial.

When providing examples of the discourses present, in some cases I only used a few paragraphs or sentences from each article, in an attempt to highlight some main points. In four cases, I conducted a full CDA on the entire article and labelled it a 'case study'. While I was conscious about using examples from each publication, certain frames or discourses were found in some newspapers more than others. In such instances, I have attempted to be as transparent about the prevalence (or absence) of such coverage so as not to mislead the reader, frequently using statistics to strengthen my point. While this summary gives a brief explanation of how the analysis was carried out, specific practices will be identified throughout the next three findings chapters where relevant, beginning with news of feminism.

2
Reporting the Women's Movement, 1968–82

Introduction

The Second Wave feminist movement takes place in the aftermath of the post-war era – a time of 'home dreams' (Parr 1995, p. 4) – where the (white) middle-class nuclear family was idealized as the norm after years of war. While many women had gained some semblance of independence and economic freedom when taking over men's jobs during the war, traditional gender roles were quickly re-established in 1945, when women were kicked 'out of the work force and into the ranch house' (Fraser 1997, p. 165). Consequently, the public sphere once again became constructed as intrinsically 'masculine', and the private sphere as 'feminine' (Macdonald 1995), re-establishing a patriarchal, gendered hierarchy. Despite women's expulsion from the public sphere, it also became clear that society was changing. Many women who had been in the paid work force during the war effort were unhappy with their postwar eviction (Bryson 2003). They started to recognize that their positioning within the home had more to do with ideology than biology and began to question the division of spheres (de Beauvoir 1989; Friedan 1963). As women's consciousnesses were raised, they began to organize and agitate for change, recognizing that biology was no longer a plausible justification for job segregation, pay differences and limited opportunities.

Women were not the first group to campaign collectively for social change during this period. The US Civil Rights movement began in the late 1950s, followed by the gay liberation and the New Left student movements. In Britain, activism was strongly focused on the anti-nuclear and peace movements. By the 1960s, women were just one of many groups who sought social change, and it is here that this study begins.

Feminism in the news

For anyone interested in women's history or welfare, the public construction of feminism is an important topic. As a result, this chapter seeks to trace the ways in which the Second Wave movement and its members were represented in 555 news articles drawn from four newspapers – *The New York Times,* the *Chicago Tribune,* the *Daily Mirror,* and *The Times.* Using both content and critical discourse analysis to sketch the emergence and decline of discourses surrounding the movement and its members, the 14-year time period (1968–82) covers what I define as the most politically active period of the Second Wave. Although not the first study to examine news coverage of feminism in the US (Ashley & Olson 1998; Cancian & Ross 1981; Bradley 2003; Lind & Salo 2002; Morris 1973a, 1973b; Rhode 1995), it is one of the first to systematically examine news of British feminism (see Hinds & Stacey 2001; Dean 2010; Morris 1973a as exceptions). Furthermore, only one study has analysed news of feminism cross-nationally (Morris 1973a), which provides insight into women's role and resistance to these roles across cultures.

Because 'feminism is never available in some pure or unmediated form' (Moseley & Read 2002, p. 234), the news media is a key site of investigation in understanding what it has historically meant to be a feminist. From this data, it is clear that public constructions of feminism have historically been fragmented, contradictory and subject to change. While at times referred to as a 'lunatic fringe', (No Byline 1972b, p. 12), comprising of 'bra-less' (No Byline 1970, p. 13) and 'bearish' women (Bender 1970, p. 147), it was also referred to as 'spirited' (Weinraub 1970, p. 3), 'powerful' (Haberman & Herron 1977, p. E3) and 'supported' (No Byline 1974c, p. 3). How does one account for these mixed messages, many of which were found within the same publication or articles, and what do they say about the role of women in British and American society? How did the media make sense of widespread calls for change, and how did patriarchal and capitalist ideologies seek to neutralize or eliminate them? These are some of the questions addressed below.

Throughout this chapter, I will demonstrate that (i) a surface-level reading indicates that supportive discourses actually attained overall hegemony, but that over time; (ii) supportive coverage was overwhelmingly limited to a liberal, reformist feminism, which promoted reform rather than a fundamental restructuring of society or radical change. This meant that radical critiques of patriarchy or capitalism were virtually absent, and the dominant ideologies remained largely intact through *adopting* (liberal) feminist principles where necessary while de-politicizing revolutionary and radical goals; (iii) oppositional frames were prominent throughout the sample and drew from a limited, but effective, range of discourses constructing feminists as deviant, unnecessary and harmful to society. This discourse reproduces itself over and over again throughout the 14-year time period; and finally, (iv) while most coverage could be said to support or oppose the movement, a smaller range of articles constructed it as complex and contradictory, demonstrating instances where journalists did not merely report the movement in black or white terms but reflected the diverse nature of the movement, its actors and their desired outcomes.

Overall trends in coverage

In total, I collected 555 articles on the women's movement and its members, of which *The New York Times* comprised the largest proportion with 210 articles (38 per cent), followed next by the *Chicago Tribune* with 183 articles (33 per cent), then by the *Daily Mirror* with 110 articles (10 per cent), and finally by *The Times* with 52 articles (9 per cent). Overall, then, it is clear that there were more articles in my American (393) than British (162) newspapers (see Figure 2.1). While it would be misleading to state that the women's movement was more important in the US than the UK, it is clear that, at least within these four publications, the movement was more newsworthy in the former than in the latter. This is likely the result of several factors. To begin, the American movement formed highly organized groups, such as NOW and the National Women's Political Caucus (NWPC), whose membership included a plethora of women who understood journalistic conventions and tactics needed for attracting media attention (Bradley 2003; Ferree 1987; Huddy 1996). Conversely, the British movement consisted of smaller, more fragmented groups, who either made little or no attempt to attract mainstream media attention or actively opposed it (Bradley 2003; Bouchier 1983; O'Sullivan n.d.). Such differences also likely account for the lower levels of coverage in the UK press.

Publication length is another likely factor in the uneven distribution of articles between nations, as British papers were, on average, significantly shorter than their American counterparts. An analysis of newspapers produced on 1 January of each year during my sample indicates that the *Chicago Tribune* and *The New York Ties* were anywhere between 50 and 150 pages long, whereas *The Times* and the *Daily Mirror* averaged between 35 and 50 pages. This is likely the result of post-war paper

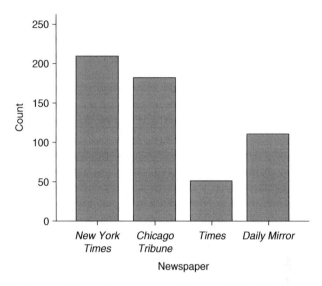

Figure 2.1 News articles on feminism by publication, 1968–82

rationing in Britain, which, while ending in 1956 (Curran & Seaton 2006; Griffiths 2006), left a legacy of shorter papers.

Cross-national differences were apparent not only in the distribution of articles per nation, but in article focus as well. In my American publications, for example, articles often referred to the movement as a cohesive whole. Common headlines include: 'Women's Movement at Age 11: Larger, More Diffuse, Still Battling' (Klemsrud 1977, p. 63), and 'Where the women's movement is today' (Kleiman 1974, p. D1). The results of such constructions are two-fold. On the one hand, rather than being viewed as individual set of beliefs, feminism was constructed as an active, often powerful, political movement with public credibility. On the other hand, by referring to *a singular* women's movement, articles ignored the diverse nature of feminist political theory, goals and tactics. This absence of context becomes problematic when feminists disagreed in public (such as at feminist conferences or over certain issues such as the ERA or abortion), as many journalists simply dismissed the movement as being fragmented, or as in conflict, and feminists as confrontational and catty.

In my British publications, on the other hand, articles were less likely to refer to *a* women's movement, and instead focused on the beliefs or activities of individual feminists or 'women's libbers'. Typical headlines included 'Purely in the name of women's liberation, our girl Deborah acts like a man for the day' (Thomas 1970, p. 11), and 'She Wants to Ban the Bra!' (James 1970, p. 12). By focusing on the individual, news coverage downplayed the universal nature of women's oppression, constructing feminism as a *personal* belief (often a fringe one at that), thereby removing it of its politics.

Genre

Genre is an important feature to analyse when doing newspaper research, as it not only dictates where a story sits in a particular newspaper, but also affects the topics covered, tone, style, headline and use of journalistic conventions in its narrative (Cottle 2003; van Zoonen1994). According to journalistic conventions, 'hard' news stories, or those focusing on politics, the economy, international affairs and other 'serious' matters, have traditionally been valued more highly than 'soft' news stories, or those set in or affecting the private sphere, and connotes non-pressing, light or unimportant events or issues (Tuchman 1978a). Because women have traditionally been excluded from the public sphere, they have also been largely absent from hard news stories, both as writers and sources. Despite this absence, scholars have noted that women's liberation provided both a 'way in' for female journalists to cover public events, and a space for women to speak as voices of authority as sources (Freeman 2001).

Because of the Second Wave's potential for providing such unique space for women's voices and serious discussion of their issues, genre was an important category in this analysis. In total, my coding scheme allowed for 11 possible genres, including: news report, news brief, feature, column, letter to the editor, editorial, backgrounder, agony aunt, photo, cartoon and women's/lifestyle section. Of these categories, news reports, news briefs and, sometimes, photos are considered to be 'hard news', whereas features and agony aunts are considered 'soft news'. Columns, letters to the editor, editorials, cartoons and photos are more difficult to categorise and, depending on the story topic, can fit into either the 'hard' or 'soft' news label. Table 2.1 demonstrates a clear tension in how feminism was reported. Overall, despite the significance of the movement, most news of feminism was found in either features (217 articles or 39 per cent) or news reports (178 articles or 32 per cent), indicating that, while considered important enough to merit news coverage, feminism is not yet considered to be in the same realm as the masculine arena of news. Consequently, the data indicates that the

Table 2.1 Genre by newspaper, 1968–82

Valid	Frequency	Percentage (%)
News report	178	32.1
News brief	30	5.4
Feature	217	39.1
Column	68	12.3
Letter to the Editor	30	5.4
Editorial	12	2.2
Backgrounder	2	0.4
Agony Aunt	1	0.2
Photo	1	0.2
Cartoon	2	0.4
Women's/lifestyle section	14	2.5
Total	555	100.0

'march from the women's page to the front page is hardly complete' (Mills 1990, p. 349).

Because the reporting of genres has well-known gender biases (Lachover 2005; Global Media Monitoring Project 2005, 2010; Ross 2007; Rhode 1995; Tuchman et al. 1978; Women in Journalism 1998), it is useful to examine the use of women as both sources and journalists within this sample. In total, 258 articles (47 per cent) were written by women compared with 168 articles (30 per cent) written by men.[1] This finding suggests that the women's movement provided women an opportunity to appear in the news, and female journalists with an important news story to report. However, while female journalists were more likely than men to cover the Second Wave, the data indicates that gender norms remained largely intact regarding story genre, although there were some advances made. For example, male and female journalists wrote an even number of news reports (66 articles each), indicating a breakthrough for women into hard news genres. At the same time, however, women were significantly more likely to author feature stories (131 vs. 62 articles), columns (36 vs. 28) and letters to the editor (11 vs. 2), which can be constituted mostly as soft news. What is interesting about these statistics is that while women were able to cross over and author hard news stories, a similar trend was not seen for men regarding soft news stories. Such patterns indicate then that while women have slowly been accepted into, and allowed to report on the public world, the same is not true of men in the 'private' world, as soft news continues to be gendered female – a trend that continues to this day (Global Media Monitoring Project 2005, 2010).

While it is easy to remain critical of women's relegation to 'soft' news stories, it is important to keep in mind Tuchman's (1978c) assertion that such stories, though perhaps not as 'prestigious' in terms of topics or page placement, provide a legitimate space for women's voices and concerns to be heard in the public sphere. Furthermore, these genres do not require conventions of objectivity or balance, and thus allow more multifaceted ways of thinking about the world (Strutt 1994), enabling journalists to explore different aspects of the movement without fear of being labelled 'biased'. Finally, because features are often long in length, they provide an important space for serious, in-depth coverage, which is often omitted in hard news reports. Consequently, while it is unfortunate that gender divisions remain firm regarding the reporting of soft news stories, I argue that little is problematic about the prominence of such stories in the first place.

News pegs

For any social movement interested in attracting media attention, it is important to understand the types of stories likely to make it into the news, and the conditions in which success is likely. Such information is vital in planning movement media strategies. For example, in addition to having a story that meets a journalist's sense news values, the amount of competing newsworthy stories in a day, and the newspapers' own agenda will determine the likelihood of coverage (Campbell 2004; Harcup & O'Neil). While interviewing journalists and editors is the optimal way to garner such information, it can also be worthwhile examining news pegs, or the 'hook' that sparked the story in the first place. In regards to longitudinal studies, recording news pegs can depict media attention cycles and may offer interesting comparisons as to differences in newspapers' agendas and notions of newsworthiness.

In total, this study documented a total of 20 different news pegs (see Figure 2.2), ranging from the more prominent protests and demonstrations (30 articles or 5 per cent of total), feminist campaigns (85 articles or 15 per cent of total), conferences/annual meetings (53 stories or 10 per cent), and 'feature' stories for which there was no obvious spark (106 articles or 19 per cent). Certain news pegs were also used to varying degrees throughout the sample period. For example, in 1975, many stories were sparked by equal rights legislation, as both the Sex Discrimination and Equal Pay Acts became enforced in the UK, and the ERA was ratified by both New York and New Jersey in the US. Interestingly, feminist conferences were rarely considered newsworthy until 1977, when the

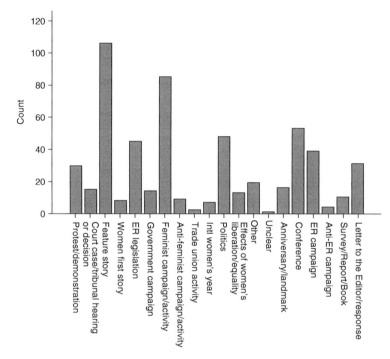

Figure 2.2   Total news pegs, 1968–82

Women's National Conference, funded by the US federal government, took place. Furthermore, feminist conferences were much more likely to be reported in the US than in Britain, where only the first women's conference held at Ruskin College in 1970 received any press coverage (Hall 1970).[2] This can, perhaps, be linked back to the tendency of my British papers to report feminism as an individual choice, disregarding the collective activism of British feminism.

Interestingly, and perhaps fitting in with the prominence of 'soft' news stories, is the large number of features, which provided no apparent 'hook' as to why the story was included in the paper. In total, features comprised 106 articles (19 per cent) and covered a wide range of topics. Examples of headlines include: 'Down on the Farm, a wife's life isn't the drudgery it used to be' (No Byline 1973b, p. 16), 'Women's Lib – Millett, Militants and Militantes' (Winton 1971, 9), 'Let's face it. A housewife's job is bloody awful' (Gomery 1970, p. 13), and 'What daughters think when mom's a drum-beating feminist' (McCormack

1973, p. B7). While it is nearly impossible to determine how such stories made it into the paper without interviewing journalists or editors, the prominence of features indicates that feminism was seen as such an important issue, and one with the ability to make it into the paper without necessarily being linked to an 'event'. This should be seen as a positive step because it means that a whole range of issues and topics, which would normally be ignored if going by traditional journalistic conventions, were given a public forum. It might also be a sign that journalists themselves (or their editors) were becoming interested in feminism, and pitched these stories on their own accordance at editorial meetings.

Framing feminism

Frame analysis is a longstanding tool used to de-construct coverage of social movements (Ashely & Olson 1998; Barnett 2005; Baylor 1996; Benford & Snow 2000; Costain et al. 1997; Couldry 1999; Creedon 1993b; Lind & Salo 2002; Strutt 1994; Rohlinger 2002). Frames help to create discourse as they determine which questions are asked, the story angle taken, the voices used (or ignored) and the problems or solutions given. When examining all 555 articles, 27 themes emerged, which, when taken together, can be broadly categorized into three main frames: support for feminism (279 articles); opposition to feminism (174 articles); and feminism as contradictory or complex (101 articles). What is notable about the range and balance of these frames is that there are a larger number of supportive frames than previous scholars have demonstrated. However, as I will go on to argue, this support largely resulted from de-emphasizing feminism's more radical goals, and presenting reformist, rather than revolutionary critiques, surrounding women's oppression/inequality. As a result, patriarchal, capitalist, racist and heterosexist ideologies were rarely challenged, thus inhibiting true liberation for women.

Legitimate feminism

Unlike previous work focusing on the largely negative representations of feminism in the news (see Dean 2010; Freeman 2001; Sheridan et al. 2007; van Zoonen 1994 for exceptions), this research found that the majority of articles could be generally labelled supportive of feminism (279 articles or 50 per cent of total). At best, these articles engaged with the women's movement, their members, actions or goals, or at worst, reported them in a manner that was not trivializing, degrading or sarcastic. Particularly noteworthy is that feminism was not always supported in my more liberal publications, particularly the *Daily Mirror* which, contrary to my expectations, consistently employed an oppositional position throughout the 14-year time period. On the other hand, I was surprised to find feminism regularly legitimized in my more conservative publications *The Times* and the *Chicago Tribune*. Such results indicate that political leanings may not always be an accurate means of judging coverage of social issues. In exploring the various ways the Second Wave was supported, this section will be broken down into three parts. The first will examine the use of legitimizing frames and techniques regarding feminism, including source use. Second, I will examine how articles engaged with women's issues, looking specifically at the problems and solutions proposed. Finally, I will end this section with a discussion of articles which constructed feminism in a complex or contradictory manner.

Feminism as a unified and effective movement

Within this sample, supportive frames were constructed in a variety of ways, including labelling feminism as a unified/effective movement (84 articles), as being 'liberating' (39 articles) or 'necessary' for women (17 articles) and through frequently engaging with its goals. Such constructions were found not only in the story body, but in headlines such as: 'It was a great day for women on the march' (Klemsrud 1970, p. 4), 'Judge Gives a Boost to Women's Lib' (No Byline 1971b, p. 16), 'Black feminists form battle line against racism, sexism' (Eason 1973b, p. 32) and 'Feminist movement gains growing support' (No Byline 1974b, p. 3). While all four publications carried supportive articles, these were particularly apparent in *The New York Times*, the *Chicago Tribune* and *The Times*. While there were various means upon which feminism was supported, one *Times* feature demonstrates this in more detail. Titled, 'Women of the world unite – in song, laughter, work and protest' (Puddlefoot 1973, p. 8), the journalist reports how feminist organizations from 28 countries worked together effectively during their three-day conference to achieve positive results:

> The conference was a cheerful chaos of song, laughter, endless discussion and punishingly hard work. It resolved itself efficiently during the last day-and-a-half into the election of an ad hoc operating committee to initiate planning for a world feminist congress in the autumn of 1974, the establishment of policy

guidelines on programme and content, and the selection of possible locations.

Here, feminism is seen to unify women around the globe, and is an effective organizer of future events. Evidence of solidarity between feminists is also found in statements such as, '[T]he task force discussing topics for the agenda had no difficulty outlining 15 main issues'. This theme of solidarity – a common legitimizing tool – was particularly noticeable during the early years of the movement, as the spirit of feminist activism grew (found in 83 articles or 15 per cent of total). However, it is worth pointing out that the notion that women could successfully work together in unity was also challenged from an early age, as journalists and opponents drew upon stereotypes of women as catty, petty and unable to get along (see also Douglas 1994). For example, the article 'Punch-up at the women's peace rally' (Hitchen 1971, p. 5) reported how 'Chairs were hurled and fights broke out at the first international women's liberation conference yesterday', leaving half of the 400 delegates not speaking to the other half by the conference's end. Such events likely attracted media coverage because they appealed to journalists' attraction to conflict in a story (Shoemaker et al. 1987) – a value that women getting along did not arouse.

Sources of support for feminism

While many articles clearly focused on feminism's positive effects on society, a more subtle technique used to legitimize the movement was through constructing feminist supporters as 'ordinary' (read, white, middle-class, heterosexual) members of society. Such constructions became increasingly important as opponents began casting all feminists as 'radicals' and 'deviants' in their attempts to de-legitimize the movement. While some radicals and socialists embraced such descriptions (or at least did not fear them), others were uncomfortable with such labels, particularly as they struggled to attract mainstream support. One consequence of this, then, was the demarcation between 'ordinary' and 'legitimate' feminists (who were traditionally feminine and often attractive) and those who opposed such conventions. This 'domestication' of feminism is a trend identified in news of feminism 40 years later (see Chapter 4; Dean 2010).

A key means of creating mainstream acceptability for the movement was to get both authoritative and 'ordinary' members of the public to adopt the feminist identity. Regarding the former, one *New York Times* news story interviewed the first female Mayor of Houston, who stated she was a 'deeply committed feminist', a member of several women's organizations and an equal rights legislation supporter (Whitmire 1981, p. A24). Furthermore, several interviews with celebrities throughout the sample focused on their feminist beliefs: 'She is one of the biggest singing stars in the world. She's also a women's libber of great dedication' (Hagerty 1975, p. 9). Having a powerful person embrace the feminist label sets a good example to the community and indicates that feminism is a positive force in women's lives. While having a feminist as the primary definer of a topic was not enough to guarantee that supportive frames were always used, many feminists clearly tried to present themselves and their cause in the best possible light.

On the other side of the coin, feminists were presented by others and themselves as 'ordinary' women, in an effort to combat claims they were elitist and out of touch with most women's lives, as it was so often claimed:

> The Equal Rights Amendment remains an elitist enterprise, led by self-righteous, over privileged feminists with easy access to the media and no broad following in the country, whose vision of America's future is rejected by the housewives in whose name they profess to speak. (Buchanan 1975, p. 20)

As Russo (1994) argued, this 'normalization' is problematic not only because it represents women's fear of losing one's femininity, or alienating (powerful) men, but because it 'leaves uninterrogated the very terms and processes of normalcy' (cited in Hesford 2005, p. 227), which are rooted in identities such as class, age, race, gender and sexual identity. A typical 'normalization' of feminists then comes from a *Chicago Tribune* feature, describing the scene at a women's trade union conference:

> Like others who have been turned off by sensationalised television presentations (especially David Susskind's) of any women's group which attempts to participate in and define and decision outside a kitchen or maternity ward, while distorting and inventing realities, I cannot help thinking of Women's Liberation today whenever the word 'women' comes to mind or is mentioned.
>
> Thus mentally encumbered, I was expecting dungareed, Army blanketed brigade of Brunhildes practicing karate chops, grunting, and screaming 'male chauvinist pig' while busting imaginary male heads – any possibly my real one.

Such was not the case. There were about 200 of them, neatly dressed, mostly in middle-class prints. They were extremely logical in their presentations of arguments for and against the Equal Rights Amendment (ERA), the main topic of their meeting. They were as feminine as any group of women you would find at a baking contest, bingo parlour, or at church on Sunday morning. But they were all working women, meat packers, clerks, machine operators, waitresses, etc. (LaVelle 1972, p. 12)

As indicated above, part of the normalization process for feminists included describing them as 'ordinary' women, frequently attractive and married, sometimes educated, and always heterosexual. Interestingly, in this case, women were described as normal *despite* their working-class status, indicating the extent to which normative femininity was rooted in issues of class.

Common normalizing statements include: 'Leonora Lloyd is married with two children' (Winton 1970, p. 9), or 'Jean Faust of New York's NOW: 37, married, attractive, a research assistant to Congressman William F. Ryan' (Lear 1968, p. SM25), and seem to have no real bearing on the story except to localize feminists within acceptable feminine parameters. Furthermore, many journalists discuss how pleasantly surprised they were to find prominent feminists beautiful and feminine:

Juliet Mitchell is twenty-nine, a university don, blonde of hair, long of leg – a woman any man would be pop-eyed with pleasure to be seen with. And she is the intellectual leader of the women's liberation movement. (Gomery 1979, p. 13)

Because the media frequently drew upon a perceived tension between homemakers and feminists (Freeman 2001), a common legitimizing strategy was to demonstrate that the movement appealed to a broad range of women, not just those seeking (middle-class, professional) careers. In fact, in the late 1970s, feminists purposively began to stress their housewife status, likely as an effort to relate to homemakers who often felt alienated and threatened by the movement:

NOW's new president, Eleanor C. Smeal, bills herself as a housewife, a description any good feminist would have disdained seven years ago. Mrs. Smeal's view, which is emerging in the organization, is that the work women do, whatever it is and wherever it is done, has value that must be recognized. (No Byline 1977a, p. 40)

While the frequent mention of women's status in the home perhaps made homemakers feel included, I argue this label is somewhat disingenuous, as Smeal was a full-time paid member of staff for NOW. Furthermore, ignoring the ways housework and childrearing have historically oppressed women is extremely problematic from a revolutionary standpoint (Mitchell 1971).

The normalization of feminists was also accomplished by differentiating between 'acceptable' and 'unacceptable' forms of feminism. One *Times* article quotes Member of Parliament (MP) Dame Patricia Hornsby, who described herself as 'a feminist not a militant feminist' (Brittain 1971, p. 12), which clearly indicates an aversion to radical politics. Similarly, a *New York Times* article writes about how Mrs. Simpson was both a 'nonmilitant feminist', and a 'happily married wife and mother' (Bernstein 1975, p. 128). The explicit legitimization of only non-radical positions has also been identified by previous movement scholars (Dean 2010; Freeman 2001; van Zoonen 1992) and is harmful to the feminist cause because it legitimizes only those who refrain from challenging traditional norms of femininity or who fail to evaluate social values and structures critically.[3] Consequently, as Freeman (2001) wrote, 'The mainstream news media are not, given their capitalist nature, revolutionary, and feminist messages tend to be eventually subsumed within the status quo' (p. 5). This means that those who are willing to raise their voices, dress unconventionally and are not traditionally beautiful are likely to be de-legitimized by the press regardless of their message. While I understand that radical views are unlikely to attract the broadbase support that many feminist supporters sought, they are absolutely necessary in pushing boundaries for social change. Consequently, revolutionary positions were either largely absent from, or ridiculed within, public discourses.

Engagement with issues

One strategy used to legitimize the Second Wave was to engage with the causes and solutions to women's subservient position in society. The data demonstrates that such context was not the norm, as only 243 articles (44 per cent of total) engaged with causes, while 175 articles (31 per cent) addressed solutions to women's inferior status (see Table 2.2). These percentages are broadly similar within each publication, although some, such as *The Times* and the *Daily Mirror* were marginally better than *The New York Times* and the *Chicago Tribune* in this respect.[4] Although these absences are significant and give further evidence to the news media's tendency to focus on surface issues rather than substantive critiques (Martindale 1989), it worthwhile to examine the causes and solutions

Table 2.2   Causes and solutions to women's inequality/oppression, 1968–82

Genre	Newspaper				
	New York Times	*Chicago Tribune*	*Times*	*Daily Mirror*	*Total*
News report	83	57	11	27	178
News brief	19	4	1	6	30
Feature	82	66	34	35	217
Column	7	34	6	21	68
Letter to the Editor	8	13	0	9	30
Editorial	7	1	0	4	12
Backgrounder	1	0	0	1	2
Agony aunt	0	1	0	0	1
Photo	1	0	0	0	1
Cartoon	0	0	0	2	2
Women's/lifestyle section	2	7	0	5	14
Total	210	183	52	110	555

when cited. For the former, these include 'sexism/discrimination' (61 articles or 11 per cent of total), 'sex/gender roles' (31 articles or 6 per cent of total), and 'patriarchy/exploitation' (38 articles or 7 per cent of total). Because sexism and discrimination are easy concepts to convey when space is limited, they were frequently employed in article headlines and body. Typical examples include: 'A chance to compare notes on discrimination against women' (Charles 1972, p. 14), 'Barnard Class Told to Battle Bias' (Cook 1980, p. B3) and 'Chicago Jaycees Urge End to End Sex Discrimination' (No Byline 1974a, p. 15). Sex/gender roles and patriarchy/exploitation were more likely to be found in the story body as these concepts are more difficult to summarize. For example, one *Times* column argued that both sexism and sex roles oppress women:

> The truth is that since the beginning of time sex discrimination has operated, making sure that girls fulfil their predetermined sex roles, indeed the brainwashing begins as soon as they are old enough to look at picture books. Women are positively discouraged from attempting to enter male dominated territory, such as politics, and only the strong in mind and body manage to break through the barriers and stay within the magic enclosure. (Short 1975, p. 7)

Perhaps because of the capitalist and patriarchal nature of the press, critiques of these systems were rare. However, out of all four publications, *The Times* proved most amenable – a particular surprise given its middle-class, conservative readership. One particular feature, 'France's feminine feminist' (Matthews 1969, p. 11), quotes feminist Evelyn Sullerot, who discussed both patriarchy and capitalism in France:

Typical of Evelyn Sullerot's approach is the way she looks at the role of the housewife. Although this role has little economic justification in the modern world, much pressure is brought upon her to maintain it. In an increasingly technological society, it is reassuring for men to keep women as their link with traditional values, bending over stewpots as their mothers and grandmothers did. And in capitalist countries, where productivity is the highest goal, women are urged to stay at home, the principal consumers in a consumer society.

Not only does this article identify patriarchy and capitalism as the causes of women's oppression, but it also argues that in order for things to change, society must reorganize itself in women's favour. Another feature article discussed how 'the women's struggle is against oppression and therefore is part of the class struggle. They are preparing for the radical cultural transformation of society – possibly even to take over power from the men, or to do without them' (No Byline 1974c, p. 3). While radical critiques were found in news articles and features, a number of columns also presented these views. One, written by British feminist Dr Anna Oakley, explodes the 'myths surrounding today's feminist woman' and de-constructs the ideologies found in feminist stereotypes:

The feminist stereotype consists of a set of assumptions about the personality and life-style of people who call themselves feminists. A feminist is not married, or if she ever was, the experience must have been an unhappy one. She is anti-children, and usually has none herself; if she has, she has rejected (and hence knows nothing about) their day-to-day care.

This rejection is symptomatic of her general antipathy to the biology of being female. She doesn't wear a bra (having of course burnt it) and she may actually be a lesbian. Personally, she is aggressive, self-assertive and independent: 'no man is an island' – no, but a feminist is [...]

A feminist doesn't do much housework because dirt and untidiness don't upset her the way they do most women. Her main aim is to make 'ordinary' women unhappy. She wants to stir up trouble in the kitchens of the world, so that her theories about the female condition become self-fulfilling prophesies.

Here, Oakley identifies several popular (anti-) feminist stereotypes, and through the use of humour and sarcasm, she demonstrates their absurdity. Yet, at the same time, it is clear that if this is how feminists are continually represented, then it is no wonder so many women (and men) reject them. While pointing out their existence is useful, Oakley's analysis strikes at the ideological heart of such stereotypes – stating that they are the result of our patriarchal society's need to keep women in their place:

> The feminist stereotype, like all stereotypes, has a few grains of truth in it, but also, like most stereotypes, it has a more subtle function: it serves to keep women in their place. A male-oriented society such as ours has an overriding need to define the nature of women. Men are people and women are women, as somebody once put it. The creation of idealised models – the housewife, the wife, the career-woman – fulfils this purpose by putting firm boundaries around women's social, economic and behaviour. The feminist woman is a clear threat to this framework. Hence the rationale for the feminist stereotype.

What is significant here is Oakley's level of analysis. By stating that feminist stereotypes are grounded in a 'few grains of truth', she affirms MacDonald's (1995) claim that they effectively mask their own ideologies. Further, Oakley identified these specific ideologies as patriarchal, noting that such stereotypes are necessary if men want to retain their dominant position in society. Such articles therefore demonstrate that, occasionally, alternative, truly critical discourses circulated in mainstream publications, demonstrating that even though newspapers operate within a capitalist and patriarchal system, they are 'not a pre-given instrument of oppression', and can be responsive to social change (Strutt 1994).

Black feminism and radical critiques

One topic that frequently employed radical critiques of patriarchy, capitalism and racism regarded news of black feminism. While their voices were few and far between,[5] they were more likely to be found in *The*

Chicago Tribune – a daily newspaper based in a city with a high black population. Many of these articles acknowledged that women's experiences of oppression were largely dependent on race, class and gender. In some instances, this provided the incentive for black women to become involved in the women's movement, while in others, it provided an excuse to separate themselves and either form their own feminist networks or remain active in the broader Civil Rights movement. For example, one *New York Times* article described how the women's movement received little support from black southern women out of fear it would drive a wedge between them and black men: '[The] role of the black woman can only be made specific and clear when the role of the black man is made specific and clear' (Reeds 1975, p. 51). Others highlighted how white men and women were equally responsible for oppressing black people, thereby problematizing universal experiences of gender oppression:

> Black women worked their fingers to the bone and black men were lynched to pay bloody homage to white ladies. Hence, it's hard to conceive how these very women could expect blacks to empathise with members of the most privileged class cults in American history – 'sacred white womanhood.' (Poussaint 1971, p. E12)

As a National Black Feminist Organization (NBFO) founder stated, 'Black women in America have the problem of being both black and female in a country that is both sexist and racist' (Eason 1973b, p. 32). While such articles rightly identified variations in women's experiences based on class and race, not all articles focused on the *tension* between the white and black movements, but on the *benefits* of collective action. For example, the article 'Problems unite black feminists' (Eason 1973a, p. C15) reported on the first Eastern regional conference on black feminism, sponsored by the NBFO. The article quotes Beth Rawles, a minority programme director for a local TV station, who stated that black women must join together to fight a three-fronted battle:

> We have to continue to work with black men to develop human rights for black people. We have to work with black women to educate ourselves that we have certain rights as women. And we have to work with the white women's movement because we have a special interest vital to our survival.

Similarly, several other articles not only identified interlocking forms of oppression, but included frameworks and solutions for how to overcome these issues. This ranged from asking women to re-evaluate their roles in society, to urging for more organized support and campaigning for women to join the black feminist movement. Not only do these articles engage with issues raised by (black) feminists, but, unlike their white counterparts, their activities were overwhelmingly constructed as a positive force in women's lives. One typical article ended with a quote from Carolyn Reed, a NBFO founder, who proclaimed, 'Feminism has made such a difference in my life. I feel that I was just playing a role before' (Eason 1973a, p. C15). Both the legitimacy afforded to black feminism and the critical perspectives employed here about the nature of women's (interlocking forms of) oppression are worth noting.

While the discussion so far has focused on a variety of tactics used to legitimize the Second Wave and its members, this section will finish with a case study of a *New York Times* feature on the then emerging movement.

Case study 1 – legitimacy in *The New York Times*

Titled, 'What do these women *want*? The Second Feminist Wave' (Lear 1968, p. SM24), this nine-page feature is found within the supplementary *New York Times Sunday Magazine* and was selected for a case study because it encompasses many of the points already raised regarding how the movement and its members were legitimized. Furthermore, it is just one of the many supportive articles found within *The New York Times,* which consistently legitimized (liberal) feminism throughout the time period. It is fair, then, to state that this article is consequently only atypical in terms of its length and level of analysis. It is also worth noting that, from a purely observational point, articles such as this, which seriously engaged with the movement in-depth, were more likely to be found near the beginning of my sample period than at the end, perhaps a result of the media's initial attempt to place the movement in context.

Because the digital database used to collect *New York Times* articles did not produce a page view, but only the article itself, it is not possible to conduct an intertextual analysis. Underneath the headline are four columns of text, and beneath them, photos of well-dressed, middle-aged white women marching with signs. One reads, 'Women can THINK as well as TYPE', while another proclaims, 'It is a woman's civil right to bear only wanted children'. The article opens with the introduction to members of the newly formed National Organization for Women, which wants 'full equality for all women in America, in truly equal partnership with men', and describes a recent demonstration:

It was billed as a black comedy, nothing elaborate. Twelve comely feminists, dressed for cocktails would crash the hearings of the Equal Employment Opportunities Commission on sex discrimination in employment. They would make some noise, possibly get arrested, certainly get thrown out, meet the press, and all the while give prominent display to large, home-lettered signs [...] To the press, they would explain that they were protesting all those prejudices and laws of the land which keep women at home and in the bottom of the job market, but exclude them from jobs that utilise intelligence in any significant way.

> This makes it clear, they would say, that women are valued not for their intelligence but only for their sexuality – that is as wives and mothers – which, stripping the matter of its traditional sacred cows, reduces the Women's Role to a sort of socially acceptable whoredom. (1968, p. SM24)

Here, the article engages with various feminist critiques – from liberals' understanding of discrimination and prejudice as barriers to women's full participation in society – to the more radical critiques of patriarchy and capitalism. Despite the plurality of feminist positions, the journalist does not frame the movement as 'fragmented', or in conflict but reports these differences in a matter-of-fact way, withholding judgements on how such differences could affect the movement. As Gallagher (2001) writes, it is 'lazy journalists' who frequently rely upon stereotypical representations of men and women, and who consequently do injustice to social movements.

What is also significant about the article is that its long length allows the journalist to go in depth and explore not only the feminists' grievances but their goals as well:

> What NOW wants, but way of immediate implementation of its goals, is total enforcement of Title VII: a nationwide network of child-care centres, operation as optional community facilities; revision of the tax laws to permit full deduction of housekeeping and child-care expenses for working parents; maternity benefits which would allow some period of paid maternity leave and guarantee a woman's right to return to her job after childbirth; revision of divorce and alimony laws ('so that unsuccessful marriages may be terminated without hypocrisy, and new ones contracted without undue financial hardship to either man or woman'), and a constitutional amendment withholding Federal funds from any agency, institution or organization discriminating against women. (p. SM24)

The breadth and depth of the movement's goals were rarely reported in later articles, as the movement became more familiar and closely associated with single-issue campaigns such as equal rights and abortion. In addition to taking an in-depth look into the movement's formation and goals, the article devoted space to combating feminist stereotypes: 'When I finally prepared to do an article on this new tide, I prepared to be entertained; it is the feminist burden that theirs is the only civil-rights movement in history which has been put down, consistently, by the cruellest weapon of them all – ridicule' (p. SM24). Furthermore, the article engaged with claims that women have nothing to be liberated from, and already hold a considerable amount of power. Feminists were given space to respond to such criticisms, noting that most of women's 'power' is in fact 'a fraud', as it 'devolves ultimately on which breakfast food to buy' (p. SM25). Consequently, the article interrogates anti-feminist claims rather than merely reporting them.

This critical engagement continues as the article discussed the radical segment of the movement – the faction often given less favourable media coverage for their contravention of traditional gender norms and revolutionary aims. However, rather than framing them as deviant, the article stated: 'Not all of the new feminist activity is centred with NOW. To its left is a small group called Radical Women – young, bright-eyed, cheerfully militant – which recently splintered off from Students for a Democratic Society' (pp. SM26–7). Though still defining its members as 'militant', the word 'cheerfully' in front of it removes negative connotations. Later on, the journalist even described the radicals as 'movement's intellectual hip', a complement to them surely.

Though it would be inaccurate to claim that the article is entirely uncritical of the Second Wave, the last word is supportive rather than dismissive, and is evident in the analysis of differences between NOW and radical feminists, particularly concerning their views on marriage, the family and the parent-child relationship. Where radical feminist Ti-Gracce Atkinson urged the abolition of the nuclear family, instead arguing children should be raised communally, three differing viewpoints were provided, with varying levels of support. For example, sociologist Suzanne Schad-Summers contended that children raised collectively were more independent and had fewer psychological problems, while Dr. Selma Fraiberg, Director of a Child Development Project remarked that these children turned out to be in no way superior to children raised in the family system. The third view was from the director of a child-research clinic who argued that all children, whether raised communally or not, have problems.

I would argue that, overall, by engaging with the movement, its members and their differences, in a serious, non-trivializing manner, the article legitimizes the movement and its members and gives fair consideration to many of their goals. Consequently, through unpacking the various ideological differences within the movement, the journalist was better able to engage with it, as opposed to writing it off as in conflict. While this article is unique both in terms of the length and depth in which it explores the movement, examples of engaging articles can be found in *The New York Times*, the *Chicago Tribune*, and *The Times* throughout the 14-year time period

In concluding this case study, it is worth noting that while the discourses present in this article (and others like) it serve feminists, it does not necessarily serve all women. Rather, this and other discourses frequently legitimize a white, middle-class, heterosexual feminism, which ignores the plight of those women whose day-to-day realities do not involve struggling to find fulfilling careers or entering top-level positions. Rather, such women are often already a part of the paid labour system (where their work has been traditionally undervalued) and often lack the education, training or opportunities required to achieve top-level positions. So while the discourse is certainly 'positive' for a specific construction of the women's movement and its members, it is lacking in terms of addressing various issues of concern to many women (e.g., ethnicity, race, sexuality, ability and age). This is a common omission found throughout all four publications throughout the sample period.

Opposing feminism

When examining past literature on news of feminism, it comes as no surprise that oppositional frames were prominent in my sample (174 articles or 31 per cent). What *was* surprising is that they only attained hegemony in one of my supposedly 'liberal' publications, the *Daily Mirror* (47 articles or 43 per cent of the paper's total). This opposition is likely because, while a Labour paper, the *Daily Mirror's* readership were mainly (working-class) men, who likely felt the quest for women's rights detracted attention from the wider labour movement (Toynbee 2010). In all four publications, however, a slew articles outwardly opposed the women's movement and worked to de-legitimize it by, for example, labelling feminists 'deviants' (43 articles), as 'ineffective' and 'unnecessary' (30 articles), and bad for men, women, the family and society (25 articles). While frames were largely determined through story body, headlines are also useful to examine, as they provide a de-legitimizing interpretive framework for which to understand the movement. Examples of such headlines include: 'Long May I Stay Unequal' (No Byline 1972c, p. 13), 'Sisterhood Is Powerful, but Not Omnipotent' (Charlton 1977, p. 132), 'Where Women Provide Their Own Discrimination' (Lester 1981, p. 9) and 'All Women's Liberationists Hate Men and Children' (Wittner 1973, p. H12). While audiences negotiate media messages rather than accept them uncritically (Hall 1980), such framing serves explicitly to harm the movement and create popular opposition.

One of the most effective means of de-legitimizing feminists and feminism throughout the sample period was to label them as 'deviants' – as lesbians, man-haters, bra-burners and aggressive women – all traits conflicting with traditional notions of femininity, and thus warned women they would be labelled subversive if they challenged patriarchal gender roles. Such tactics are not unique to my four publications and have been identified by previous movement scholars as well (Bradley 2003; Freeman 2001; Hesford 2005; Pingree & Hawking 1978; Scharff 2010). Furthermore, what is particularly powerful and dangerous about such discourses is that they *adapted* feminist critiques where necessary, de-politicizing and incorporating them into their own rhetoric. Hence, the ideology allowed *some* support for feminism, so long as it was not of the 'radical' (and thus revolutionary) or 'militant' type – a process of negotiation used to maintain patriarchal hegemony.

Deviant feminism, deviant feminists

Because frame analysis takes into account how its key players are represented (Kitzinger 2007), it assumes that such constructions contribute to the overall understanding of an issue, event, group, individual or social movement. As a result, if feminists are constructed in a 'negative' manner, the movement itself also inherits these negative connotations. An example of this is found in a feature about American choreographer Agnes de Milles, who, when asked about feminism responded: 'I believe in equal rights, but the thing I don't like about feminism is really the feminists. There's a sexual kink in every one of them. No question. I don't hate men. I adore them' (Lawson 1976, p. D1). This passage de-legitimizes feminism (and feminists) because of their supposed hatred towards men and their lesbian tendencies. On an ideological level, a rejection of marriage and heterosexual unions threatens patriarchal and capitalist power, as marriage and the family have long been recognized as one of the key sites of women's exploitation and oppression (Bouchier

1983; Mitchell 1971; Stacey 2002). As radical feminist Ti-Grace Atkinson argued:

> The institution of marriage has the same effect the institution of slavery had. It separates people in the same category, disperses them, and keeps them from identifying as a class. The masses of slaves didn't recognize their condition either. To say that a woman is really 'happy' with her home and kids is as irrelevant as saying that the blacks were 'happy' being taken care of by Ol' Massa. She is defined by her maintenance role. Her husband is defined by his productive role. (Lear 1968, p. SM28)

Consequently, in order to retain hegemony, the discourse must construct the actions and the actors as 'deviant' or 'other'. This tactic was consistently reproduced throughout my sample period, demonstrating its historic effectiveness.

What is worthwhile noting, is that even though lesbians are often *discussed* in my sample, their *voices* are rarely used, giving rise to the argument that the media marginalize and de-legitimize voices outside dominant and elite circles (Shoemaker & Reese 1991), reproducing heterosexist discourses that ignore the various ways gays and lesbians have been unjustly treated in society (Freeman 2001).[6] Discourses of lesbianism were generally only used when anti-feminists and pro-family supporters raised the issue, as many (non-radical, heterosexual) feminists avoided the topic, recognizing that supporting homosexual rights was considered 'dreadful politics' (Margolis 1977b, p. 2). Additionally, when the lesbian issue was raised, news articles mostly focus on surface level details such as their 'deviant' lifestyles or appearances rather than on issues such as sexuality, human rights or gender role socialization. As one feature, covering a women's movement meeting, noted of its members:

> Neatly coiffed and demurely dressed, with their laps full of questionnaires and check-lists, these middle-aged women hardly look like the partisans they are. Far less do they resemble radical lesbians, the prototype, as some of their adversaries would have it, of their rank. (Bennetts 1978b, p. 25)

While constructing feminists as deviant played a large role in the maintenance of oppositional frames, it is also useful to examine how the movement itself was represented. When analysing the quantitative results, it becomes clear that several news stories labelled it 'ineffective' (30 articles), or 'unsupported' (10 articles), often claiming that the Second Wave was dying or dead, regardless of reality. Obituaries for feminism have appeared so regularly since the Victorian era that writers have labelled such claims 'False feminist death syndrome' (Smith 2003, n.p.). This syndrome is also apparent in my sample. For example, in 1976, *Daily Mirror* columnist Marjorie Proops wrote: 'It's all over bar the shouting. The battles have been fought and some of them were won. But the sex war women have waged for so long has now been lost'. Proops goes on to suggest women should 'give up trying to pretend we've won, when it's patently clear we've lost' (p. 16). In stating that the movement was dead, the discourse serves to limit the ways it could be talked about, and allows for an easy dismissal to any counter-discourse. This means that any legitimate breakthroughs and changes (both in the law and in people's consciousness) could be more easily ignored.

Marginalizing feminism

In addition to claiming that feminism is dead, ridicule, humour and condemnation were popular tools for opposing the movement and helped construct it as fragmented, radical, lacking progress, or an outright failure. Previous social movement scholars have also documented similar discourses (Barker-Plummer 2000; Gitlin 2003; Rhode 1995; Sheridan et al. 2007), noting that women are particularly the target for denigration and humour when they are old, fat, lesbians or women of colour (Butcher 1981 cited in Conboy 2006, p. 127). While the prevalence of such rhetoric was not quantified in this study, there is plenty of qualitative evidence available, particularly within *Daily Mirror* columns. One such column describes a 'Women's Enslavement Movement', that arose 'to counter this dangerous threat to women's comfort and security' (Ward 1972, p. 6). Here, the columnist Christopher Ward created a mock scenario of one of the Women's Enslavement Meetings, where members 'were heavily veiled to conceal their identities in case of reprisals from their liberated sisters, and they all wore short skirts, suspenders and black fish-net stockings'. The use of ridicule is an effective tool to demonstrate that Ward (and countless others) believed women had nothing to be liberated from, in their comfortable lifestyle as stay-at-home wives:

> A 'Mistress' whose mini-skirt wasn't quite long enough to conceal her black satin panties was the next to speak. She said: 'I entirely agree with our Chairlady.

'My husband came home from the office one night last week and burst into tears. He said he couldn't bear to exploit me any longer and pleaded with me to get a job too.

'How could I tell him that if I worked I wouldn't be able to spend afternoons with my lover?' (1972, p. 6)

While humour was one tool used to ridicule the movement and its goals in the *Daily Mirror*, other publications used more direct objections. One *Times* journalist declared: 'I would question some of their most publicized priorities and others, I would say, were downright silly' (Glynn 1981, p. 9). Such editorializing leaves little space for alternative perspectives on the movement.

Source use

Because frames are largely constructed by source use, it is worthwhile to examine whose voices are prioritized, and what message they bring. When examining the total number of sources, women were quoted 1055 times, compared to 342 quotes from men.[7] This finding is significant because Hall et al. (1978) and Becker (1967) argue that it is the powerful, whose high status and top positions privilege them to become 'primary definers' of topics. However, because women do not usually occupy powerful positions in society, their voices are often omitted (Gallagher 1981; Zoch & Turk 1998). These results, however, indicate that the Second Wave provided a unique opportunity for women's voices to be prioritized in the news. When specifically examining source identity, it becomes apparent that women's movement members were the primary definers (403 quotes), followed next by members of the public (229 quotes), journalists through the use of scare quotes (209 quotes), while surprisingly, anti-feminists/pro-family members were one of the least quoted groups (56 quotes). However, having a large number of feminist sources does not automatically ensure that the movement will be constructed in a positive manner. In fact, this research demonstrates that several prominent feminists were quoted making statements *against* the movement or other feminists – a de-legitimizing tool that was even more effective than the use of anti-feminist voices. An example of this can be seen in the *Daily Mirror*, which included a story on Betty Friedan, often labelled the mother of the women's movement, declaring the movement was dead:

Betty Friedan, the woman who twenty years ago tried to set the female world alight with burning speeches and burning bras, admits today that she's bitter, utterly disappointed and near to despair.

Two decades after the bright and hopeful beginning, she says of the feminist revolution: 'From all sides, now, they are tolling the bell to mourn the death of the women's movement in America.' (Proops 1977, p. 9)

When someone as prominent as Friedan claims feminism is dead, it becomes very difficult indeed for counter-positions to gain credibility. From a critical perspective, it is also worth noting that very few voices in all four publications were from what Ehrenreich describes as 'working-class' – or:

[A]ll those people who are not professionals, managers or entrepreneurs; who work for wages rather than salaries; and who spend their working hours variously lifting, bending, driving, motoring, typing, keyboarding, cleaning, providing physical care for others, loading, unloading, cooking, serving, etc. (1995 cited in Richardson 2007, p. 137).

This finding supports the assertions that the working-class are consistently under- or mis-represented in the news (Richardson 2007), and is particularly noteworthy in the *Daily Mirror,* a publication whose readership was predominantly working-class. This absence is perhaps in part explained by many tabloid papers' aspirational stance, meaning that they were likely to adopt many middle-class values and voices.

In many cases, middle-class voices were used specifically to frame feminists as a bunch of women 'discontented with their marriages, their families and sexual conventions' (Baker 1978, p. 19) and out to ruin housewives' good deal. In addition, the use of middle-class female voices opposing the movement constructed a view that women's liberation was not only bad for women, but that it was unwanted as well:

Is the Women's Liberation Movement inadvertently in danger of doing more harm than good to women they aim to liberate?
The answer to this question could be a definite YES [*sic*].
A report by a Finnish doctor of social sciences, Elina Haavlo-Mannila, reveals that many wives who have no careers feel threatened by the women's lib movement [...]
But all this talk about their status has made some of them restless and guilty. They're wondering whether they, too, oughtn't be out there fighting along with their sisters getting liberated.

Strongly as I come on for justice for women, admiring as I am about the selfless efforts of the few to improve the lot of the many, I'd be very sorry indeed if contented stay-at-home wives began to question their values and the role they play.

If a woman is happy to stay home and be a loving wife and mother she's entitled to do so without guiltily worrying whether she should engage in the battle for freedom. (Proops 1971, p. 11)

Backlash and postfeminism

Contrary to popular belief, discourses of backlash and postfeminism did not emerge in the wake of the Second Wave but can be found throughout the 1970s during the movement's height, and vary cross-nationally as a result of unique socio-cultural contexts and the ways the women's movements evolved. That postfeminist discourses emerged in the beginnings of the Second Wave indicates the extent to which patriarchal and capitalist ideologies contested feminist ideologies from an early stage, suggesting that feminism's eventual illegitimacy and notions of its redundancy were not constructed overnight, but took years to achieve hegemony.

While it is difficult to pinpoint one definition of postfeminism (Genz & Brabon 2009), I argue that it is a specific type of anti-feminism. Rather than merely rejecting the movement, postfeminist discourses 'incorporate, revise and depoliticise' (Stacey 1987 cited in Gill 2007, p. 268) feminism because its goals (appear to) have been achieved (Gerhard 2005, p. 40; McRobbie 2007; Tasker & Negra 2007); it is thought to be dead or dying; or has failed women, creating a stream of new 'problems' for them (Faludi 1992; McRobbie 2007). Similarly then, 'backlash'is also a specific type of anti-feminist discourse, and is often used interchangeably with 'postfeminism' to describe a whole new range of problems that feminism created for women, men or the family (Faludi 1992). However, despite this similarity, I argue that there are subtle differences. Backlash indicates that where feminist goals or tactics were once supported, they have now *gone too far*, and the public has no choice but to reject them. Backlash also says, 'you may be free and equal now ... but you have never been more miserable' (Faludi 1992, p. 1). Because of this overlap, I will only use the latter term when I am specifically referring to discourses stating that feminism is bad/harmful for women, has gone too far or has made women miserable.

The first thing to note when examining postfeminist discourses in the US and the UK is that they largely reproduce themselves over and over again, each time presenting themselves as a new phenomenon. For example, Faludi (1992) recounts news stories documenting the rise in female criminals – a 'new trend' that also emerged several times throughout the 1970s in the *Daily Mirror* (Davies 1973; Smith 1976). As Faludi goes on to note, rather than reacting to women's improved status, such discourses act as a 'pre-emptive strike that stops women long before they reach the finishing line', (p. 14) and are thus redeployed throughout periods of feminist activism.

A second trend worth highlighting is the variance in postfeminist discourses between the two nations – the likely result from the Second Wave's differing histories and tactics in pursuing goals such as equal rights. In Britain, for example, the Equal Pay and Sex Discrimination Acts came into effect in 1975, providing the grounds to claim that *all* women were now equal, and that feminism was unnecessary (Bouchier 1983). In the US, however, the ERA was debated for ten years before being defeated in 1982, meaning a wider range of arguments were needed to convince society of women's supposed equality and of feminism's irrelevance. Thus, each nation's varying legislative successes and failures explain one of the main variations in postfeminist discourses, including the US' 'legitimate goals, illegitimate movement discourse', and Britain's 'women's inequality? No problem' discourse.

Legitimate goal, illegitimate movement

The earliest and most prominent postfeminist discourse found in both *The New York Times* and the *Chicago Tribune* was what I have termed the 'legitimate goal, illegitimate movement' (LGIM) discourse. Emerging in the mid-1970s, it is classically postfeminist in that it incorporates feminisms' (positively constructed) goals, while depoliticizing and rejecting the movement itself. A contemporary example of this discourse today would be the 'I'm not a feminist, but ...' statement, where people declare their support for equal rights, abortion, government child care facilities and other ideals, all the while rejecting the feminist label. In both instances, the discourse suggests that specific goals can be or have been achieved without feminism's help, and while similar constructions were widely documented by Faludi (1992), the LGIM discourse is different because it seems to genuinely accept and promote equal rights, as opposed to constructing them as detrimental to women, men and society at large. The likely explanation for this difference is that the LGIM discourse emerged in the mid-1970s, before equal rights could really be said to have been 'won', perhaps indicating that rhetoric relaying its consequences was not yet in circulation. Regardless of the cause, such assertions are clearly postfeminist and *actively* acknowledge feminist goals, while attacking the movement or rendering it unnecessary (Gill 2007; McRobbie 2007).

One article that explicitly embodies the LGIM discourse is from the *Chicago Tribune*, titled: 'The Lady Is a Closet Feminist' (Landis 1974, p. D1). The word 'closet' here draws meaning from the then emerging gay rights movement, implying that one's identity (in this case, as a feminist) is hidden because of society's general intolerance to it. The journalist goes on to describe a woman whose husband 'does the grocery shopping and the vacuuming, but she'd never admit it to her bridge group'. However, despite her support for equal rights, 'she's a model of unquestioning femininity, every hair in layered place, gleamer and lip gloss perfect, clothes not bursting her husband's budget but fashionable. No one would suspect that beneath this tranquil exterior beats the heart of a closet feminist'. Here, the author accepts the notion that to be a feminist is to be some sort of deviant – something to hide from society. Furthermore, feminism and femininity are not perceived to go hand in hand, as most feminists are thought to have 'failed' as women, are 'unattractive, unshapely, too smart, aggressive, demanding, altogether social misfits'. Such words are powerful tools used to de-legitimize the movement through discrediting its members. However it is important to note that this discourse goes beyond a simple rejection of feminists and is more complex. While the article acknowledges a dismissal of 'women's libbers', it expressly recognizes the legitimacy of several goals, particularly equal rights:

> It has taken her a long while to get where she is. When the most recent wave of feminist consciousness raising started in the early '60s, the bra burning turned her and a lot of other respectable ladies off [...] But slowly the feminist movement started taking on signs of recognition: The President and other politicians began carefully adding the words 'and women' to their speeches. Women began to enter law and medical schools in unprecedented numbers. And the media began highlighting the unique and outstanding tasks women were accomplishing outside the home. How could anyone argue with 'equal pay for equal work?'

Even as the article continues to acknowledge women's improved status and changing gender roles ('he does the shopping and vacuuming, she goes to the lumber yard and helps file their income tax'), these feminists are still described as 'closeted', suggesting that while feminist goals might be acceptable, to be 'outed' as a feminist was not:

One 45-year-old executive secretary, a closet feminist, surprised her boss of 20 years recently when she asked to be admitted to the corporation management training program. Another one, a single teacher, has submitted her application to be assistant superintendent of her school district. Both disavow any sympathy with the 'women's libbers.'

In addition to denying the feminist label and highlighting it as 'other' through the use of scare quotes, this passage demonstrates the juxtaposition between 'equal rights supporters' and 'feminists'. At no point does the article try to explain who or what feminists are, or what they believe, and it certainly does not challenge the feminist stereotype but uses more colloquial, derogatory language such as 'women's libbers' to define them, even as the journalist appears to be fairly accepting of feminism. Perhaps equal rights were not demonized because they struck a chord with people. As the journalist reasoned, 'How could anyone argue with equal pay for equal work?' It is in passages like these that we witness hegemony at work. Gramsci (1971) states that ideologies strive to retain dominance through a process of negotiation, mediation and compromise. As a result, one can expect to witness alterations in dominant ideologies over time as they negotiate with and contest against counter-hegemonic ideologies in a battle to convince the public they are best equipped to fulfil the public's interests and needs. In this particular case, patriarchy – which organizes sexual differences ideologically (by stating that masculinity and femininity are 'natural'), and hierarchically (where masculinity is dominant and femininity is subordinate) – appears to be in a process of negotiation and compromise with liberal feminist demands. It is willing to accept that women might be entitled to equal pay and opportunities but refuses to allow more radical feminist critiques of gender roles that could erode male dominance. As a result, equal rights are viewed as acceptable, but (radical) feminism is constructed as a threat to the social order and is de-legitimized as a result.

While the LGIM discourse was prevalent in the US, I found no equivalent in my British publications. Instead, the most common postfeminist discourse was the sentiment, particularly in the *Daily Mirror*, that women are already equal.

Women's inequality? no problem

As a result of the relatively early passage of both the Equal Pay and Sex Discrimination Acts in 1975, it became common to find *Daily Mirror* articles pronouncing women equal to men, and therefore the Second Wave as unnecessary or redundant. When going back to the problems and solutions to women's inequality/oppression 'asked' of the text, 'sexism/discrimination' was the most common response. Such response is particularly problematic because it argues that women's subservient position in society is an *individual*, rather than a *structural*, problem. In doing so, it removes the need to question society's (patriarchal, capitalist, racist, heterosexist) values and instead directs attention at reforming individual values (Bradley 2003). The second most common response, which is perhaps more problematic, was that there was, in fact, 'no problem' at all, because women were already equal (25 articles). Twenty-one of these articles were from the *Daily Mirror,* and while clearly not hegemonic (14 per cent of all *Daily Mirror* articles), its presence is notable.[8]

Contrary to the LGIM discourse, the women's inequality? No problem (WINP) discourse is classically postfeminist, in that it 'takes feminism into account' by stating women have already achieved equality so further action is unnecessary (Gerhard 2005; McRobbie 2007; Tasker & Negra 2007). While the Sex Discrimination and Equal Pay Acts enabled journalists to insist on feminism's redundancy, there was also evidence in the *Daily Mirror* that these sentiments had existed prior to this legislation – perhaps as part of a pre-emptive strike against feminism. One letter to the editor that acts as a riposte against the formation of the women's movement explained:

> We hear a lot about the Women's Liberation Movement. Liberation from what? Don't these women, mainly young and unmarried, enjoy being feminine?
>
> I'm 44, and I have always thought that women enjoyed being as attractive and desirable as possible.
>
> And from a financial viewpoint, women have never been so well off, nor had such equality of opportunity. Are these liberationists merely frustrated females? (Mrs.) D.M.M., Kettering, Northants (No Byline 1970, p. 9).

By focusing on the fact that women have never had such 'equality of opportunity' rather than on why these 'frustrated females' are still fighting and what they want, the letter de-legitimizes their goals by stating that there is nothing wrong in the first place, and therefore nothing needs to change. Furthermore, playing women off one another (feminine and attractive vs. unfeminine and ugly) is one of patriarchy's most effective tactics in maintaining hegemony (Levack 2009). Such arguments subvert feminist critiques by labelling the movement redundant while reinforcing patriarchal ideologies through stereotyping feminists as unfeminine, single, and 'frustrated', implying that the two do not go hand in hand, and that femininity should be their primary concern.

While such pre-emptive strikes were common, later articles `took feminism into account' by documenting how women's quest for equality was so successful, men were now the ones in need of a liberation movement. 'Year of the Burning Y-Front' (Hall 1978, p. 13) opened by stating: 'Look out girls! Downtrodden men are after something you have already got – equality. Moves are afoot to make 1979 the Year of Men's Lib. Bonfires of Y-fronts could soon be burning in the streets'. Others comment on how women had achieved equal rights but were not willing to accept equal responsibilities: 'You can't have it all your own way, girls' (Wilson 1972, p. 25) deplored how women unfairly demanded equal pay and treatment even though they were not performing equal work. Such sentiments could also be said to fit into a larger 'backlash' discourse akin to ones identified by Faludi (1992), where a series of new 'problems' for women, men and society were identified. A further discussion of backlash can be found in the next chapter, which deals specifically with equal rights and their supposedly 'negative' consequences.

Though the above examples demonstrate various ways in which the women's movement and its members were de-legitimized, particularly through the use of postfeminist discourses, one of the most powerful and pervasive tools found within all four publications, but particularly within the *Daily Mirror,* were discourses stating that feminists subverted 'natural' gender roles. This will serve as my second Case Study. While I focus specifically on two *Daily Mirror* articles, I could have easily substituted them with countless others and drawn similar conclusions. The first article used is a feature interviewing 11 year-old Linda Greally (see Figure 2.3), who argued that that equality between men and women is wrong, and the second is about housewife Adrienne Roosenbloom, who explained why she does not want to be a man (see Figure 2.4).

Case Study 2 – the *Daily Mirror* and women's 'natural' role

Located on page 12, between an advertisement for stencils and a centrefold article, and above a cartoon, this article is prominently placed on the page, running about a third of a column wide and the full vertical length of the page. At the top of the article sits a photo of Linda Greally, the 11-year-old who thinks that 'it's wrong to be equal', as the article's

Figure 2.3 'It's wrong to be equal' *Daily Mirror*

headline states (Evans 1970, p. 12). In the photo, Linda is looking off camera wistfully, chin on her hand. She looks innocent, and the caption reads, 'Women are different'. The combination of headline, photo and caption sets the tone for the article and sums up a major discourse within both this article and this publication in general – that men and women are innately different – and that it is therefore wrong for women

Figure 2.4 'Why Adrienne doesn't want to be a man' *Daily Mirror*

to try and change their 'natural' roles. This discourse is prioritized in the article, as Linda's is the only voice present, resulting in an unchallenged opposition to 'women's libbers' and the defence of current gender roles. As Gitlin (2003) argued, the absence of alternative voices is an important part of the hegemonic process, where dissenting views are marginalized or routinely ignored, and is demonstrated in the passage below:

> Men would be hopeless at home. They wouldn't know how to work the electrical things and it would be very unfair to children to have men around them.
>
> Mothers understand children better. If a boy ran home crying because he'd had a fight and got hurt a father would tell him to go back and hit harder next time, whereas a mother would have the sense to comfort him and tell him not to fight if he's going to lose [...]
>
> Men and women are very different you know. Women like to talk about cooking and fashion and men like to discuss football and money, which is best talked about outside the home.

Linda here (re)produces ideology surrounding traditional gender roles and the belief that men are poor nurturers ('it would be unfair to children') and helpless around the house with domestic duties, and that they (and certain topics of discussion) belong in the public sphere. Linda argues that equality is bad not only for women and men, but also for the children, who have no choice in the matter yet have to suffer the consequences. The construction of gender roles as 'natural' within this and other publications is dominant, and could be referred to as a 'metanarrative' or a 'master frame'. These remain hegemonic because they are both pervasive and credible beyond empirical scrutiny (Koenig 2004, p. 3) and are seen to stem from biological differences between the sexes, rather than as social constructs. This gender essentialism – often fuelled by popular psychology – gained momentum in the 1970s and 1980s, and provides powerful biological arguments against changes in gender roles by constructing human nature as fixed (Fine 2010; Hasinoff 2009).

A similar ideological construction can be seen in the second of many *Daily Mirror* articles. This article, titled 'Why Adrienne doesn't want to be a man' (Palmer 1976b, p. 7), features housewife and mother Adrienne Roosenbloom, who emphatically states that a woman's job is to stay home and care for her husband and children. This is one of three articles on a page titled 'inequality: part two on how women lost the sex war' with a photo of a thumb pointing down, indicating the publication's opposition to equal rights. Next to the article on Adrienne is a column where the author brags about his outward chauvinism through the title: 'I'm a pig and proud of it!' (Hagerty 1976a, p. 7), followed directly below from a response from his wife on why she is happily married and hopes their son grows up to be a male chauvinist pig, too (Hagerty 1976b). When examining the overall page then, the articles' placement already positions it in opposition to women's liberation. Featuring a photo of Adrienne and her two small children, the caption reads: 'Adrienne Roosenbloom: "A mother's job is with her children," ' and sums up Adrienne's argument that men and women have different roles to play in society (men provide for the family while women nurture it). This position not only places women in a subordinate state of motherhood but also idealizes this role through arguments of biology and destiny (Anderson 1999; p. 41). Accordingly, Adrienne argues that men and women should be content with their differing roles:

> Adrienne Roosenbloom is a housewife and a mother. And proud of it.
> She doesn't want to be independent or equal and says: 'I've no time for women who dump their kids and go out to work.'
> She would rather be at home, caring for her family, than out fighting for female freedom [...]
> It is most important for a mother to bring up her own children. A mother's job is with her children and wife's is with her husband. (Palmer 1976b, p. 7)

Once again, the discourse serves to naturalize gender roles and demonize anyone who states otherwise ('I have no time for women who *dump* their kids and go out to work'). Throughout the article, Adrienne constructs differences between men and women as 'natural' and seeks to demonize and label 'deviant' anyone who challenges these roles: 'You either stay single and be independent or you get married and look after your family'. The discourse presents middle-class values and ignores those women who cannot afford (or who choose not) to stay home to look after their families. Additionally, Adrienne suggests that while women might not have equality, they are certainly not second-class citizens. Instead, she insists, 'We have a different role to play and we should be content with it'. What Adrienne ignores is that the role women play is one of subservience to men, where their (sexual) labour is exploited. The discourse also reinforces the traditional private/public binary where (middle-class) women are *tolerated* in the public sphere until they can find a man who can support them.

Consequently, their labour outside the home is therefore understood as temporary. When examining the narrative and 'what makes the story hang together' (Deacon et al. 1999), it becomes clear that both articles oppose feminism based on the premise that women are not suited to take part in the public sphere – their place is within the domestic sphere as carers or nurturers.

In any news story, the use of sources plays an important role in the overall narrative or frame, and indicates what view or position is being supported (Ross 2007; Tuchman 1972). Both articles provide evidence of how 'ordinary' members of the public's voices are used to oppose 'women's libbers' (as they are often referred to). If read in this way, then not only does the use of Linda and Adrienne's voices tell us that the women's movement is rejected and understood as unnatural, but that this is a view widely held by most 'ordinary' women. That such views are found within the predominantly working-class *Daily Mirror* is perhaps, at first glance, paradoxical. However, as one *Chicago Tribune* article explains: 'the blue-collar wife has spent much of her life dependent on a man for her security and happiness', and strongly believes in the 'family unit' as a means of survival (Winter 1974, p. D3). Perhaps as a result, one should expect the support of traditional gender roles in such a publication.

Because gender roles were deeply entrenched and thought of as 'natural', many people began to question what women need liberating from in the first place. As Linda Greally put it:

> I really don't see why those liberation ladies are so unhappy and want to change everything. If they can vote for who they want to be Prime Minister and choose the man they want to marry, then, really, they're having their fair share, aren't they?

However, at one point, Linda briefly suggests that it would be nice to have economic independence (which she views as being the result of necessity rather than choice), though she quickly asserts that the benefits do not outweigh the costs:

> Some women of course have to find a career for themselves. In a way, it's nice for them since they can just go out and buy a carpet without having to ask anybody.
> But those ladies must feel envious of wives who have nice husbands who would buy the carpet for them.
> I think those liberation ladies are a little bit silly.

Interestingly, independence here is understood in terms of consumer freedom, where a woman is able to purchase whatever she chooses without having to rely on or consult her husband. While economic independence was an important message of the Second Wave, it went beyond merely purchasing power and extended to one's ability to support oneself so as not to be forced to remain in abusive or unhappy marriages (see de Beauvoir 1989).

While this article is not latent with explosive language about the 'women's libbers', or 'bra-burners', it is ideologically rich in other ways and is a good example of how discourses reinforced women and men's 'natural' gender roles, thus constructing the women's movement and its members as illegitimate, deviant and 'silly'. If, as Richardson (2007) suggests, we rely on the discourses present to reveal something about the society in which they were produced, then it becomes clear that a hegemonic discourse, at least within this newspaper during my sample period, 'portrays the dominant [masculine] codes as reasonable and right and the alternative [women fighting for equal rights – or worse] as insignificant' (Beck 1998, p. 145), thus upholding patriarchal, capitalist and heterosexist ideologies.

Complex feminism

The final and smallest frame in the sample (101 articles, or 18 per cent of total) includes those articles that constructed feminism as a complex or contradictory movement. Within this frame, there are two types of articles. The first are those that present feminism in a contradictory manner through the use of dualisms, where any view must be accompanied by an opposing view, and fulfils journalistic norms of 'balance'. However, one consequence of always presenting an oppositional view is that questions around how knowledge and meaning are produced are ignored (Strutt 1994). In keeping with notions of balance, journalists uncritically (re)present dichotomies, as any analysis derived from the journalist's own expertise would be viewed as bias (Creedon 1993b; Strutt 1994).

The second type of story here is where balance is not adhered to, but feminism is still presented as a complex social movement. Such articles are particularly noteworthy because they provide evidence that journalists were at times able to construct issues in a more diverse frame than merely good vs. bad, and report on grey aspects of the movement, and thus avoided minimalizing constructions. For example, going back to news on black feminism, rather than merely reporting it as in conflict with white feminism, many articles engaged with their concern that gender was not the only, or predominant, form of oppression for some women, but that race, too, oppressed people in different ways. As one article articulated, the 'traditional role of the Southern white woman as "decoration" for her husband, contrasted with the black woman's traditional role as servant and manual worker' (Reeds 1975, p. 51). Consequently, rather than merely criticizing the white feminist movement for excluding black people, such articles explored reasons behind differences and demonstrated the diversity within feminist political theory and activism.

While many of these articles carried a mixture of supportive or oppositional positions, the overall narrative is more difficult to judge and often includes mixed messages. From a critical perspective, while I would prefer to see 'positive' news of feminism, the reality is that the Second Wave was a complex movement, at times espousing contradictory messages (men are our friends, vs. men are the enemy). Such articles could consequently be said to represent more accurately the nature of the movement, and therefore should be viewed as an alternative to hegemonic journalistic conventions.

Summary

This chapter explored the various ways the Second Wave and its members were represented in four mainstream daily newspapers during the movement's most active political period. A mixture of content and critical discourse analysis was used to elucidate national, cross-national and longitudinal variances and similarities of news of coverage and to analyse what these say about British and American society between 1968 and 1982. That feminism has been represented in a diverse, often contradictory, manner in this sample is perhaps unsurprising, given the movements' differing size, means of organization, political ideology, efforts into public promotion and use of spokespeople. Such differences were brought to light with the help of cross-national comparisons that highlighted, for example, the differing nature of feminist organization between the two nations. Highly organized in the US, a majority of articles focused on the activities of major feminist organizations such as NOW, the NWPC, the NBFO, or other anti-feminist groups (Happiness of Women). Evidence of similar highly organized groups was absent in the UK, where, Ferree's notes, informal networking groups were more common (Ferree 1987). Here, only a handful of articles constructed the movement as a cohesive organization (such as the Six Point Group, the Fawcett Society, or smaller conscious-raising groups consisting of neighbourhood women), or followed specific movement events or demonstrations. Rather, articles often referred to singular feminists or 'women's libbers', a term suggesting more of an individual acceptance of beliefs in women's rights than a cohesive movement – a problematic construction for those who want to foster collective social change.

Despite these cross-national variances, three main frames emerged in the construction of feminism: those of support (279 articles or 50 per cent), those of opposition (174 articles or 31 per cent) and those that constructed feminism as contradictory or complex (101 articles or 18 per cent). One of the biggest surprises to emerge from this research is the prevalence of supportive frames, particularly in two of my supposedly conservative publications – the *Chicago Tribune* and *The Times*. Such findings indicate that political leanings are not necessarily the best means of judging how social issues will be reported, and perhaps suggests that decisions by individual editors or journalists at times can have an impact. Despite overall support for the movement and its members, I cannot help but be critical of the fact that much coverage legitimized a narrow conceptualization of feminism (read, liberal, middle-class, heterosexual and reformist) at the expense of more radical or revolutionary versions. While I understand that the watering down or silencing of radical voices is an inevitable part of social movement development (Davis 1991), labelling certain ideas as radical (and thus deviant) serves to draw 'boundaries around women's aspirations', and inhibit moves towards greater social change (Freeman 2001, p. 247). Furthermore, the legitimization and de-legitimization of certain forms of feminism can be understood as part of the hegemonic process where dominant ideologies must incorporate counter-ideologies and dissenting voices if they want to remain in power (Gitlin 2003; Gramsci 1971). In this case, patriarchy and capitalism made concessions for liberal, reformist feminisms that, for the most part, failed to challenge the hierarchical nature of society. Consequently, despite women's growing acceptance in the public sphere, gender roles, and thus gendered hierarchies, remained largely intact, while any ideas that challenged the social structure became labelled 'radical' and were demonized by (liberal) feminists and anti-feminists alike.

As a result, while not numerically dominant, I would argue that oppositional frames attained cultural hegemony, particularly in regards to 'militant' or 'radical' feminism. These discourses were constructed through the use of patriarchal, capitalist, racist and heterosexist ideologies that upheld a normative femininity which was white, middle-class, heterosexual and located primarily within the private sphere. Specific tactics included labelling anyone in breach of these norms as 'deviant', often through the use of ridicule and humour; of postfeminist discourses that acknowledged, engaged with and ultimately depoliticized feminism by arguing its goals had been achieved; and a focus on gender essentialism which discredited social explanations for the organization of society, while upholding oppressive binaries such as masculinity/femininity, private/public sphere and consumer/producer, claiming they are natural and 'fixed'.

Finally, a smaller number of articles constructed the movement and its members as complex and diverse, recognizing that there was no single, uniform women's movement, and that identities such as gender, race and class oppressed women in different ways. While perhaps one could argue that such articles 'sat on the fence' in their judgements regarding the movement, I am more optimistic that through seeking understanding, rather than 'balance', the Second Wave was more accurately represented.

3
Reporting Equal Rights, 1968–82

[A] central tenet of feminism is that gender relations hold power relations. Any increase in power for women must therefore decrease power for men – it is thus understandable why they [men] reject it. (Edley & Whetherell 2001, p. 439)

Introduction

Feminists have long sought greater legal, social and economic rights for women. While they recorded many successes throughout the nineteenth and twentieth centuries, including the right to vote; own or inherit property; and hold judicial, political or civil office, systemic inequalities persisted in both the US and UK. As a result, gaining greater social, legal and economic rights not only became a major focal point for activism in the Second Wave (Anderson 1991; Bouchier 1983; Bradley 2003; Margolis 1993), but also in how the movement became defined (Bradley 2003). This chapter examines how 'equal rights' – defined in the broadest sense – were publicly constructed in *The Times*, the *Daily Mirror*, *The New York Times*, and the *Chicago Tribune* during the movement's most active political period, 1968 to 1982.

Although British and American feminists sought equal rights through various means, they achieved differing levels of success for their efforts. In terms of legislation, Britain passed two equal rights Acts relatively quickly. In 1970, Parliament approved the Equal Pay Act, which stipulated that employers must pay equal wages to men and women if engaged in the same work, or work of equal value.[1] Five years later, the Sex Discrimination Act was also passed, preventing employers from discriminating against a person based on sex or marital status. Along with this latter Act, the Equal Opportunities Commission (EOC) was established as a governing body meant to oversee employers' compliance with the new legislation.

What is also noteworthy about the history of equal rights campaigns in the UK is the prominent role played by trade unions. While there is ample evidence that the unions did not always support equal pay (see Davis, n.d.), many women came to feminism through such organizations, which raised their consciousness about the injustice of performing similar work while receiving a fraction of the pay. Trade unions were also powerful bodies to be reckoned with at the time because of their ability to pressure employers, lobby the government and mobilize large groups of working-class men and women (Coote & Campbell 1982, p. 37).[2] As a result, they, along with feminist MPs such as the Labour Party's Barbara Castle, were instrumental in passing equality legislation in the UK. The absence of larger, explicitly 'feminist' interventions and activism will be discussed in more detail throughout this chapter.

The US and the Equal Rights Amendment

While trade unions also played an important role in equal rights campaigns in the American women's movement,[3] large feminist organizations such as NOW and the NWPC were also at the forefront of highly publicized campaigns for equality. Although a form of equal rights legislation was passed in 1963, many feminists did not believe it was far-reaching enough and joined campaigns to pass the Equal Rights Amendment (ERA).[4] Although tabled each Congressional session since 1923, the amendment, which sought to alter the federal Constitution and guarantee equality under the law regardless of gender, finally passed through both houses of Congress in 1972. Initially given a seven-year deadline in which ratification was required by a minimum of 38 states, it received a controversial three-year extension in 1978, the year before it was due to expire. Despite the amendment's extension, it was eventually defeated in 1982, requiring ratification from only three more states.

News of equal rights

Since the emergence of the Civil Rights movement in the mid 1950s, equal rights have played a prominent role in the news (Butler & Paisley 1978), with the Second Wave being only one of several new social movements interrogating and challenging oppression and discrimination in

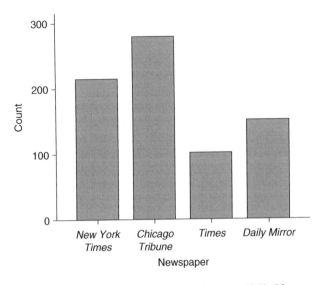

Figure 3.1   News articles on equal rights by publication, 1968–82

society. After searching the digital databases, it was perhaps unsurprising that 747 articles were gathered (see Figure 3.1), each dealing with women's (in)equality, suggesting that as a topic, 'equal rights' was considered more newsworthy than 'feminism'. Typical headlines include: 'Women Turn to Courts to Gain Rights' (Margolick 1982, p. A21), 'Firm Stand on Equal Pay for Women' (Wigham 1969, p. 8),'Bus Girls Demand a Fare Wage' (Connew 1976, p. 13) and 'Equal Rights Approved in Maine: Seven to Go' (No Byline 1974c, p. S9). Once again, the statistics demonstrate that more articles were published in the US than Britain (494 vs. 253 articles), likely as a result of the national ERA campaign, which intertwined with formal institutions and organizations such as the law, federal and state politics, employers and unions, which are regularly reported in the traditional news 'beat' system (McCarthy et al. 1996; Mills 1997).

Cross-national comparisons

Similar to news of the Second Wave, equal rights were addressed through different lenses in each nation. My American publications focused heavily on pro- and anti-ERA campaigns, and while much was written about the amendment's progress, amount of support, its benefits and drawbacks, there was less general discussion about the merits or pitfalls of equal rights more generally. The debate in these publications, therefore, was not about whether women should be (or are) equal to men, but whether the best way to achieve equality (or protection) was through a constitutional amendment. For example, the editorial, 'Fasting for the ERA' (Editorial 1982, p. A4) argued:

> From the beginning, the ERA has had both justice and precedent on its side. Women have been discriminated against, with the full support of the law, since this Republic was founded. Even today, President Reagan's belief to the contrary, there are state and federal laws that saddle women with an inferior status. Constitutional amendments were required to secure the rights of black Americans, and another was needed to admit women into the democratic process. One can hardly object to another constitutional amendment to confirm the nation's commitment to the legal equality of men and women.

Here, the ERA was seen as just one more necessary piece of legislation to guarantee women the equality to which they should be entitled. In contrast, one oppositional letter to the editor insisted that the ERA would erode protections that are currently afforded to women and the family and should therefore be rejected:

> Without ERA, women will have the choice of giving their time to their families and caring for others, instead of being coerced into taking care of themselves (as they would have to if society does not protect them in the nurturing role). It is impossible to protect wives and mothers by writing identical, interchangeable, unisex laws as would be required by ERA. ERA would have created a new need for women to work outside the home as a result of undermining the wife's legal right to support, as the family ceases to be the basic unit of society. Without these laws homemaker wives have no share in that wealth. (Letter to the Editor 1980, p. A2)

Neither of these articles discusses the benefits or drawbacks of equal rights themselves, but instead focuses on how women are best served or protected.[5]

In contrast, the *Daily Mirror* and *The Times* addressed equal rights through a much broader lens than equal rights legislation alone, although this constituted part of the coverage. Examples include: 'The

Wise Woman's Guide to Equality' (Burton 1975, p. 5), 'Unions warn on equal pay for women' (Law 1974, p. 11) and 'Where women provide their own discrimination' (Lester 1981, p. 9). Rather than debating the benefits or drawbacks of equal rights legislation (it was assumed to be a logical means of enforcing women's rights), these articles focused on the merits or drawbacks of equal rights themselves. While equal rights were frequently supported in *The Times*, the *Daily Mirror* tended to produce stories discussing the various ways in which feminism would harm or had harmed society. For example, the column 'Where have all the ladies gone?' (No Byline 1972a, p. 11) lamented women's loss of 'ladylike' qualities as a result of their many 'new-found freedoms'. Another insisted that equality would turn women into 'little more than men without penises' (Bedford 1971a, p. 9), which, in turn, would cause men to lose their 'natural' desire to protect them. These articles insist not only that such changes are unwanted and negative, but also that as women continued to gain equality, their feminine virtues – highly prized in a patriarchal society – would be lost.

Individual vs. collective change

A common occurrence in many of my American articles was their frequent reporting of large organizational efforts (feminist or otherwise) to pass (or oppose) the ERA. Examples include: '100,000 Join March for Extension of Rights Amendment Deadline' (DeWitt 1978, p. 11), '3,000 Heed Call to "Join Us, Sisters" in March and Rally Here for Equality' (Johnston 1972, p. 54), 'Equal Rights Plan and Abortion are opposed by 15,000 at Rally' (Klemsrud 1976, p. 32) and '6,000 March on Capitol for ERA' (Fritsch 1976, p. 3). Because many hundred protests occur each year, 'it takes an enormous movement of people through an area to make a strong news story', meaning that only the largest demonstrations were likely to receive coverage (Cochrane, personal interview, 2010). One of the American Second Wave's strengths was its ability to convene large crowds of people and, consequently, attract media attention. Conversely, because Britain lacked such an ongoing equal rights news peg, articles tended instead to track *individual* women's experiences of (in)equality – a factor likely accounting for the lower overall number of articles in this sample. However, this is where the similarities end and intra-national differences emerge. Within the *Daily Mirror*, articles focused on women's attempts to use the Equal Pay or Sex Discrimination Acts to effect change. When examining news pegs, 14 articles (9 per cent of the paper's total) reported on tribunals, court cases or hearings, while 38 articles (25 per cent of the paper's total) were classed as feature stories about women using the new legislation to attain equal pay or access to previously banned spaces. Examples of such articles include: 'Judge Gives a Boost to Women's Lib' (No Byline 1971, p. 16), 'Waitress clears up pay dodge' (Davies 1976, p. 5), 'Bank Girls in Pay Battle' (No Byline 1976, p. 4) and 'Battling blonde calls the law in to fight for equal pay' (Daniels 1976, p. 7). Judging from news coverage, both Acts passed with little apparent controversy in the *Daily Mirror* and *The Times* and received widespread support before and after their passage, particularly from trade unions and MPs.[6] For example, there is evidence that equal pay legislation was demanded at the 1969 Trades Union Congress (TUC) meeting, which unanimously passed 'a motion calling on the Government to act immediately on the principle of equal pay for equal work' (No Byline 1969b, p. 8). Even after the 1970 passage of the Equal Pay Act, union leaders continued to campaign for women's equal rights, arguing: 'The passing of the Equal Pay Bill earlier this year will not by itself give women equal pay. The unions must make it a reality' (Jones 1970, p. 4). According to journalism scholars, conflict is an important news value (Galtung & Ruge 1965; Harcup & O'Neill 2001), and perhaps these Acts' lack of conflict prevented them from gaining widespread media attention. In fact, while references to both Acts can be found scattered throughout coverage, most accounts emerged after 1975 and report on individual or small groups' attempts to gain equal pay or opportunities in male-dominated spheres. In such instances, individual women were pitted against employers, bars or clubs, thus providing a sense of conflict that fit with news conventions. For example, the lead to one such news report writes: 'Eight angry bank girls claimed yesterday that their bosses don't balance the books properly when it comes to pay' (No Byline 1976, p. 4).

Where the *Daily Mirror* covered court cases, tribunals and women's attempts to utilize both Acts, *The Times* in contrast employed features (32 articles or 31 per cent of the paper's total) to explore women's new roles in society, particularly in international contexts. Such coverage indicates the paper's awareness that feminism did not only occur in Western countries. For example 'Women: equality in cities but not in rural areas' (Mukherji 1973, p. XI) explored women's status in India, and 'Principal Roles For Women' (Appiah 1969, p. VII) focused on women in Ghana. Other countries examined include: Bangladesh, Belgium, Canada, China, Egypt, Finland, France, Iran, Japan, Lebanon, Kuwait, Russia, Spain, Sweden, Thailand and Turkey. While a more detailed discussion of international coverage in *The Times* will be addressed in

Case Study 4, it is worth pointing out that there is a very strong focus in both its national and international coverage on women's equality and status. For example, 'Women win their way to higher public posts' (El-Calamawy 1969, p. 7) discussed Egyptian women's increased move into paid employment and higher education, while 'Drive to lure more women on to labor market' (No Byline 1971a, p. 4) noted Sweden's use of women to fill labour shortages. Both British papers demonstrate a stronger focus on labour issues than their US counterparts, which is unsurprising given that the latter had a comparatively weak labour movement (Jacoby 1976; Margolis 1993, p. 388).

Another key difference between *The Times* and the *Daily Mirror* is that the latter tended to focus on how 'ordinary' women were fighting for equal pay, while the former reported on equal rights stories involving 'elite' members of society. Such differences support the distinction between newspaper formats in the UK, where the tabloids tend to report on personal stories, often from a layperson's perspective, while the broadsheets report institutional stories and thus rely on voices of authority (Conboy 2006; Macdonald 2000). Examples of this elite focus in *The Times* includes coverage of how government campaigns were established to evaluate women's roles in British society, assessing what could be done from a policy angle to improve them. One such article, titled: 'Women at work: the five wasted years' (Gibb 1981, p. 11), relayed a House of Common's session on how the government's past economic and social policies had marginalized women and outlined strategies to improve their situation. Other articles involved interviews with prominent feminist politicians, or even political parties, such as, 'Belgium: A women's party goes into battle' (Bywater 1974, p. 9) or 'France's Feminine Feminist' (Matthews 1969, p. 11).

Gendered newsroom?

In regards to the overall number of male and female journalists, there was no significant gender divide when reporting equal rights (see Table 3.1). In total, women authored 312 articles (42 per cent), compared to 235 by men (32 per cent).[7] This indicates that, unlike the Second Wave, which was overwhelmingly considered a 'woman's story' (Molotch 1978), equal rights was a topic more inclusive of men. However, despite greater parity in overall figures, gender divides regarding genre remain clear. For example, men were still more likely to write news reports (110 articles or 43 per cent) than women (72 articles or 28 per cent), indicating that when pressing equal rights stories emerged, or when

Table 3.1 Journalist gender by genre, 1968–82

Genre	Journalist gender			
	Male	Female	Unclear/unknown	Total
News report	110	72	76	258
News brief	3	1	32	36
Feature	69	139	38	246
Column	38	49	4	91
Letter to the Editor	9	37	22	68
Editorial	4	0	24	28
Backgrounder	0	1	1	2
Agony aunt	0	2	1	3
Photo	0	0	1	1
Women's/lifestyle section	2	11	1	14
Total	235	312	200	747

they involved traditional party politics, the economy or legislation, they remained part of the masculine domain. Conversely, women were more likely to write features (139 vs. 69 articles), letters to the editor (37 vs. 9 articles) and columns (37 vs. 9 articles), reinforcing gendered genre norms that 'soft' news is women's domain (see also Global Media Monitoring Project 2005, 2010). Furthermore, while some have argued that the rise of 'opinion journalism' represents a decline in journalistic quality (McNair 2008), postmodernists believe that there is more than one 'correct' way to view the world, which includes subjective perspectives and personal experiences (Bryson 2003, p. 233). As one editor argued:

> Who would live in a community where the only 'facts' that could be expressed were those certified by a higher authority? [...] The challenge is to find new voices and to give space to people who are not just the easily recognized political and civic leaders. (Phillips 1990 cited in Wahl-Jorgensen 2002, pp. 76–77)

Consequently, columns and letters to the editor provide a potential forum to challenge gendered notions of what constitutes 'news', creating a space where personal matters can become politicized (Phillips 2008). That equal rights stories were not always written in the traditional, (highly valued) inverted pyramid style, where 'facts' and authoritative voices construct the narrative, should be viewed as a step forward for feminist theorists who reject notions of balance and objectivity for their reproduction of normative accounts of reality (Hissey & Strutt 1992). Instead, I argue that alternative formats such as features and columns can provide greater opportunities to challenge current journalistic norms and conventions by affording more space and context to issues than hard news stories can provide. Furthermore, soft news stories are not bound by requirements of objectivity or balance, and do not necessarily seek to create dualisms required from hard news (Strutt 1994).

Framing equal rights

In order to better examine the nuances of coverage, and explore how feminist goals of equal rights were constructed, frame analysis will once again be utilized as a means of organizing the results. After analysing 28 themes present in coverage, I identified three main frames: support for equal rights (512 articles); opposition to equal rights (122 articles); and equal rights as contradictory/complex (113 articles). The rest of this chapter explores these frames in more depth, analysing the range of discourses present. Overall, I argue that while the amount of support equal rights received is both laudable and a step towards more structural forms of change, liberal feminist perspectives are privileged throughout all four papers and are problematic because they ignore systemic inequalities in society. Consequently, the discourse demonstrates the hegemonic function of the mass media, which, as a capitalist, patriarchal institution, absorbs the most palatable aspects of equal rights (such as legislative changes or calls for 'equal pay for work of equal value'), while rejecting radical calls for reform or revolution.

Support for equal rights

Although the Second Wave movement was not always publicly supported, it is encouraging to see one of its main goals, equal rights, achieving widespread support throughout this sample. In total, 512 articles supported equal rights through constructing them as beneficial for women, men and society in general (33 articles or 4 per cent of total), as being generally supported (82 articles or 11 per cent of total), as only fair (13 articles or 2 per cent of total) and as providing new opportunities for women in the public sphere (45 articles or 6 per cent of total). Examples of such supportive headlines include: '1,000 women march for equal pay' (No Byline 1969a, p. 2), 'Men join women on equal rights' (Pratt 1974, p. 3) and 'ERA: keystone to other rights' (No Byline 1978, p. A28). As one suffrage argued in a *New York Times* feature, equal rights are 'just as much for men as it is for women. A society that is more just and fair and equitable is going to help men just as much as it is going to help women' (No Byline 1977b, p. 41).

Sources of support

Within this sample, a wide range of sources were used to legitimize equal rights, both as 'authorized' speakers and as 'ordinary' members of the public. In terms of the former, one of the most prominent endorsements came from ten *Chicago Tribune* editorials, all of which supported the ERA throughout its ten-year ratification period. Having editorial support is significant because, in theory, the editor is largely responsible for the overall tone of the publication.[8] Therefore, if the editor openly endorses the ERA, it is likely that many articles within the publication will follow suit.[9] An example of such outright support can be found in one editorial that reasoned: 'The Equal Rights Amendment to the United States Constitution comes up on the Illinois Senate calendar Tuesday for the third time and we urge its ratification. Thirty-four states have ratified the amendment. Four more are needed. A rejection by Illinois could be fatal' (Editorial 1975, p. A2). This paragraph clearly demonstrates support for equal rights, not only from the editor's perspective (and therefore representative of the publication), but also from the other 34 states that already ratified the amendment. The article further constructs supportive frames through engaging with its reasons for support: 'We have heard the rhetoric, pro and con, and find no compelling reason why ERA should be rejected'. Though perhaps this endorsement sounds half-hearted, the editor argues that it should ultimately be supported because of substantial public approval: 'The people of Illinois approved this constitution in December, 1970. If there were objections to the equal rights provision, they were next to inaudible'. Another editorial also used determined supporters as a reason to pass the ERA:

> The ERA's supporters have five more years in which to get the necessary total of 38 states to ratify it. If they fail to win approval this year, they will keep coming back until they succeed. A great deal of valuable legislative time will be wasted in needless debate and rancor in the meantime. Why not approve ERA this year? (Editorial 1974, p. 14)

Here, the editor views the ERA as not only a beneficial piece of legislation, but as an inevitable one. Similar supportive sentiments were echoed by a number of prominent citizens in both countries, including politicians, celebrities, feminists and academics, and by a range of 'ordinary' (though predominantly white, middle-class) men and women. The latter is evident in the following feature article:

> Dolly Malloy is a bright 21-year-old who is studying hotel management at the University of Houston. She believes in equal legal and economic opportunities for women, and in the right of women to make their own choices, including the choice of whether to have an abortion. (Margolis 1977b, p. 2)

Liberal notions of equality

One of the most notable findings from this sample was the predominance of liberal theory when discussing women's equality (see also Bradley 2003; Freeman 2001; van Zoonen 1992). These articles frequently included arguments stating that human potential should not be determined by biological sex (or age, class or ethnicity) and that women should be granted equal social, political, legal, sexual and economic rights as men. In many cases, as will be discussed below, legislative measures (as opposed to the radical restructuring of society) were seen as the most effective means of rectifying these inequalities. Previous research has also demonstrated that few journalists were capable of framing radical or socialist demands outside the boundaries of liberal democracy and the capitalist system (Freeman 2001, p. 239). Consequently, articles focused on how equal rights were necessary, fair and being unjustifiably denied to women.

The liberal values embedded within this discourse likely assisted its widespread acceptance, as such values were already prominent in the US and UK (Bradley 2003). Furthermore, such values hardly challenged dominant ideologies perpetuated by capitalist news organizations and their sources and were thus easily adopted. That said, while common in all four publications, liberal notions of equality were clearly dominant in some more than others. For example, this discourse constitutes 60 per cent of *New York Times* articles, 51 per cent of *Times* articles, 36 per cent of *Daily Mirror* articles and 24 per cent of *Chicago Tribune* articles. An illustration of this discourse can be found in the following article:

> Miss Manning considers the [feminist] movement a true revolution and says that in the year 2020, 'Each human being regardless of race, color, creed, national origin, or sex will have the chance to realize

his or her full potential without the artificial barriers of the sex role.'
(Coleman 1970, p. F9)

Liberal critiques often engage with the concept of sex roles – the false
belief that women and men are innately different, and it is this difference that provides the impetus for unequal treatment (Jaggar 1983).
By stating that human potential is sexless, artificial barriers (such as
discrimination) prevent women from achieving their full potential.
However, these views have been criticized because they ignore the fact
that *gender roles* remain intact long after men and women have been
granted equal opportunities, and thus have firm ideological roots that
cannot be legislated away (Code 1997). Additionally, the focus on sex
roles is problematic because these liberal critiques ignore the working-
class and minority women, who have been given 'equal opportunities'
to work alongside men and yet are still 'discriminated' against by having their work classified as less skilled, and receive less pay and fewer
overtime opportunities as a result. However, despite the theoretical
weaknesses of liberal arguments, publications should be applauded
for positively engaging with problems and solutions suggested by
equal rights advocates. The existence of such context is significant
as it is often missing from social movement coverage (Kerner 1968;
Martindale 1989).

Liberal problems and solutions to women's inequality

As noted in the previous chapter, most news articles failed to analyse
both the causes (401 articles or 54 per cent of total) and solutions (479
articles or 64 per cent of total) to women's subordinate position in
society. When present, however, sexism and discrimination were once
again the most commonly cited problem (112 articles or 15 per cent of
total), while legislative changes were the most frequent solution in all
four publications (87 articles or 12 per cent of total).[10] Both concepts are
rooted in liberal theory and argue that when women are discriminated
against (rather than being oppressed or exploited, which have radical
connotations), their human potential is ignored. Such sentiments are
found in one *Daily Mirror* feature:

> In America they call themselves WITCHES (Women's International
> Terrorist Conspiracy from Hell). In Holland they are known as the
> Dolle Minas.
> Here in Britain they are simply members of the London Women's
> Liberation Workshop, the Fawcett Society, the Six-Point Group or the
> Status of Women Committee.

> They are all part of a revolution that is sweeping the Western world
> with strident demands for equal rights for women [...]
> All are dedicated to removing what even the least militant mem-
> bers of the movement call grossly 'frustrating and humiliating dis-
> crimination against women.'
> The Six-Point Group, set up in 1921, and the Status of Women
> Committee have worked out that the worst inequalities are economic,
> legal, moral, social, occupational and political. (James 1970, p. 12)

As witnessed in the article above, discussions of sexism and discrimination require no underlying critiques of ideology or gender roles, but
instead implores individuals to re-think their 'misinformed' views.
Furthermore, not only was it commonly believed that women had been
legally discriminated against for years, but that such unfair practices
could only be remedied by equal rights legislation:

> Equality is a basic constitutional right which must be guaranteed
> to all Americans. A constitutional amendment is the only perma-
> nent insurance women will have of equal opportunity in education,
> employment, credit, retirement plans and numerous other areas
> (Rasberry 1982, p. A13).

Articulation of 'isms' is often found within liberal discourse – from
racism to ageism to heterosexism – which laments the unfair treatment of individuals because of unenlightened individual prejudices –
prejudices that many believe can be legislated away. Liberal discourse
places so much faith in legislative solutions that, according to NOW
Director Kathy Rand, within 25 years of its passage, the ERA would
successfully remove all sex stereotypes, enabling society to see men
and women as 'individuals and respect them for their own capabili-
ties and talents. Men and women will be truly liberated in the sense
that all options will be open – socially, psychologically, legally – and
they will be free to fulfil themselves any way they choose' (cited in
Proston 1975, p. C1). Unfortunately, however, *oppression*, which is the
root of hierarchical rankings in society, cannot be legislated away
and requires more structural changes in *ideologies*. Consequently, discourses surrounding sexism, discrimination and legislative changes
at best uphold oppressive ideologies and, at worst, fail to challenge
them. Furthermore, women often hold jobs in which there are no
male equivalents, and therefore cannot earn 'equal pay' because no
man is performing 'equal work'. In fact, several UK articles recognized

this loophole in the years after equal rights legislation was passed: 'Millions of working women have been conned by the Equal Pay Act, says a report out today. Their wages can't be raised to men's rates because there aren't any men doing the same work' (Todd 1977, p. 14). Consequently, despite passing equal rights legislation, British women continued to 'clear up pay dodges' (Davies 1976, p. 5), call in 'the law in fight for equal pay' (Daniels 1976, p. 7) and get a 'raw deal' from their 'mean' bosses (Law 1977, p. 5).

Oppositional frames and discourses

While it is clear that the majority of news articles supported equal rights or constructed it as a legitimate goal, there still existed a number of articles that countered such claims. In total, 122 articles (16 per cent) employed oppositional frames regarding equal rights, although a closer examination of the data indicates that the majority of these articles were found in the *Daily Mirror* (55 articles or 37 per cent of all oppositional articles). Given its association as a Labour newspaper, its clear rejection of equal rights for women is surprising, although, as previously noted, this can perhaps be explained by its high male working-class readership, who likely felt threatened by the loss of their breadwinner status. Furthermore, as British journalist Polly Toynbee suggested, equal pay for women might have been negatively perceived as an unnecessary diversion to trade unions' ability to improve work conditions and pay for men (Personal Interview with Polly Toynbee, 2010).

While such causes are impossible to determine without speaking to ex-staff members, some of the more common themes running through many of these texts were that equal rights were unwanted (34 articles) or would harm the family, society, men and women (58 articles). In several cases, a mixture of discourses were present, as I will demonstrate in Case Study 3.

Case study 3 – 'natural' gender roles, 'real' women, and equal rights in the *Chicago Tribune*

Titled 'All Women's Liberationists Hate Men and Children' (Wittner 1973, p. H12), this four-page feature of anti-feminist and anti-ERA campaigner Phyllis Schlafly was published in the *Chicago Tribune's* Sunday magazine (see Figure 3.2). The top half of the article is split into three columns. The first portrays the article headline, and next to it is a photo of Schlafly, eyes down, reading an article. With her hair done up and wearing a nice coat modestly buttoned up to her neck, Schlafly's appearance

"All women's liberationists hate men and children"
Dale Wittner
Chicago Tribune (1963-Current file): May 20, 1973; ProQuest Historical Newspapers Chicago Tribune (1849 - 1986)
pg. H12

"All women's liberationists hate men and children"

By Dale Wittner

A typical male chauvinist muttering? No, a few words from Phyllis Schlafly, an Alton housewife who has undertaken a 12-state crusade against Women's Lib ("a bunch of bitter women") and the Equal Rights Amendment ("a fun fight") on behalf of "the other 97 per cent of American women."

The oak-and-marble dignity of Illinois' Capitol rotunda was violated for a day. A bright and noisy storm of women, delegations pro and con, had assembled from all over the state, armed with neighborhood petitions and conflicting placards. "ERA is A-Okay," proclaimed one. "ERA is *Not* the Way," contradicted another. Secretaries had phoned in sick to be there. Housewives brought their children, and coeds cut class. A grandmother came all the way from Chicago by bus. Some of the women brought little bribes of fudge and homebaked bread to help persuade the lawmakers.

A year ago such commotion was beyond prediction. The proposed Equal Rights Amendment (the ERA of the women's signs) had breezed thru Congress with hardly a whisper of opposition. Twenty-two states ratified it in such fast and quiet succession that the approval of 16 more required to attach it to the United States Constitution appeared certain. If anything, ERA seemed unnecessary, after the fact — a trophy acknowledgement of years of small victories already

won by women. But now, in state houses from Nevada and North Dakota to Florida, scenes like the one in the Illinois rotunda occur almost weekly. The amendment has been meeting unexpected resistance from women who think it would take away more than it would give them.

Considering that there was barely one chair for every 20 women waiting outside the House chamber that day in Springfield, it was curious that when Phyllis Schlafly arrived, a chair immediately became empty. Automatically it was hers. She was a colonel at a command post. When the others had questions, they came to the chair to ask her.

Phyllis Schlafly does not want perfect equality with men and is convincing a lot of other women that they don't want it either. Her trip to the state capital from her home in Alton, was the shortest of her year-long campaign against ERA, less than a two-hour drive. Other trips had taken her as far as Arizona, Georgia, the Carolinas — a dozen states in all. Wherever she appeared, busloads of angry house-

wives and worried mothers showed up too. Of the 12 states she has targeted so far, not one has gone on to ratify the amendment. Nebraska, whose legislature had rushed to be the second to ratify ERA last year, changed its mind this year. After listening to Mrs. Schlafly at a special breakfast meeting the lawmakers took the unprecedented step of voting to rescind their ratification.

"That's not too bad a track record for an amateur," she is fond of saying.

Just how "amateur" Phyllis Schlafly really is has become a sore point among her political foes. They have charged that as founder and chairman of the Committee to Stop ERA, she is getting money secretly from such unlikely coalitions as organized labor and the John Birch Society, the Roman Catholic Church, and the Ku Klux Klan. Mrs. Schlafly vehemently denies getting money from any of them. "I *give* to the church at mass each Sunday, tho. I don't suppose my

detractors would approve of *that* either.

"These women on the other side have worked for years for this. They know how much money they have spent. All of a sudden they see ERA stopped, and they have come to the conclusion that I must have out-spent them to do it. That really isn't true. All I did was write a few articles and go on a few television shows and articulate the views of the other 97 per cent of American women."

If her popularity is hard to understand, a little biography makes it at least plausible. For more than 20 years she has been active in Republican politics. Once she was given an award by the Illinois Federation of Republican Women for traveling 100,000 miles for the party — all within the state. In 1964, she wrote a thin volume called "A Choice Not An Echo," boosting Barry Goldwater for the Presidency, which sold three million copies. Since then she has issued a newsletter modestly called "The Phyllis Schlafly Report." It goes out to something less than 10,000 conservative subscribers

16 ▶

Figure 3.2   'All women's liberationists hate men and children' *Chicago Tribune*

◀ *12* **Schlafly**

"A man's first significant purchase is a diamond. . ."

willing to pay $5 to hear from her 12 times a year. She has become an expert on the Pentagon and national defense, authoring three hawkish books on the subject, and has found time to have six children and hold each of them out of first grade so she could "teach them all how to read properly, by the phonics method, at home."

"Oh, I ran for Congress once too," she reports, hurrying past that bad defeat to a happier subject. A closer contest was her bid to become president of the National Federation of Republican Women during the recovery-from-Goldwater

21 ▶

◀ · **Schlafly**

Schlafly's views

On her own fight against ERA: "I'm having a ball. It's a fun fight. I've been in a lot of fights that have been grim and bitter and tiresome and tedious. But this is a fun fight. The girls really enjoy it."

On the nature of "real women": "Marriage and the home is the greatest liberation for women. It's security, fulfillment, achievement, and emotional satisfaction. It's what they want . . . . Not only are women physically different from men, they are emotionally different. They may say they like their job and they want a career and all that. And—oh sure, I know—they say they like all kinds of intellectual things and all that. But there is something they will not do that men must do—make everything take second place to their career . . . . For women, home and family come first . . . . They can't help it. That's the way they are."

On women in politics: "Look at Congress—only a dozen women. That's not discrimination. That's the price it takes. . . . All those night meetings, shaking hands, all those miles."

Where Kate Millett found repression stretching back to prehistory, Mrs. Schlafly discovered the most fortunate of historic accidents. A few paragraphs later: "The institution of the family is advantageous for women for many reasons. After all, what do we want out of life? To love and be loved? . . . . A man may search 30 to 40 years for accomplishment in his profession. A woman can enjoy real achievement when she is young — by having a baby."

For less fortunate women elsewhere, she offered sympathy. She grew up in the Depression in St. Louis, and her family was "terribly poor," she remembers. "My mother went to work to support the family and did so for years when my father was unable to get a job. The best thing my parents gave me was the desire for a college education — and not a dime to pay for it." The desire, tho, was enough. As a student at Washington University during World War II, she earned her diploma, a Phi Beta Kappa key, and a graduate scholarship to Harvard, all in just three years and while working 48 hours a week on the night shift at the St. Louis ordnance plant—as a gunnery and ballistics technician.

Right or wrong (and her femme opponents have strong arguments), she spells out the main reasons why she's against the ERA, which she says would wipe out the financial obligation of a husband and father to support his wife and children; wipe out laws that protect only women against sex crimes such as rape; make women subject to the draft and combat duty equally with men; wipe out the right of a mother to keep her children in case of divorce; lower the age at which boys can marry; wipe out the protection women now have from dangerous and unpleasant jobs; and wipe out a woman's right to privacy.

"In other civilizations, such as the African and American Indian," she says, "the men strut around wearing feathers and beads and hunting and fishing while the women do all the hard, tiresome drudgery. . . . This is not the American way because we were lucky enough to inherit the traditions of the Age of Chivalry.

"In America, a man's first significant purchase is a diamond for his bride, and the largest financial investment of his life is a home for her to live in. American husbands work hours of overtime to buy a fur piece or other finery to keep their wives in fashion, and to pay premiums on their life insurance policies to provide for her comfort when she is a widow.

"I don't want to give that up," she says earnestly. "I don't think most women do." ■

Figure 3.2 Continued

◀ 16 **Schlafly**

Schlafly's views

On Women's Liberationists:
"The real division between women doesn't have anything to do with whether they are educated or uneducated or black or white or rich or poor or old or young or married or single. The only thing it has to do with is whether they are happy or

bitter. . . . The liberationists are a bunch of bitter women seeking a Constitutional cure for their personal problems. . . . To them children are a terrible nuisance. They are not planning on having any themselves and if by accident . . . well, they favor an abortion."

---

period. She was narrowly beaten in a bitter fight. But the consolation prize was something she would use well later — a network of loyal, conservative contacts reaching down to the precinct level of every state.

After more than two hours of delays, the hearing finally began. The 23 men and one woman of the Illinois House Executive Committee listened, first to testimony from the proponents and then to the opponents. The star witness in both lineups came first — Jill Ruckelshaus to report that President Nixon realizes women might have to be drafted but he favors ERA

committee approved, the full House would not and ERA would be stopped in Illinois for the second year.

Later, over a single glass of sherry at a Springfield restaurant, she noted: "I wasn't the least bit interested in the Women's Liberation Movement or ERA until about a year and a half ago. A friend once invited me to come to Connecticut to debate some libber. "I had to do some research and started reading their literature. That's when I realized how destructive these people are—destructive of the family, of values that I think are important. All of them hate men and children, you know."

When she returned from Connec-

anyway; then Mrs. Schlafly to announce that most women don't want to be drafted no matter what the President wants.

The arguments were more complicated than that, of course. But when it was over everyone agreed that not one member of the committee had changed his or her mind. By a predicted 13-to-11 ballot they approved the ratification proposal and sent it to the full House, a small defeat for Stop ERA but an expected one. Just as surely as the

ticut, she went to her typewriter and wrote the 4,000 words of Volume 5, Number 7 of "The Phyllis Schlafly Report," a manifesto that would cornerstone her counter-revolution.

"Of all the classes of people who ever lived, the American women is the most privileged," she began. "We have the most rights and rewards and the fewest duties. Our unique status is the result of a fortunate combination of circumstances . . ."

22 ▶

Figure 3.2 Continued

indicates that she is a middle-class woman between 40 and 50 years old. The third column includes a caption for the photo stating:

> A typical male chauvinist muttering? No, a few words from Phyllis Schlafly, an Alton housewife who has undertaken a 12-state crusade against Women's Lib ('a bunch of bitter women') and the Equal Rights Amendment ('a fun fight') on behalf of 'the other 97 per cent of American women.' (Wittner 1973, p. H12)

The prominence of this caption with the headline positions equal rights (and women's liberation) as unsupported, deviant and illegitimate, thus providing an interpretive framework when reading the story body (Hall et al. 1978). Furthermore, the article opens with a description of the 'battle' between pro and anti-ERA forces:

> A bright and noisy storm of women, delegations pro and con, had assembled from all over the state, armed with neighborhood petitions and conflicting placards. 'ERA is A-Okay,' proclaimed one. 'ERA is *Not* the Way,' contradicted another.

While pro-ERA forces are understood to have gained an early victory, the article remarks that the amendment had recently met 'unexpected resistance from women who think it will take away more than it will give them'. From this point on, the anti-ERA position, voiced by Schlafly, dominated the article.

Through the use of military metaphors, Schlafly is introduced at the end of the second column, described as a 'colonel at a command post. When the others had questions [about the ERA], they came to the chair to ask her'. The high-ranked position afforded to Schlafly asserts her importance in this particular battle, as well as her effectiveness in the field: 'Of the 12 states she has targeted so far, not one has gone on to ratify the amendment'. While most oppositional articles in the US focused on a rejection of the ERA rather than equal rights in general, Schlafly is an exception: 'Phyllis Schlafly does not want perfect equality with men and is convincing a lot of other women that they don't want it either'. One side box on the last page includes a section titled 'Schlafly's views'. Within this is a subsection titled 'On the nature of "real" women', where she goes on to proclaim:

> Marriage and the home is the greatest liberation for women. It's security, fulfilment, achievement, and emotional satisfaction. It's what

they want [...] Not only are women physically different from men, they are emotionally different. They may say they like their job and they want a career and all that. And – oh sure, I know – they say they like all kinds of intellectual things and all that. But there is something they will not do that men must do – make everything take second place to their career.

Here Schlafly acts as a spokesperson for what (real) women really want, using biological determinism to outline (supposed) fundamental differences between men and women – that women are designed to put their careers second and are happiest in the home. Yet, while arguing that women do not want to pursue intellectual matters, Schlafly is described as being an avid Republican (and very effective fundraiser), the author of a monthly newsletter subscribed to by 10,000 members, a former Congressional candidate and an author of six books. Surely such activities require some sort of intellectual engagement – an irony noted by the journalist. Additionally, in the late 1970s, Schlafly returned to university where she attained a law degree to better understand the legal ramifications of the ERA. By claiming that she knows what 'real' women 'really want', Schlafly not only contradicts herself by occupying a prominent place in the public sphere, but she de-legitimizes those who do want a career and are not willing to put it second for their family (implying that this is unnatural). The discourse therefore patronizes equal rights supporters by stating that only *think* they know what they want, but because women are *biologically* different from men, it is only a matter of time before they realize they would be happiest at home.

In addition to promoting traditional gender roles, the discourse is problematic because it ignores issues of class, race and sexuality. Schlafly overlooks the fact that many (lesbian, middle-class and minority) women work out of necessity and neither have, nor may they want, a male breadwinner to take care of them. Instead, she turns her attention to the danger 'equal rights' poses for (white, middle-class, heterosexual) women's privileged position in society:

'Of all the classes of people who ever lived, the American woman is the most privileged,' she began. 'We have the most rights and rewards for the fewest duties. Our unique status is the result of a fortunate combination of circumstances [...] The institution of the family is advantageous for women for many reasons. After all, what do we want out of life? To love and be loved? [...] A man may search 30 or

40 years for accomplishment in his profession. A woman can enjoy real achievement when she is young – by having a baby.'

Proclaiming that having a baby is the surest way to achieve fulfilment alienates those women who cannot or choose not to have children and says nothing about the fact that many women abort or give up unwanted pregnancies each year. A child is not always a blessing for those who cannot afford or are not mentally prepared to have one, and Schlafly's views de-legitimize those who attempt to find fulfilment in other ways, suggesting that it is only secondary at best to raising children. Such views fit in with DePaulo's 'mythology of maternal superiority', which is based on the idea that single-parent and non-parenting women's lives are deficient (cited in Negra 2009, p. 61). Furthermore, this line of argument says nothing of how women can achieve fulfilment once their children grow up and leave the home. However, despite my objections, the success of Schlafly's campaigns indicates that her message resonated with many American men and women.

One common tactic in many anti–equal rights articles was to discuss the consequences such newfound freedoms would bring. For example, Schlafly constructed the stay-at-home wife as receiving the better end of the bargain, noting that equal rights would represent a negative turn in women's comfortable lives:

> 'In other civilizations, such as the African and American Indian,' she says, 'the men strut around wearing feathers and beads and hunting and fishing while the women do all the hard tiresome drudgery [...] This is not the American way because we were lucky enough to inherit the traditions of the Age of Chivalry.'
>
> 'In America, a man's first significant purchase is a diamond for his bride, and the largest financial investment of his life is a home for her to live in. American husbands work hours of overtime to buy a fur piece or other finery to keep their wives in fashion, and to pay premiums on their life insurance policies to provide for her comfort when she is a widow.'
>
> 'I don't want to give that up,' she says earnestly. 'I don't think most women do.'

This backlash discourse, which will also be further addressed in the chapter, is exemplified in when Schlafly argues that the ERA would:

> [W]ipe out the financial obligation of a husband and father to support his wife and children; wipe out laws that protect only women

against sex crimes such as rape; make women subject to the draft
and combat duty equally with men; wipe out the right of a mother to
keep her children in case of divorce; lower the age at which boys can
marry; wipe out the protection women now have from dangerous
and unpleasant jobs; and wipe out a woman's right to privacy.

Such statements support previous studies noting that the ERA has been
framed as an act that would weaken women's legal protections (Costain
et al. 1997). If constructed in this manner, then it is no wonder that
many (middle-class) women reacted so violently to the ERA (and perhaps equal rights in general). However, it should be noted that many
'privileges' the ERA would supposedly erode were based upon specific
gender ideologies. In the case of mothers keeping their children after
divorce, this relies on the false belief that women are better nurturers
than males, thereby making it unnatural for fathers to gain custody.
With regard to 'protective' legislation, this is historically based on the
notion that as actual or potential mothers, it was in the public's best
interest to regulate women's hours and working conditions in order to
preserve the species (Jacoby 1976). Wage differences were also based
on assumptions that women's smaller size and strength in relation to
most men meant they were less useful members of the workforce and
thus legitimized pay differences (Mitchell 1971). Such statements make
it evident that Schlafly's views on women are firmly rooted within capitalist, patriarchal and heterosexist ideologies, where women were positioned as 'different' (and subsequently subordinate) to men as a sex and
a class.

Furthermore, by wrongly associating her privileged position to that of
most American women Schlafly indicates the extent to which she was
deeply out of touch with the realities of millions of American women's
lives – particularly in the post-war era, when more and more women
worked out of choice or necessity (Coote & Campbell 1982; Lewis
1992). Though Schlafly offered her 'sympathy' to those 'less fortunate'
women, she engaged with traditional liberal discourses indicating that
it is up to each individual to improve their situation. Coming from a
working-class background, Schlafly attributed her climb up the social
ladder to her intense desire to succeed and to her strong work ethic. In
this sense then, she ignored the fact that poverty is cyclic and very difficult to escape. Additionally, she credited her hard work (rather than
a financial scholarship) as the reason she escaped a working-class life,
further entrenching the idea that individual (rather than social) change
is needed.

In summary then, this case study sought to highlight the various ways in which equal rights were de-legitimized, constructed as unwanted, unnecessary and detrimental to American women. As with news of feminism, oppositional discourses largely relied on a traditional construction of gender roles, stating that women who defy them in their quest for equal rights (particularly feminists) are deviant, do not represent most American women and will end up living unhappy and unfulfilled lives. Though these frames and discourses were addressed in this particular *Chicago Tribune* article, they are typical of those found throughout all four publications.

Problems and solutions

While this chapter has already discussed some of the problems and solutions posed regarding women's inequality/oppression, two in particular were useful for constructing an overall oppositional frame. The first stated that women had the *opportunity* to become equal but were merely *self-limiting,* thus shifting the focus from a societal problem (which is inherently sexist, racist and homophobic) to an individual problem (which can be overcome with enough hard work and determination). While only the main problem in fourteen articles (2 per cent of total), the statistic does not account for one-off remarks or lesser discussions about why women are unequal. For example, though the headline for *The Times* feature, 'Where Women Provide Their Own Discrimination', indicates that women were the main reason for their inequality, the article body actually focused more on gender roles as the problem and was coded as such. Here, Joan Lester, MP, discussed why so few women are in public posts:

> Girls are conditioned away from 'men's' occupations even before they start school, and education does little to widen their horizons.
>   It is also hard for parents, however emancipated, not to transmit their own outlook to their children. What a child perceives in the home affects her attitude almost from birth. Father is still the breadwinner, mother's career is secondary, and especially in working-class homes, a managing director is out of the question [...]
>   We need to look at our educational system and challenge some of the conventional beliefs about our sex. Society's concept of femininity teaches that women who go into what are traditionally men's jobs are unfeminine, and we should show what rubbish that is [...]
>   Although discrimination plays a part, it is not nearly as great as many women profess to believe. The harsh truth is that women do not try in the same numbers as men because they believe succeeding

is so much more difficult. Women provide their own discrimination, which they have been taught from birth. (Lester 1981, p. 9)

Therefore, while 'women as the problem' emerged in many articles, this category is not reflected in the quantitative statistics and must be addressed through qualitative means. This is further evident in one *Chicago Tribune* article featuring the first female to run for a public post in her area. She was asked whether she thought discrimination prevented women from entering politics, and responded: 'No, I don't believe women have been discriminated against', before adding that 'They haven't shown enough desire to run for office' (Zahour 1971, p. S1). In both instances, the problem is therefore not the workplace or society but women's lack of desire.[11] Such notions are elaborated in another *Times* article where advertising executive Ann Petrie outlined her views on why there were so few women management positions:

> Ann Petrie is obviously wanting to wake up some women in advertising to the possibilities open to them, if only they would push harder. 'My advice would be for them to get all their qualifications, and exploit any talent they may have and go all out for what they are after.
>
> 'But in advertising, as in many other professions, some women are their own worst enemies. I was told they showed very little interest in courses leading to professional qualifications, giving the impression that they regarded it as a job for the moment only until they married. In view of this, one forgives a male employer for any prejudice he might have against employing women!' (Symon 1971, p. 8)

This passage supports previous research arguing that individual (as opposed to social) changes are often suggested when women's needs were not satisfied by the workplace (Rhode 1995). Furthermore, the article used economic sensibilities to justify discrimination against women as their work was framed as temporary – something to fill their time until they found a husband and bore children (their 'natural' calling). It is also significant that the journalist takes for granted the statement (from an unnamed source) that women show 'little interest' in professional courses rather than following this up to verify such claims. What the article fails to take into account is that many women choose the homemaking path, not because they are lazy or uninterested in advertising, but because this is what they have been conditioned to do since birth. Therefore, rather than questioning why women might 'choose' home over family (and therefore assuming it is a 'natural' choice), traditional gender ideologies remain intact, and a discourse forms stating that women are lazy, uninterested or better suited as wives and mothers.

Backlash

Zald and Ash (1966) argued that if a social movement becomes successful, it is likely to witness a backlash and increased hostility from some members of the public. Whether the Second Wave's backlash occurred because of its success is difficult to confirm, but it is clear that this discourse was present in all four publications, particularly the *Daily Mirror*,[12] which consistently de-legitimized feminists and their goals throughout the 14-year time period.[13] While my longitudinal study demonstrates that few *Daily Mirror* articles ever supported feminism or equal rights, many articles with the backlash discourses gave off the *impression* that they once had, but that the movement had finally gone too far.[14] In many cases, articles acted as a comeuppance to women for welcoming feminism into their lives.

While backlash discourses can be found throughout the sample period in the UK, it became much more prominent in my US publications towards the early 1980s. By that time, the British Conservative Party's Margaret Thatcher had already been elected Prime Minister, and the decade was marked by a deep economic recession with high unemployment. There was also much hostility towards women competing for limited jobs with men. In the US, the early 1980s was when Republican candidate Ronald Reagan was elected President, and the ERA was defeated. Both Thatcher and Reagan's ascents to power were seen as an indication of a wide-scale return towards conservative values and beliefs (Faludi 1992). These included the importance of family values – which were often seen as incompatible with feminism and equal rights. Particularly in the US, Reagan's election was widely interpreted as a signal of society's rejection of the women's movement, providing the media authority to claim that a backlash was occurring. An example of this can be found in a *New York Times* article titled, 'Feminists Dismayed by the Election and Unsure of What Future Holds' (Bennetts 1980, p. A13), which began with a discussion about how the election of Reagan was 'a total disaster' for advocates of women's rights, and was followed by quotes from feminist and pro-family leaders who debated what the election meant for the women's movement. While Phyllis Schlafly, leader of an anti-ERA campaign proclaimed the election was: 'a decisive defeat for the ERA and for the feminist movement', even equal rights proponents agreed. Senator McGovern, who lost his seat in the election and was a supporter of women's rights added:

> People were reluctant to come out and admit they wanted to put women in their place, but there was a strong current of that running through much of what happened [...] The 'family' issue raised by the right wing was a code word for putting women back in the kitchen and stripping them of any decision on the question of abortion, and forcing them back into the old orthodox roles.

What is ironic about the popularization of backlash discourses around this time is that they emerged as feminist activism in the US increased, when groups such as NOW made one last attempt to pass the ERA. Such contradictions indicate that an ideological battle was being waged over the public construction of feminism, between those claiming it was dead or dying (therefore post-ing it, and pro-moting patriarchal and capitalist ideologies) and those claiming it was still relevant and necessary (and attempting to challenge these ideologies).

While such articles tended to focus on the change of sentiment surrounding feminism, other backlash discourses claimed it had 'gone too far'. This rhetoric indicated that society was finally willing to fight back against feminism's 'irrational' claims, and was commonly found in the *Daily Mirror*, and the *Chicago Tribune*. This discourse is summed up well by the column 'One Big ERA Problem: NOW's Manners Turn People Off' (Thimmesch 1978:, p. C2). Here, the ERA was constructed as losing support, not because of its content, but because the tactics employed by feminist supporters had 'offended large groups of fair-minded Americans with a display of bad manners and bigotry'. These included 'attacking Mormons and Catholics by lumping them with the Ku Klux Klan, Nazis and Communists, because elements in their churches oppose ERA'. The columnist closed the article by stating that while the ERA was desirable, feminists and their tactics certainly were not. Articles such as this are clever because they de-politicize feminism without even engaging with what it really means. It is also appears to be open to feminism, but is sadly forced to reject it because the movement itself is unreasonable. As Faludi writes: 'Identifying feminism as women's enemy only furthers the ends of a backlash against women's equality, simultaneously deflecting attention from the backlash's central role and recruiting women to attack their own cause' (1992, pp. 12–13).

While backlash can be discussed more generally, we can also break it down and examine how it constructed consequences society now faced for women's increased equality. These include consequences for the family, men and women.

Consequences of equal rights – the family

As demonstrated in case study 3, a common means of opposing equal rights was through a discussion of its supposedly negative consequences. One common sentiment, as seen in the following *New York Times* column, was that equal rights (and, specifically, the ERA) would ruin the (traditional nuclear) family. The column began by outlining the importance of the family:

> The family was once our basic social institution. The husband was the provider [...] While many women were employed as teachers, or as household help in families sufficiently affluent to afford this cost, relatively few women were independently employed in jobs which men had historically depended upon and filled.
>
> The housewife was the guardian of her children. She provided them their early education and initiated them into the principles of religion, respect for others, care of physical property and the work ethic. (Shoemaker 1975, p. E17)

The use of language describing the family in idealized terms ('the housewife was *guardian* of her children') is significant and reiterates the rigid, but 'special', status afforded to women in the home.[15] However, rather than critiquing narrowly defined gender roles, the columnist endorsed them as an ideal model, likely because they provided a sense of security and control during this time of social change. Additionally, the columnist indicated that any 'increase in women's leisure time, courtesy of new household products, have enlarged their interests', making them more 'enchanted with alcohol and other women's husbands'. As a result:

> The increasing attendance of women in college would be applauded if it included the realization that without the family our society loses substance. There are many brilliant women. I am not suggesting that many have not done well in the professions and in business. I do submit that when women become so intrigued with women's liberation and the Equal Rights Amendment that family and children become secondary, and our values are distorted. (p. E17)

Once again, this article uses notions of 'natural' gender roles to suggest that, while women certainly are *capable* of excelling in higher education and in paid employment, it is *unnatural*, as they are needed within the confines of their family, who *suffer* from neglect because of women's new interests. What the article fails to question is why the well-being of the family and children resides solely on women's shoulders. And what of families with no mother, or of working-class families who rely on two-incomes? While columns are not subject to the same journalistic conventions as news reports, such as balance and objectivity, they still have an obligation to provide sustained evidence to support their claims (even fear-mongering ones). What is striking about these narratives is that they are similar to those identified by Faludi in the 1980s, when the US government warned that a rise in 'female autonomy' was leading to the collapse of the family (1992, p. 73). Such warnings demonstrate how dominant ideologies consistently reproduced a limited range of patriarchal and capitalist discourses, used to maintain women's unpaid labour in the home, and under-paid labour outside of it. As scholars note, modern capitalist economies are dependent on the continued underpayment of women (Wolf 1991), meaning that women's minimal (if any) contribution to the household income provides the impetus for men to claim dominance over women, both financially and ideologically.

While the importance of traditional nuclear families was found in both my American and British publications, differences emerged in how these discourses were constructed. In the US, it was often from a religious point of view. Catholics, Mormons and Protestants spoke out against equal rights, arguing that they were a slippery slope to eroding the family, downgrading the mother's role and making it more difficult for women to stay home and raise children. In Britain, however, religious voices were almost entirely absent. Instead, equal rights' consequences for the family were constructed by politicians, 'ordinary' men and women and journalists. It is important to note that lobby groups and the religious right played a much larger role in the US than Britain, and have long been considered a force to be reckoned with on many political issues (Bouchier 1983). While equal rights were often constructed as harmful for the family, many articles specifically focused on how they were negative for men.

Consequences of equal rights – men

The *Daily Mirror* was the publication most likely to construct equal rights as bad for men, perhaps because of its high male readership. Article headlines supporting this view include: 'We are just slaves, says Mr. Men's Lib' (James 1973, p. 7), 'Men's Lib Champ Tony Gets the Boot' (King 1977, p. 5) and 'At last – its men who are feeling the pinch' (Thomas 1970, p. 17). All of these texts focused on how men suffer as women reap the benefits of equality. One example of this discourse, explicitly stated in the *Daily Mirror,* can be found in a column by Christopher Ward. In it, he described the then, newly emerging Women's Liberation Movement, but commented that: 'what is liberation to women is often enslavement to us men, and what's good news for them is bad news for us'. Ward commonly used humour and ridicule – techniques noted by previous movement scholars as well (Barker-Plummer 2000) – to combat both feminism and its goals. In this particular article, Ward mused:

> I hadn't realized just how much bad news we men have suffered until I came across this Liberated Woman's Appointment Calendar and Survival Handbook, which is rapidly becoming the pocket book of every bra-burning American lady.
>
> Every day this diary records the anniversary of some past female victory, which we men have been suffering for ever since.
>
> I mention here some of the more prominent landmarks in the history of Women's Liberation so that, while women celebrate them, we men can treat them as days of mourning of our formerly great sex. (Ward 1970, p. 7)

This discourse is particularly destructive as it evokes the metaphor of 'war of the sexes' and argues that equal rights cannot be good for *both* men and women, but must benefit one at the expense of the other. Therefore, as long as women continue to 'win' their rights, men can only expect to 'lose' theirs. This is further exemplified in another column, where Ward stated: 'Until quite recently, I've been an ardent supporter of equality for women, but now I find myself turning against the liberation movement. Far from just wishing to liberate themselves from the limitations imposed on them by men, they now seem hellbent on turning the tables and clapping the very same shackles on us' (Ward 1971, p. 10). Interestingly, this discourse (and others like it) can be considered postfeminist in that it claims feminism has gone too far and encourages a return to 'better' times when men were dominant.

Consequences of equal rights – women

In all four publications, a specific discourse emerged stating that equal rights were bad for women. Such sentiments were constructed through various means. As seen in case study 3, this could be seen in terms of moving away from an age of chivalry. In one article, women's equality was blamed for a rise in men becoming 'more romantic' after a few drinks – implying that male sexual aggression towards women was their own fault (Buchan et al. 1979, p. 16)! Others, such as 'Life for Soviet Woman Is All Hard Work and Little Status' (Shipler 1976, p. 8), and 'Soviet women given day off from "liberation"'(Binyon 1978, p. 8), discussed the double burden equal rights brought for women, who were now expected to work *and* still take care of the family. However, these articles failed to mention that equal rights should *also* mean women's access to employment and education, and men's responsibilities with child rearing and domestic duties. Such discourses clearly indicate that while women might be breaking into the public spheres, gender ideology remained largely intact. Another range of articles cautioned that equal rights were paving the way towards a unisex society. As one *Chicago Tribune* source articulated:

> 'I enjoy being a woman, and I'm sure that 99 per cent of other women feel the same,' she wrote. 'I don't want to dig ditches or empty garbage as women in Russian do. I don't want my daughters drafted. As far as I'm concerned, the passing of the Equal Rights Amendment would mean the downfall of womanhood.' (Wolfe 1973, p. 33)

This concern about the move to a unisex society and the erosion of femininity is common in many articles, and led to a series of sensational claims, particularly in the *Daily Mirror*. Here, articles traced the effects of equal rights through a rise in female alcoholics 'Drinks Danger in Women's Lib' (No Byline 1973a, p. 7), balding females, 'Baldness can send wives right off their heads', (Bedford 1971b, p. 3) and female violence and bullies, 'Menace of the gymslip bullies', (Davies 1973, p. 11), 'Girl thugs' (Palmer 1976a, p. 1) and 'The violent sex' (Smith 1976, p. 7). This last article explored the unforeseen dangers in the following paragraphs:

> More dangerous than the male [...] that's the new breed of women criminals.
>
> Britain's top policewoman said yesterday that the growing number of women thieves and muggers could eventually plunge Britain into a jungle.
>
> And she suggested that one reason for the dramatic upsurge in these crimes might be women's liberation [...]

'In the countries where emancipation is the greatest, the women participate more in crime,' she said.

One opinion is that, owing to their improving status and their release from commitments of home and family, they are able to exercise latent greed and viciousness.

Another viewpoint is that women, bewildered because of the rapid alteration of their life-style, are now insecure and uncertain, and that later this crime trend will be eradicated. (Smith 1976, p. 7)

All of these articles are concerned with apparent shifts in gender roles and femininity. Women, it seems, were taking on more 'masculine' characteristics which is constructed as abnormal, deviant and harmful. Even though the article concluded with a quote from a female police commander stating that not even a rise in female criminals should be reason enough to turn back 'the tide of liberation', the article has already undermined equal rights by focusing on the negative impact equality *really* has. Additionally, I would argue that the logic in some of these arguments is flawed. For instance, it is unlikely that equal rights would provide women *more* time to commit crimes, as their entry into the paid workforce did nothing to free them from the burdens of domestic duties. If anything, therefore, I would argue that many would women have *less* time (and energy) to commit such crimes.

While it is worth noting the various discourses within this oppositional frame, it is also important to examine which voices are used in these articles and what they reveal about the flow of power in both nations.

Voices of opposition

As scholars note, it is important to examine the use of sources in news stories, as they can reveal positions taken (Ross 2007; Tuchman 1972) and indicate who has the power and authority to define issues (Becker 1967; Hall et al. 1978). When examining oppositional discourses, certain source patterns emerge. In many cases, 'negative' or unsupportive stories were written by, or included the opinions of, columnists, members of the public (including letters to the editor), 'normal' (but mainly middle-class) women and unsympathetic journalists. Such diverse voices could be used to indicate that opposition to equal rights was not limited to one segment of society – and demonstrate the pervasiveness of capitalist and patriarchal ideologies, which struggled to keep women subordinate. Even though the *Daily Mirror* carried the largest proportion of oppositional discourses, a wide range of voices were used in all four publications.

As to be expected, my broadsheet publications frequently constructed oppositional frames and discourses through quoting authority figures. As Ericson et al. (1987) argued, the news is a 'representation of authority' (p. 3), meaning 'ordinary' citizens' voices are few and far between. For example, one *Chicago Tribune* article reported on how several male legislators 'openly admit they find the whole notion of female independence and equality threatening', before claiming that 'They're [women] not equal, they're not the same as men' (Roberts 1979, p. E4). At no point during the article were 'ordinary' members of the public's voices heard. Similarly, one *Daily Mirror* column quoted MP Ronald Bell proclaiming to the House of Commons that: 'Of course women are inferior second-class citizens and ought to be treated as such' (Proops 1973, p. 9).

As discussed in the last chapter, female voices were powerful tools in the construction of oppositional frames and discourses, as they provide evidence that women themselves were uninterested in equality/feminism. In doing so, equal rights supporters were frequently marginalized through suggesting they were ignoring their 'natural' roles as wives and mothers. One *New York Times* article focused on lawyer Margaret Mahoney, who, despite her professional status, rejected the ERA. Instead, she labelled equal rights opponents and homemakers as 'unsung heroes' who resent being told they are 'second-class citizens' (Kifner 1976, p. 69). What is noticeable about this quote (and many others like it) is that Mahoney strengthened her position by identifying with homemakers first, and professionals second (if at all), to justify a wider opposition to the ERA. Phyllis Schlafly also regularly employed similar tactics, as seen in case study 3, where she prioritizes her housewife status (despite her plethora of extra-curricular activities) and used this identity to strengthen her opposition to the ERA, and equal rights more generally.

Another common pattern throughout this chapter is the lack of working-class, minority or lesbian voices, issues or concerns. However, despite this overall 'symbolic annihilation' (Tuchman 1978b), there are a few exceptions regarding working-class voices that merit attention. This mainly involves news stories about trade union activism, but the catch here is that stories quote union leaders rather than union members.[16] Trade union stories appeared relatively frequently in both the *Times* and the *Daily Mirror* and constituted their own news beat within these publications.[17] As previously noted, trade unions played a large role in campaigning for equal rights in the UK, and these efforts were documented in several news articles throughout the sample (Beecroft 1969; Jones 1970; Law 1974; No Byline 1969b, 1976c). As one *Daily Mirror* article reported:

> The battle for equal pay is only half won. That was the sombre message hammered home to the unions before the TUC packed its bags and went home yesterday.
> Mr. Jack McGougan, secretary of the Tailors and Garment Workers was first to sound the warning.
> He told the delegates at Brighton: 'The passing of the Equal Pay Bill earlier this year will not by itself give women equal pay.
> 'The unions must make it a reality.' (Beecroft 1969, p. 4).

While US newspapers also had a history of reporting on labour issues, there is an overall absence of references to trade unions (known as labour unions) in the *New York Times* and the *Chicago Tribune*. While such absences could be linked to decreasing labour union membership, and thus of news coverage in the 1970s and 80s (Erickson & Mitchell 1996, p. 405), I would argue that a more likely explanation is that the women's movement and other women's organizations were largely responsible for campaigning for equal rights in the US (Bouchier 1983; Jacoby 1976). Because many of these groups comprised middle-class (white) women, there is an overall lack of working-class (also known as 'blue-collar') female voices. However, when these voices were present, they were normally constructed in opposition to feminists or equal rights supporters. One letter to the editor argued that, rather than liberating working-class women, the ERA would do them more harm than good: 'The Equal Rights Amendment will not help women in industrial jobs. I wish "libbers" could see what they have done to us women in factories in Ohio. Maybe they were trying to help, but they and their "equal rights" have made things worse for us' (Letter to the Editor 1975, p. A2). The letter went on to describe how the ERA, in eliminating protective legislation, would force women to lift heavy loads, rather than their current maximum – a 'pile of paper'. That employers would begin forcing employees, regardless of their gender – to engage in work they are physically incapable of doing is ludicrous and appears to be lost on the letter-writer. However, having a blanket rule stating that no woman, no matter how physically capable, cannot do the same work as a man is unfair to those who wish to participate in such jobs.

This and other articles therefore construct equal rights as not only detrimental to women but as out of touch with their lived realities. This particular letter writer chastised 'women's libbers', who 'in their eagerness to, perhaps, get their boss' jobs as office managers, are most generous in giving away those precious distinctions so badly needed by their harder-working sisters on the assembly line' (1975, p. A2). Another *Chicago Tribune* feature remarked that feminist organizations 'don't speak' for working-class women, particularly regarding issues of birth control and abortion, who are overwhelmingly Catholic and have large families (Winter 1974, p. D3). Furthermore, while middle-class feminists were said to picket over 'the price of steak', working-class women were interested in 'day to day survival'. Consequently, these and other articles constructed feminism and their goals as elitist and out of touch with millions of (working-class, minority) women. While unfortunate in some ways, these articles rightly identify the folly of assuming all women experience similar forms of oppression and should therefore be united in the same goals. While few and far between, such articles opened up space for alternative voices (feminist or not) to critically analyse the diversities in women's lives and should therefore be applauded for bringing forward a variety of voices and analyses of the human condition.

While this discussion focused on a variety of ways in which equal rights has been de-legitimized, it is now time to examine those discourses where the case was not so black and white, and where contradictory or complex discourses and frames emerged.

Complex discourses and frames

While most of this chapter analysed how articles used either supportive or oppositional frames and discourses regarding equal rights, I wish to devote some space here to those texts where equal rights were not framed in black or white terms, effectively demonstrating how the battle between opposing discourses ensued not only within each publication or country but within individual articles as well. These complex, contradictory and sometimes controversial articles are useful to examine because they provide evidence of multiple, competing discourses surrounding equal rights and can be used to see how these discourses were deployed by different groups.

This section will therefore discuss articles that framed equal rights as a controversial issue, and those that included a mixture of supportive and oppositional discourses.

Equal rights as controversial

In total, 113 articles (15 per cent of total) framed equal rights as controversial or complex, with the vast majority (100) belonging to my US sample.[18] That equal rights legislation was passed early on in the UK with little apparent controversy likely accounts for the glaring absences of this frame, whereas equal rights and the ERA were hotly debated throughout this sample period in the US. Consequently, many US articles constructed equal rights as a controversial topic, often noting little else about amendment. This frame was particularly prominent in the *Chicago Tribune*, where a series of articles were devoted to two issues regarding the ERA. Such articles were likely prominent in this publication because Illinois was one of the three states targeted by ERA supporters in their quest to ratify the amendment in the late 1970s and early 1980s.

The first controversy addressed concerned a dispute over the number of votes needed within the Illinois state legislature to pass the amendment. While most states required a simple majority (51 per cent), the Illinois Constitution stipulated that a three-fifths majority was needed. Therefore, a battle ensued between those who wanted the number reduced to 51 per cent and those who felt that it was only fair to keep it as it was. A typical article relayed the dispute:

> Because the Illinois Senate has acted on the Equal Rights Amendment to the federal Constitution, supporters of the amendment said yesterday they are going back into court for a decision on whether a three-fifths or simple majority is needed for passage.
>
> Earlier this week, a three-judge federal panel dismissed a challenge to the three-fifths voting, saying that both branches of the legislature had not yet acted on the issue. That same day, the Senate did act.
>
> Last year, ERA supporters produced 95 votes in the House to ratify the amendment, but House Speaker W. Robert Blair (R., Park Forest) ruled that three-fifths, or 107, was needed. (No Byline 1974d, p. C13)

Therefore, articles such as this actually say very little about the ERA itself, aside from the fact that it has created controversy.

Although equal rights legislation was not necessarily constructed as controversial in Britain, many articles pitted both supportive and oppositional frames against one another, thus producing a frame of complexity. An example of this can be found in a *Daily Mirror* article describing a (now famous) tennis match between Billie Jean King, a Wimbledon champion and feminist, and Bobby Riggs, a former tennis star who opposed women's rights. The match was labelled the battle between the 'libber versus the lobber' (Wright 1973, pp. 20–21), and the article included both discourses of support for women's rights and the belief that 'women are at their prettiest when they're barefoot and pregnant at home'. Similar constructions were found in *The Times* coverage, particularly concerning its international features, which, I argue, overwhelmingly constructed equal rights in contradictory terms (see case study 4 below). Such articles are interesting to examine because they often begin by constructing equal rights as a positive force in women's lives:

> Anyone visiting Ghana during the recent general election would have remarked on the vital role played in them by the women of Ghana. All through the election campaigns, working in party offices, on propaganda vans and in the well-organized women's branches, as election officers and polling agents with the same voting rights as men, they took a full part in choosing the new Government. (Appiah 1969, p. 7)

Here, as in many other articles, the new freedoms afforded to women are constructed as positive changes for women, men, children or society in general. At the same time however, while noting women's equal roles in public life, rather than being 'liberated', many articles soon focused on the double-burden that women now faced of work in the public and private spheres. Equal rights then, were constructed as a double-edged sword – while greatly benefitting women in some ways, they were also a burden that women must bear. As the article on Ghana's women went on to report:

> Few people will deny that women work much harder than the men. Going through a village in the early morning you will see the men sitting out in the sun with their chewing sticks or smoking long after the women have left for the farm. In the evening the women carry home immense loads of wood and foodstuffs, their babies on their backs, while the men, if they can, walk home unimpeded except for their machete of gun. Once, I visited a village near Kumasi where they make beads – carefully pouring the ground powder into small clay moulds, inserting a stick I the middle of each and firing them in the ovens. I asked one man if the women ever did this work. He looked up in horror and said: 'Oh no! They are far too busy.' I doubt if he realized the implication of his remark. (p. 7)

Because the contradictions present in such articles are ideologically rich, they will serve as the focus of my fourth case study. In this particular article about Finnish women, equal rights are constructed in contradictory ways, not because they are viewed as a burden, but because they are seen as something that is available to women in theory but not in practice.

Case study 4 – women's equality internationally in *The Times*

This case study will examine the contradictory nature of equal rights in one *Times* feature. The article headline sums up equal rights' paradoxical nature well. Titled, 'Women: freedom but no power' (Kolbe 1970, p. 4), it examined the modern role of Finnish women in society. One of two articles regarding Finnish life, it occupied the middle of the page, sitting beneath an article discussing a rise in the standard of living in Finland, above a photo of girls 'enjoying eurhythmic exercises', and next to a photo of two old women gossiping at a Salvation Army Canteen. Even the photos demonstrate the contradictory nature of the article – young women trying new things vs. old women in stereotypical roles ('gossiping'). In addition to the contradictions apparent in the visual layout and the headline, the article opened with the following paragraph:

> The Finnish woman is in a paradoxical situation – perhaps unique in the world – in that she has more rights than she dares use. She works hard but demands relatively little. In theory she can attain a high position in society, but in practice the sphere of her influence is limited.

That the article clearly outlines the paradoxical nature of equal rights for women is not unique to *The Times*. Many other articles also begin with an opening paragraph discussing the new 'freedoms' afforded to women (see the example of women in Ghana above). In addition, similar to other articles, this one quickly addressed the drawbacks associated with using such equal rights ('she has more rights than she *dares* use'). These paradoxes do not stop in the introduction, and the article continues with the following paragraphs:

> In the eyes of the law women are equal to men. In theory they earn similar money for a similar job. But women are rarely found in senior professional positions in spite of the fact that the level of female education is high and more than half the students in colleges are girls.

The fact is that women have freedom but not power, and the gap between the official equality and unofficial discrimination can be seen in other ways. For example, important appointments are often made not at official meetings but during unofficial gatherings in the sauna or elsewhere.

In this passage, the article engaged with a main cause of women's inequality – discrimination – stating that it is experienced at an unofficial level (the manner in which appointments and nominations are made) and is prevalent, not just because it is widespread, but because women do not demand better. 'The Finnish woman is indispensable on the labour front and is often underpaid, since she is not easily drawn to militancy'. Here, as in other examples previously discussed in this chapter, women were to blame for their own discrimination merely because they were unwilling to improve their own lives. By placing individual women, rather than society, as responsible for eliminating gendered hierarchies, the discourse does two things. First, it perpetuated notions of traditional gender roles by stating that Finnish women were unlikely to resist their position because they were 'naturally' passive, feminine and demure. Second, the article reinforced liberal rhetoric of the 'self-made man or woman', who alone was responsible for improving their position in society. Therefore, rather than critiquing Finnish society for its patriarchal nature, the article constructed individual women or men as self-limiting, stating that anyone could improve their lot, if or when they changed their minds and acted.

That Finnish women simply had not yet decided to become equal was further emphasized when the author noted that although women dressed fashionably, chose their own boyfriends, engaged in premarital relations, ultimately they idealized traditional family roles that placed them as 'the guardian of the home, bustling mother and loving partner who brings him his slippers and clean shirt'. This subservient position is thus constructed as a choice women make, rather than something they are socialized into. Here, therefore, lies a key paradox – while equality was at women's fingertips, they *rejected* it for traditional roles. Once again, this construction served patriarchy and capitalism, both of which benefited from traditional gender roles. That the article engaged with these individualistic critiques, rather than cultural ones, is unsurprising, as the failure to de-construct gender roles further perpetuates men's dominance over women, and capitalism's exploitation of female workers through paying them lower wages at work and nothing at home. However, despite the fact that these overarching systems are served by the discourse, counter-discourses also emerge in this article, most notably when the author identifies the contradiction between the emerging women's movement (which she labelled a 'sensible, objective movement, supported by many men and far from any extremist "woman power" sentiments') and qualities most respected in a mother according to a prize-winning poem. In this poem, mothers were idealized as 'a cloudborne Madonna carrying a 20-kilo baby in her arms, or an exhausted ruin of a woman who has sacrificed herself for her many children'. Here, the author seems puzzled that women would choose the latter role, stating that these images were 'disheartening', though she provided no details as to what a more suitable model would entail. The contradiction is embedded in the final paragraph, where the author suggested that, despite the dominance of traditional women's roles and their unequal place in society, 'It is still good to be a woman in Finland, and it is getting better every day'. The contradictory mix of discourses stating that although equal rights are available to women, they reject them for traditional gender roles, demonstrates the ideological battle that took place in the quest to frame equal rights. Like the previous chapter, framing equal rights as contradictory or complex should be seen as a sign of progress – that journalists are moving away from simple black-and-white dichotomies and taking into account various nuances and paradoxes within society and men and women's places within it.

Summary

Through the use of content and critical discourse analysis, this chapter explores the nuanced ways in which equal rights were represented, and addresses cross-national differences and similarities in coverage. These nuances were the result of differing socio-political contexts; the ways in which equal rights were sought after; and the format, readership and political leanings of the publications in which they appeared. One of the most noticeable features from my sample is that, similar to the Second Wave, equal rights were addressed through different lenses in the US and the UK. In the former, this was done mainly through the proposed ERA, which was first presented by Congress to state legislatures for approval in 1972 and was defeated ten years later. The UK, on the other hand, experienced no such equivalent ongoing news peg. Instead, it addressed equal rights in relation to individual attempts to use equal rights legislation (as in the *Daily Mirror*) or through features on how women were coping with newfound equality (as in *The Times*). The difference in lenses also accounted for other qualitative cross-national differences. For example, most discussion in my US publications focused on the merits or drawbacks of equal rights legislation only, whereas in the UK, articles explored the opportunities and problems equality posed for various institutions and members of society. Perhaps because liberal theory was so ingrained in the US, and public debates over equality were waged during the Civil Rights Movement a decade earlier, people bypassed such discussions. In the UK, however, the public might have been so preoccupied discussing equality between classes that the topic of gender had never really emerged. Furthermore, passing equality legislation early on gave people the time to ponder the effects of such changes and their effect on society.

Another notable difference is the prominence of supportive discourses and frames, which achieved hegemony in all of my publications except for the *Daily Mirror*. Here, equal rights were continually rejected and delegitimized throughout the 14-year time period – a surprising finding given that the *Daily Mirror* was a well-known Labour newspaper and a strong supporter of the trade unions. Another surprise was that my two conservative papers, the *Chicago Tribune* and *The Times* overwhelmingly supported equal rights (legislation). Once again, these results indicate that in times of social change, traditional affiliations of 'conservative' or 'left-leaning' might not be the best predictor in how a publication will report social issues. Perhaps interviews with editors and journalists would have been able to shed light on these findings.

Liberal discourses prevail

While the overall amount of support for equal rights is laudable, I argue the overall prominence of such discourses is problematic, placing the burden on individuals to improve their position in society, omitting a discussion of the need for collective social change. Such discourses consequently ignored the capitalist and patriarchal nature of society and the fact that these ideologies were so deeply ingrained that they could not merely be legislated away. Consequently, while equal rights legislation theoretically opened up many doors for women, it did not go far enough to merit lasting change. For example, even when men and women were granted equal educational and occupational opportunities, people's beliefs in women's 'natural' abilities or callings remained largely stagnant, varying from woman to woman, depending on skin colour, age, physical ability, ethnicity and sexual orientation. Furthermore, despite over 40 years of equality legislation in both nations, capitalist structures have not parried out men and women's pay, nor have they ended women's exploitation in the home or raised the status of 'women's work'. My position on the discourses present is thus cautionary. While I am critical of liberal theory for its inability to bring structural change, I do believe that accepting the principal of equal rights is a positive step towards fundamental change. As Chafetz & Dworkin write, structural change is more likely to develop 'where women's educational and occupational status more closely parallels men's and where a greater proportion of women are in the labor force' (1986 cited in Margolis 1993, p. 396).

Gender roles and women's (in)equality

Where liberal theory was used to gain support for equal rights, a limited repertoire of discourses were used to oppose and de-legitimize any need for a redistribution of social, political and economic power between men and women. Here, as in the previous chapter, notions of 'natural' gender roles played a prominent role in constructing equal rights as harmful for women, men, society and the family. Such discourses provided a particular challenge for social activists because they are extraordinarily difficult to combat. How does one 'prove' that men and women are socialized differently or that biology is an unsuitable explanation for women's 'choice' to give up careers each year and return to the home? For those seeking to uphold societal inequalities, biology is a simple, effective answer. What is notable about these discourses is that they played an important role in the overall backlash to feminism that became highly theorised from the 1980s onwards (Faludi 1992), highlighting the range of problems that equal rights supposedly created for men, women, the family and society in general.

Complex equality

While clear use of such discourses and ideologies emerged in many articles, not all presented equal rights as a black-and-white issue, and equal rights were at times framed as complex, contradictory and controversial in both nations, although they were constructed in different ways. For example, in the US, articles often captured disputes between ERA foes and supporters, or discussed overall support for equal rights but a rejection of the ERA. In the UK, on the other hand, articles at times focused on the availability of equal rights, but women's refusal to accept them, 'preferring' traditional roles. While not all constructions should be seen as an improvement on the conventional 'duelling sources' format, used to create the illusion of balance and objectivity, they at least more truthfully reflected the ways in which opposing ideologies contested one another in an effort to attain (or retain) hegemony.

Overall however, whether the article supported, opposed or was somewhere in between regarding equal rights, the analysis revealed not only that a limited range of discourses were used across all four publications, but also that oppressive ideologies, such as patriarchy, capitalism, racism and heterosexism, have persisted, despite widespread acceptance that women should be afforded equal opportunities and rights as men.

4
Reporting Feminism in 2008

Wave feminism

[F]or anyone born after the early 1960s, the presence of
feminism in our lives is taken for granted. For our generation, feminism is like fluoride. We scarcely notice that we
have it – it's simply in the water. (Baumgardner & Richards
2000, p. 17)

Introduction

Forty years after the initial surge of Second Wave activism, to what
extent is feminism still on the public's agenda, and how has it been
constructed in the press? While some continue to overlook the plethora of feminist activism that has persisted since the 1980s, others
have recognized, if not embraced, the presence of this Third Wave
movement. Because the current status of feminist activism is highly
contested and debated, this chapter seeks to examine how it was
constructed 2008, paying particular attention to what it is thought
to stand for, who can be considered a feminist and what issues it is
thought to combat in contemporary society. As a result, this chapter
examines news of feminism in 2008 in eight British and American
newspapers.[1] While the chapter continues to draw upon the original
four publications – *The New York Times*, the *Chicago Tribune*, the *Daily
Mirror*, and *The Times* – four new ones were added to give a broader
look at the range of discourses of feminism in circulation. These
include the conservative *Washington Times* and *Daily Mail* (Bush 2002;
Conboy 2006; Edwards 2002), and the more liberal *Washington Post*
and *The Guardian* (Dean 2010; Decter 2002; Edwards 2002; McNair
2009; Sutter 2001; Taylor 1993).

Feminism in the news

Unlike First Wave Feminism, which has been largely associated with suffrage, and Second Wave Feminism, which was linked to equal rights, reproductive freedom and an end to sexual violence against women (Bouchier 1983; Bradley 2003), some have argued that the Third Wave lacks a single goal or identity that unites the movement (Henry 2004; Redfern & Aune 2010). Others, such as veteran Second Wave feminist Muriel Fox, stated that 'Most of us who were in the Second Wave still say we are still in the Second Wave, not the Third Wave, because the major issues haven't been resolved' (Personal Interview 2010). While some Second Wave organizations, such as NOW and the Fawcett Society, are still active today, a whole range of new organizations have since emerged, both off- and online.[2] But to what extent are these feminist enclaves recognized, and how are they constructed in the press?

Throughout this chapter, I will demonstrate that, once again, feminism was predominantly supported in all of my publications except for the *Daily Mail* and the *Washington Times,* where oppositional frames dominated. What is noteworthy, however, is that even when feminism was supported, it was often done through a defensive position, arguing that feminism was *not as bad* as people believed. Furthermore, when exploring oppositional articles in depth, it appears as though the range of discourses used to de-legitimize feminism during the Second Wave's height have changed little, indicating the extent to which patriarchal, racist, heterosexist and neoliberal discourse continue to thrive in both nations. Finally, a third frame recognized the complexity inherent in feminism, particularly in attempting to define what feminism is and who can appropriate this label. Such articles demonstrate that questions about what feminism means are still open for debate – and should be viewed as an opportunity for growth.

Overall trends in coverage

Overall, the 2008 data demonstrates that 443 articles with the keywords 'feminism', 'feminist', or variation of 'women's movement' were published in my eight newspapers, with an almost even number of articles per nation (212 in the US vs. 231 in the UK).[3] One notable change in trends is the proportionate growth of British news of feminism, which could be due to a number of factors, an important one being the increased length of British newspapers over the past twenty years (Curran & Seaton 2003), providing more space in which feminism could be addressed.[4] Other forms of feminist activism, notably the Greenham Common peace protests, continued to attract news media attention in the 1980s and 1990s, which perhaps secured feminism a more prominent place within popular discourse. Although the number of articles per nation is fairly even, a closer examination of the data reveals large variances between publications (see Figure 4.1). For example, *The Times* published 82 articles (19 per cent of total), followed closely with 78 *New York Times* articles (18 per cent of total), and 74 *Guardian* articles (17 per cent of total). At the other end of the scale, the *Daily Mirror* carried a mere 23 articles (5 per cent of total), while *The Washington Times* carried 35 articles (8 per cent of total). The disparity in figures indicates the extent to which discourses surrounding feminism were not equally distributed among newspapers, and signals that as an ideology, feminism carried more weight in some publications over others. In this

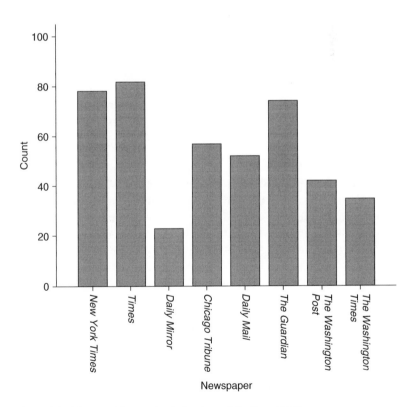

Figure 4.1 News articles on feminism by publication, 2008

particular case, while the *Daily Mirror* was once famous for supporting and advocating labour issues, it now caters to middle-aged women
interested in celebrity gossip (Niblock 2008). On the other hand, *The
Washington Times* perhaps ignored feminism because it conflicted with
the paper's 'zealous, uncompromising commitment to conservative
principles' (Edwards 2002, p. 63) and its general anti-feminist stance
(Decter 2002).

Genre

Because genre impacts the style, tone and narrative of a story (Cottle
2003), it can indicate whether or how ways of articulating feminism
have changed over time. In fact, a comparative examination of the data
demonstrates that patterns have changed dramatically since the Second
Wave, when most stories were classed as either features (29 per cent) or
news reports (32 per cent). In the current sample, however, there was
a significant increase in features (15 per cent increase) and columns
(16 per cent increase) and an even bigger decrease in news reports (25
per cent decrease). While this study is not representative of all news, it
lends credence to the argument that there has been an historical shift
from straight reporting to interpretation and commentary (Franklin
1997; McNair 2008; Niblock 2008). In fact, *Daily Mirror* editor Richard
Wallace stated in 2007 that 'today's newspapers are not necessarily
about news', and that it was 'no secret' that he had moved the *Mirror*
down a 'more magazine-style road, and skew a degree of content to the
35-plus working woman' (cited in Niblock 2008, p. 48). Consequently,
nearly all stories on feminism within this publication were in some
way related to celebrity culture, lifestyle or consumption – a worrying
trend for many feminist scholars who feel that such shifts remove feminism of its politics (see Cole & Crossley 2009 for a recent discussion).
For example, in one column regarding British pop star and soccer wife
(also known as a WAG – wives and girlfriends) Cheryl Cole's refusal to
leave her cheating husband, Polly Hudson lamented:

> Every word Cheryl uttered to the shabby newspaper goes against eve-
> rything I thought she was and believed in it. She has let us all down –
> or maybe we were total mugs for believing she was different to all the
> other WAGs in the first place.
>   She billed herself as Miss Independent, the kind of girl who returns
> a Bentley her bloke buys her because she's got a car she bought with
> her own money.

Someone who refuses to let her husband's career take precedence over hers, which is why the couple aren't currently Madrid-based. A woman with such admirable self-belief, strong morals and feminist principles that she wouldn't stand anyone disrespecting her. (Hudson 2008, p. 10)

While such celebrity-focused stories are expected in tabloids such as the *Daily Mirror*, even *The Guardian* editor Alan Rusbridger admitted that the 'quality press' increasingly includes celebrity-driven and other 'soft' news stories (cited in Franklin 1997, p. 10).[5] Examples of 'soft' headlines from British broadsheets include: 'Can a feminist really love *Sex and the City*?' (Wignall 2008, p. 18); 'Old lady Madonna: Even veteran pop icons can't avoid the usual stereotypes and slurs against ageing women' (Williams 2008, p. 35); 'Mini Skirt or Burka, That's My Right' (Bourke 2008, p. 23); and 'The day a feminist icon resigned as my mother' (Driscoll 2008, p. 3). Because many, though not all, 'softer' news stories are generated by issues or trends as distinguished from current events, it is fruitful to examine what 'sparked' these stories in the first place.

News pegs

As during the height of the Second Wave, news of feminism was sparked by a range of different events or issues in 2008. These include court cases or tribunals (17 articles or 4 per cent of total), feature stories (53 articles or 12 per cent of total) and surveys or research (20 articles or 5 per cent of total). However, three categories emerged that merit closer inspection: popular culture, politics and feminist activism. In the first two cases, attention is given because of their prominence, but the final category is addressed because of its worrying absence.

Popular culture

As Third Wave feminists have noted, feminism is a topic closely associated with a wide range of issues, concerns and campaigns (Redfern & Aune 2010; Valenti 2007). Consequently, it was no surprise to find this diversity reflected in news coverage. From the article tracing feminist and small business owner Rosie Boycott's reluctance to hire young women of child-bearing age in 'The queen feminist thinking twice about employing young women' (Boycott 2008a, p. 3) to analyses of US vice presidential candidates Hillary Clinton and Sarah Palin's feminist credentials in 'Sarah Palin: A Feminist Triumph or the Most Underqualified Vice President Ever?' (Paglia 2008, p. 6) to the ethics of beauty pageants in 'Ignore the Po-Faced Feminists. Why Shouldn't Brains Celebrate Beauty?' (Moir 2008, p. 30) to discussions about identity politics in 'Ranking race against gender is the first step towards fundamentalism' (Younge 2008, p. 31), feminism was related to a multitude of topics.

One topic in particular, however, which emerged time and time again throughout this sample, was the relationship between feminism and popular culture. In total, 115 articles (26 per cent of total) either discussed feminism or employed a feminist lens in analysing celebrities, books, television programs, films, the performing arts, music and more.[6] Typical headlines include: 'Why do so many female artists put themselves in their work – often with no clothes on?' (Greer 2008, p. 28), 'Is Carrie Bradshaw a feminist? More importantly, am I?' (Fordham 2008, p. T2 7), 'A knack for putting feminism on film' (Finn 2008, p. B4) and 'Bond girls are feminist icons!' (Weinberg 2008, p. 49). Not only do these articles often provide a feminist lens through which to evaluate cultural texts, they also demonstrate that feminist discourses are no longer the reserve of academia and have permeated popular culture. In assessing the value of a book, film, actor, art display or performer, journalists and commentators now frequently analyse the extent to which feminism has shaped or influenced the content. For example, the following *Guardian* feature does not merely trace the rise of female comediennes (which could be seen as a feminist victory) but focuses instead on the growing number of those who identify as feminists:

> [Sarah] Haskins is just one of many US comedians to have emerged in the past few years who share a defining trait. They're feminists. And this is particularly interesting when you consider that feminists are generally characterized as humorless, given to dusting off our protest signs while ominously discussing patriarchy. This stereotype is ridiculous, of course, but it has been around since at least 1911 – when the *New York Times* ran a headline attesting to 'A suffragist's lack of humour.' And while women have regularly used wit to communicate political messages in the meantime, feminist comedians have never before been so visible. (Valenti 2008b, p. G2 14)

While many articles addressed the prevalence of feminism (or feminists) in popular culture, others employed a feminist lens to analyse the merits of a particular text or performer. Regarding Stephanie Meyer's *Twilight* series, one feature explained:

> The allure of 'Twilight' lies in its combination of modern sensibility and ambience with traditional ideas about gender. Bella has broad appeal; as many girls can appreciate, she likes watching reruns of 'The Simpsons' while she nibbles on Pop-Tarts. But the twist is that Bella's ideas about gender roles are decidedly unfeminist. The pairing of a modern setting and traditional gender roles is unusual in children's and teen literature. More often, modern books communicate a modern view of gender: beginning in early childhood, for example, girls read the 'Dora the Explorer' series and grow into adolescence with books such as 'Esperanza Rising' and 'The Breadwinner.
> Despite all the modern accoutrements in the 'Twilight' saga, the girls are still girls, and the boys are traditional men. More specifically: The lead male characters, Edward Cullen and Jacob Black, are muscular and unwaveringly brave, while Bella and the other girls bake cookies, make supper for the men and hold all-female slumber parties. It gets worse for feminists: Bella is regularly threatened with violence in the first three books, and in every instance she is rescued by Edward or Jacob. (Sax, 2008, p. B07)

While at first glance the close link between popular culture and feminism might appear worrisome given that there are still more 'serious' feminist issues (such as domestic violence and subsidized child care) that have yet to be resolved, the examples above demonstrate that popular culture can provide journalists an opportunity to address pressing social, political and cultural issues – such as gender roles and oppressive stereotypes. For example, when Sony was about to release 'Fat Princess' – a video game in which an overweight princess is kidnapped and forced to eat cake, feminism provided the language through which the game could be critiqued (No Byline 2008a, p. 24).

Politics

While the majority of articles were sparked by popular culture, the second largest group were those regarding traditional party politics. This includes articles on government legislation (7 articles or 2 per cent of total), campaigns (9 articles or 2 per cent of total), politicians or political parties (24 articles or 5 per cent of total) and the US general election (90 articles or 20 per cent of total). This last category in particular sparked a range of stories in both nations, as Democrat Hillary Clinton and

Republican Sarah Palin are self-identified feminists. In stories address-ing both feminism and politics, the tone, genre and formats varied. While news reports carried more factual headlines such as: 'Gingrich calls Palin threat to feminists, slams media' (Ward 2008, p. A03) and 'For women voters, age gap emerges' (Parsons 2008, p. 1), features, col-umns and letters to the editor were more sensational: 'Fear and loath-ing of Palin; Feminists can't stand too much of a good thing' (Fields 2008b, p. A21), or 'The F-card won't wash: Sarah Palin is disastrous for women's rights, no matter how Republicans frame her as a feminist' (Valenti 2008a, 34).

While the British press carried several stories on the US election, only a handful focused on the role of (feminist) politicians or legis-lation at home – a finding also mirrored by recent research (Aune & Redfern 2010; Ross 2010). For example, one *Times* article reported how the Labour Party deputy-leader Harriett Harman 'has always been dedi-cated to furthering the cause of women', before noting 'We are making progress, but we have further to go' (Thomson & Sylvester 2008, p. 33). Harriet Harman was one of a limited number of female politicians who attracted British media attention, although her feminist stance was at times used against her. When speculation grew about her intentions to run as the Labour Party leader, several articles focused a joke she made regarding her feminist reputation, stating that were she to be elected: '[A]ll the men would want to flee the country' (No Byline 2008b, p. 8). Consequently, through a combination of dismissive comments and an overall lack of coverage, it appears that feminism and politics were not always seen as compatible in my British publications. Further evidence of this can be found in several columns discussing proposed changes to laws regarding victims of domestic abuse. In cases where such victims murdered their abusive partners, Harman had proposed that defend-ants would be allowed to plead provocation or fear of future attacks:

> Effectively, what Harman and the ultra-feminist lobby want is a license for women to kill.
> For thousands of years, one of the pillars of Judeo-Christian civili-zation has been the ethical injunction, 'Thou shalt not kill.'
> But now, radical female modernisers think that this moral edifice can be pulled down and replaced with a perverse new moral code which holds that women can murder as long as their sense of victim-hood is sufficiently powerful. (Pizzey 2008, p. 12)

Significantly, this diatribe was written by Erin Pizzey, who established one of the UK's first domestic violence shelters for women – although it should be noted that despite such seemingly feminist credentials, she has not necessarily been known to support the Sisterhood.

Feminist activism

Although it was common to find articles relating feminism to popular culture and politics, few explicitly or routinely covered feminist activities, protests or even formal organizations, *The Guardian* being the only exception. However, such articles were few and far between and fail to truly grasp the extent to which feminist organizations and activities persist in many British and American cities (see Redfern & Aune 2010 for a recent discussion). In total, only 10 articles (2 per cent of total) primarily focused on feminist campaigns or activities, in contrast to 275 articles (50 per cent of total) during the Second Wave. While some might argue that this difference is logical given that feminism is often thought of as 'dead' (McRobbie 2009; Smith 2003), feminist groups and activism have sprung up around both countries in recent years (see Baumgardner & Richards; Redfern & Aune 2010; Valenti 2007). For example, during a personal interview, Sian Norris, Bristol Feminist Network's press officer, discussed how the group regularly contacted the national and local media, sending out press releases for events (such as Take Back the Night marches and research on representations of women in the media). However, despite these efforts, she argued: '[I]t's mainly the local press that covers us. If it doesn't happen outside of London, it doesn't get covered' (Personal Interview 2010). Similarly, Finn MacKay, founder of the London's Women's Liberation Network also acknowledged the group frequently contacted the mainstream media but had more luck with community-based news organizations than national ones (Personal Interview 2010). The lack of national news coverage, identified by Third Wave feminists and by the quantitative results in this study, raises questions about why feminist activities were not considered newsworthy. When posed this question, Kira Cochrane, feminist and deputy weekend editor for *The Guardian,* responded:

> I think that a very large amount of feminist activity, thought and campaigning is regularly reported in the news section, but generally in the context of stories on a particular feminist issue. So, for instance, you often find quotations from groups such as Women Against Rape in news articles about the low rape conviction rate; quotations from members of Object [a feminist organization] in news articles about lap dancing clubs; quotations from members of The Fawcett Society in news articles about women's representation in Parliament, etc, etc. Feminist campaigning groups are very well-represented in *The Guardian* in this regard, I think. It's quite rare for

any single piece of stand-alone campaigning – a march, protest, etc – to be reported in the news pages of any newspaper, I would guess, unless it reaches the scale of, say, the anti-Iraq war protests, or some of the anti-globalisation protests that have taken place over recent years. I don't think this is due to any sense that feminism is dead, but simply that, in an age where there are thankfully quite a lot of regular protests, on quite a lot of disparate issues, it takes an enormous movement of people through an area to make a strong news story. (Personal Interview 2010)

Such remarks indicate that it is not necessarily that feminist activities have become less newsworthy per se, but that the scale of event is a more important factor in determining whether they will be included in the national or major metropolitan news.[7]

In addition to uncovering what 'sparked' news of feminism, it is worthwhile to examine how feminism is discursively constructed within a range of issues today.

Issues associated with feminism

As an ideology that has spanned centuries and continents, feminism, perhaps unsurprisingly, lacks one universal and historic definition. This means that views regarding the causes and solutions to women's oppression; identifying strategies; and determining the best means for achieving social change over time and space vary. While this research does not seek to 'prove' what feminism stands for, part of the 'storying' of feminism in a Western context entails uncovering how it has been publicly constructed over time, and analysing what it is *seen* to fight for. While the Second Wave became largely defined by battles for equal rights, pay and sexual and reproductive freedom (Bouchier 1983; Bradley 2003; Bryson 2003; Coote & Campbell 1982), it is less clear what issues feminism is associated with contemporarily. A scan on some of the more prominent feminist websites such as NOW, Feminist Majority, The Fawcett Society and Object demonstrates that Second Wave goals are still very much at the forefront today. While 129 articles (29 per cent) failed to link feminism with any specific issue, the other 71 per cent were spread out over a wide variety of topics, including work/life balance, domestic violence, prostitution, religion, gender roles and infidelity (see Table 4.1). This suggests that, publicly at least, feminism's meaning has become more fractured and diverse over time, extending its reach to a wide variety of issues (see also Redfern & Aune

Table 4.1   Issues associated with feminism, 2008

Valid	Frequency	Per cent
Not applicable	129	29.1
Equal rights/pay/opportunities	52	11.7
Sexism/discrimination	50	11.3
Oppression/patriarchy	9	2.0
Abortion	13	2.9
Child care/birth	3	0.7
Individual choice	10	2.3
Objectification	5	1.1
Appearances	34	7.7
Domestic Violence	5	1.1
Work–life balance	8	1.8
Sexual abuse/assault/harassment	4	0.9
Women in office/politics	42	9.5
Sexual freedom	9	2.0
Personal empowerment	19	4.3
Gender roles	19	4.3
Religion	6	1.4
Created new problems for women/men	20	4.5
Infidelity	2	0.5
Solidarity	1	0.2
Prostitution	3	0.7
Total	443	100.0

2010). Examples of such diversity were found within the following articles: 'The one-night stand generation' (Appleyard & Smith-Squire 2008, p. 42); 'She's thrown in the wet wipe...and turned the clock back 30 years' (Jones 2008a, p. 28); 'Feminist contempt for prostitutes' (Letter to the Editor 2008a, p. 33); and 'In Turkey, Students Test a New Policy on Head Scarves' (Knickmeyer 2008, p. A10). Despite the plurality of issues related to feminism, two main themes emerged: equal rights, pay and opportunities (52 articles or 12 per cent), and objectification, sexism and discrimination against women (50 articles or 11 per cent).

Objectification and sexism

One of the most widely discussed topics relating to feminism was the continued or increased presence of objectification, sexism and discrimination against women (50 articles or 11 per cent of total). While these issues were addressed in a number of news stories, they were particularly prominent throughout Hillary Clinton and Sarah Palin's candidacies. For the latter, whose attractiveness was frequently commented upon, a

'Sarah Palin sexism watch' emerged after doctored images of the candidate's head on a 'rifle-toting model in a stars-and-stripes bikini' began to circulate (Cochrane 2008e, p. G2 16). Manufacturers also released a 'naughty schoolgirl' and blow-up Sarah Palin sex doll (Walter 2010, p. 121), which were fortunately critiqued in much coverage: 'For better or worse (I would say the latter), Palin is the highest-profile female politician in the world now, which makes the constant objectification of her particularly galling' (Cochrane 2008e, p. G2 16).

While Palin undoubtedly received the majority of objectifying coverage, other commentators criticized the media's focus on Clinton's clothes, hair, weight and cleavage:

Like a magnet – was it the pantsuit? – Clinton drew out the nation's misogyny in all its jeering glory and put it where we could all get a good look at it. 'Iron my shirt' hecklers. Buyers of Hillary Nutcrackers. Vats of sexist nastiness splattered across the comments sections of hundreds of blogs and Web sites. It's as if every obscene phone caller and every exhibitionist in America decided to become an amateur political pundit. (Pollitt 2008, p. 19)

Although many authors took partisan positions in the election, several were able to look beyond traditional party divides and critique the media's sexism towards both women:

Supporters of both women [Palin and Clinton] claim they were the victims of sexism, ranging from overweening interest in their wardrobes to unfair suspicion of their policy platforms [...]
    But [Gloria] Steinem argues that even the sexist heckling at Clinton rallies and the negative treatment from cable television hosts had had a positive effect in opening the eyes of a younger generation of women to sexism.
    'Lots of women in their 20s and 30s were shocked and appalled,' said Steinem. 'It awoke them to a problem that they thought had been solved.'(Goldenberg 2008, p. GH7)

While unfortunate that many articles were blatantly sexist towards either candidate, they also provided a focal point for which commentators could highlight and discuss pervasive social inequalities and oppression. As one letter to the editor commented: 'Seeing Senator Clinton as an ancillary to her husband rather than her own person, minimizing her professional experience, and commenting on how she looks and sounds are quintessential sexism' (Letter to the Editor 2008b, p. A22).

Equal opportunities, discrimination and the glass ceiling

In addition to documenting the persistence of sexism and objectification in news coverage, issues surrounding equal opportunities and discrimination were also frequently addressed – often through the metaphor of a glass ceiling – the idea that women, regardless of ability, are prevented from reaching the top echelons of employment because of their gender. This topic received a fair amount of media attention, particularly after Clinton's concession speech where she declared that the 18 million votes she received to become leader of the Democratic Party represented the same number of cracks in the proverbial glass ceiling (Goldenberg 2008, p. GH7). While this topic was raised in regards to the election, it was also identified as a problem in everyday workplaces:

'Having worked in corporate America for 20 years, I find, as much as women have had some movement up, the glass ceiling is still very strong,' said Ms. Phillips, the performance artist. 'Even in publishing where most of the workday jobs are done by women, most of the executives are men,' she said. 'It's frustrating. You do feel a sense of a boy's club that keeps women out.' (Hartocollis 2008, p. B1)

Such sentiments recognized the collective nature of women's oppression, although few articles provided solutions on how to break through the ceiling, leaving the impression that this is a problem that might never be solved.

Another range of articles discussed instances where women were granted equal rights as men. For example, the *Daily Mirror* reported on 'exciting news from Sweden', where female soccer players launched a campaign demanding the right to remove their tops after their team scored a goal (No Byline 2008e). Another article along similar lines explained:

Feminism, some men may argue, has its downsides – particularly when it means they have to share the housework.
But few would protest against the latest victory for women's rights.
Ladies in Copenhagen will now be allowed to swim and walk around topless in public pools.
The decision is the result of a year-long campaign by a pressure group, the Topless Front, which says women should be treated the same as bare-chested men. (Oscarsson 2008, p. 19)

While most articles, even the ones above, acknowledged inequalities between the sexes (laws prohibiting them from removing articles of clothing in public), others reproduced claims that sexual discrimination was a 'feminist myth'. For example, one study on the matter insisted that pay gap between men and women:

> [H]as nothing to do with discrimination by employers. Instead, the difference in salaries between male and female workers came down to 'individual lifestyle preferences.' The choice of millions of mothers to put children before careers was the chief reason given for the disparity between men and women that emerged after 30, the IEA's paper said. (Doughty 2008, p. 47).

Consequently, while structural inequalities in pay were widely acknowledged, a discourse of individual blame, identified in Chapter 3, persisted.

Work–life balance

Although work–life balance was associated as feminism's main issue in only eight articles (2 per cent of total), issues surrounding time management regularly appeared throughout the sample. While most discussed the difficulties that journalists or 'ordinary' sources had managing a successful career and raising a family, others focused on high-profile people. For example, one *Daily Mail* feature argued that in stepping down from her Cabinet position, MP Ruth Kelly 'in one fell swoop, made it OK for men to continue to treat female politicians and co-workers and bedmates as the hormone-driven hysterics they always suspected they were' (Jones 2008a, p. 28). Palin also came under fire for her choice to run for Vice President while caring for an infant with Down syndrome (see Letter to the Editor 2008f; Marcus 2008). Such high-profile cases raised questions on whether women really could 'have it all' as feminists suggested (Boycott 2008b, p. 14). Even the discussion of whether or not this is ever truly possible serves to limit feminism's potency and has been long used as a backlash tactic (Faludi 1992).

Framing feminism

Similar to the previous two chapters, three main frames emerged in the 2008 sample: those of support, opposition and complexity. This section seeks to unpack these frames, exploring the range of discourses employed, sources used and context given. While it is apparent that many of the discourses in circulation in 2008 are strikingly similar to those employed during the Second Wave, particularly regarding discourses of backlash and postfeminism, there has also been the emergence of neoliberal discourses used to promote feminism through rhetoric of personal freedom, empowerment and choice. Also new to this sample is the noticeable rise of radical critiques of patriarchy, capitalism, racism, ageism and other interlocking forms of oppression, indicating that such counter-hegemonic views have slowly gained acceptance in public discourse. Finally, discussions about what feminism meant in 2008 and who could consider themselves to be a feminist, helped to construct the frame of feminism as complex. Such frames are important because they inform society about where the movement is contemporarily, and where it might be heading.

Legitimizing feminism

When examining news of feminism in 2008, I was once again surprised by the larger-than-expected number of articles legitimizing it. In total, 245 articles (51 per cent of total) could be described as employing supportive frames, representing a slight increase (5 per cent) since the movement 'ended'. Furthermore, such findings support a recent study stating that most young women identify with feminist ideals or label themselves feminists (Zazlow 2009).[8] Examples of supportive headlines include: 'This wittering beauty queen is so wrong – we do still need feminists' (Jones 2008b, p. 26); 'Feminism is a force in US politics' (Letter to the editor 2008c, p. 37); 'Don't blame feminism for male predicament' (Letter to the editor 2008d, p. 18); 'Feminism isn't a four-lettered word' (Smith 2008, p. 7); and 'Here's looking at you and your babe: taking a whack at female stereotypes' (La Rocco 2008, p. B9). What is notable about these headlines, and many similar ones, is that while certainly supportive of feminism, they legitimize it from a defensive position (see also Dean 2010). For example, the letter to the editor 'Don't blame feminism for male predicament' challenged an article blaming feminism for many of society's problems:

> Kathleen Parker's article raises pertinent questions about our changing society (Where have all the real men gone? News Review, last week). To blame the demise of the real man (she never defines what this is) on feminism is a cheap shot. She laments the prevalence of the metrosexualised man and perfumed ponies, but men wore wigs, makeup and tights in the 17th and 18th centuries. (2008d, p. 18)

Similarly, 'Feminism isn't a four-lettered word' combated arguments that all feminists were 'man haters who wore dungarees' (Smith 2008, p. 7). Such defences, however, are unlikely to hold when competing with sensational (and enduring) stereotypes of feminists as man-hating lesbians (Scharff 2010). For example, in one column, British activist Bea Campbell was described as a 'crop-headed, lesbian feminist member of the National Association of Irrationally Furious Women Against Everything' (Rifkind 2008, 13). That imagery of lesbians continue to thrive in 2008 (though one could argue that such stereotypes still circulate today) indicates that 'feminism's challenge to conventional constructions of femininity and heterosexuality are still not over' (Scharff 2010, p. 838). Furthermore, with such discourses in circulation, it is no wonder then that many articles began from a defensive position, although I would argue it would take a massive public relations campaign or a significant shift in society's views of gender to challenge these stereotypes, which have held cultural currency for so long.

Positive connotations

Throughout this sample, there were many examples where feminism was constructed as a desirable identity or as an ideology that had positively affected society (61 articles or 14 per cent of total). The prominence of such sentiments contrasts with research indicating that feminism causes 'problems' for women, men or society (Faludi 1992; McRobbie 2007; Tasker & Negra 2007). For example, when discussing her West End production in *The Guardian*, playwright Joanna Murray-Smith explained:

> My intention in writing *The Female of the Species* was to devise a lively, funny play about feminism, among other things, and more specifically, about the legacy of those Second Wave feminists whose courage, stamina and occasionally infuriating intellect have changed society forever. (Murray-Smith 2008, p. G2 28)

Another article – a news report – highlighted research that women who described themselves as feminists were 'more forgiving' when commenting on over- and underweight women's appearances, and were less likely to believe that 'the most important thing for women is to be thin'. Such views were said to lead to a healthier body image and a happier life (Nagourney 2008, p. F6).

Similar to the previous chapters, the adoption of the feminist identity by celebrities and cultural or political elites was once again a common legitimizing tool in 2008. For example, American comedienne Margaret Cho noted how she would be 'insane' not to be a feminist, given that she worked in a male-dominated field and hoped to be paid and treated the same as men (Valenti 2008b, p. G2 14). In some instances, news that certain (mostly male) celebrities considered themselves feminists was enough to merit publication. As one *Guardian* news in brief noted:

> Speaking of feminists, it was almost as much of a joy to find the *Entourage* star Adrian Grenier declaring himself a feminist in last week's G2 as it was to hear Jack Nicholson making the same claim earlier this year. So which other fabulous male feminists are lurking in celebrity-land? A quick search uncovers Alan Alda and, um, Hugh Hefner, who once described himself as 'a feminist before there was such a thing as feminism.' (Cochrane 2008a, p. G2 17)

That such announcements were considered newsworthy implies that the embracement of a feminist identity was not yet the norm, particularly for men.[9]

One surprising space where the feminist identity was legitimized was in obituaries – both paid-for announcements and news reports. An example of the latter included:

> Ruth Vilaca Correa Leite Cardoso, a Brazilian anthropologist who carved out a career as one of her country's most respected intellectuals and feminists before rather reluctantly becoming its first lady, died June 24 at her home in Sao Paulo. She was 77. (Rohter 2008, p. B7)

The announcement of feminist deaths accounted for 25 stories (6 per cent of total), indicating that the feminist identity was an important part of their legacy. What is interesting, particularly with the paid-for obituaries, is that the label was used not only for famous feminists but for 'ordinary' people, too. The following announcement was typical: 'SCHWARTZMAN–Ruth, May 29, 1916 – June 11, 2008. Beloved mother and grandmother, dedicated feminist, socialist and idealist, Ruth came out of the cauldron of the Depression dedicating her life to empowering workers' (No Byline 2008c, p. A29).

Feminist media workers

As feminist Jo Freeman (1975) argued, unlike other social movements, feminists have long had journalist advocates on their side. Even prominent feminists such as Gloria Steinem became an integral part of the Second Wave after covering it for *New York* magazine (Fox 2010). In this sample, *The Guardian* was undoubtedly the most sympathetic to feminism, as it employed writers such as Kira Cochrane, Zoe Williams, Julie Bindel and Jessica Valenti, who all actively embraced the feminist label (and have been or are currently involved in feminist activism).[10] As

Cochrane acknowledged, the paper's liberal, left-leaning stance makes it 'natural that it would be sympathetic to issues of women's equality, and employ writers who reflect that' (Personal Interview 2010). While other publications such as the conservative *Daily Mail* generally opposed feminism, certain writers such as Liz Jones were responsible for what little supportive coverage existed (12 articles in total). Such findings indicate that, despite a publication's overall position on a topic, individuals may at times have some freedom to promote alternative views.

Postfeminist discourses

A recent trend in the field of feminist media studies is the analysis of postfeminist discourses in popular culture. Commonly identified themes include empowerment, self-improvement, consumption and a return to the home (Genz & Brabon 2009; Gill 2007; McRobbie 2007; Negra 2009; Tasker & Negra 2007; Varvus 2007; Walter 2009; Whelehan 2005). While admittedly, these discourses were not nearly as rampant as I had expected, their presence was noticeable in all eight publications. For example, 38 articles (9 per cent of total) primarily linked feminism to neoliberal themes of personal choices, sexual freedom or consumption.[11] Common sentiments included the notion that 'Feminism counts for nothing if it is not a guarantee of choice' (Betts 2008, p. G2 10), while another argued, 'Isn't the point of feminism to give women the power to choose what to do with their lives?' (No Byline 2008d, p. A12). Such views open up space to claim that anything is feminist – so long as it is freely chosen – and are problematic because they allowed women to claim feminist credentials while rationalizing and excusing patriarchal or capitalist practices that oppressed them. This includes convincing women that it is acceptable to adhere to limiting notions of female beauty or sexuality and to judge their value based on such notions (Varvus 2007). As Crittenden (2001 cited in Varvus 2007, p. 54) stated, 'The big problem with the rhetoric of choice is that it leaves out power. Those who benefit from the status quo always attribute inequalities to the choices of the underdog'. For example, the article quoted above discussed a young woman's pleasure in her 'freedom' to wear high heels, indicating that they were symbols of 'sexual power and independence' (Betts 2008, p. G2 10). From a critical perspective, it is absurd to believe that empowerment and freedom can simply be purchased. Consequently, the discourse not only reinforces capitalism but places further restrictions on notions of beauty and femininity, which are already closely linked to age, ethnicity and class. This question of choice is also probed in the feature: 'Do good feminists bake cupcakes? A new breed of young women is embracing the 1950s house-wife' (Groskop, 2008, p. G2 16). This article fits in with wider themes of domesticity, retreatism, or 'going home' narratives identified by other scholars (see Brunsdon 2000; Hollows 2006; Negra 2009; Stacey 1986) and asks what forms of traditional feminine activities liberated women can perform without promoting or reinforcing patriarchy and gendered hierarchies. As Baumgardner & Richards asserted (2000), the media like to keep women in a state of anxiety or punishment about their choices, ranging from which activities to participate in, to cosmetic decisions to family planning. Feminists have long grappled with questions surrounding the acceptability of performing domestic tasks. While some have argued that baking for fun is a form of false consciousness and is one step away from domestic enslavement, others insist that it provides an innocent, temporary escape from women's hectic lives (for a discussion, see Hollows 2006, p. 106). While this feature provides no easy answer to the acceptability of young women's fascination with 1950s style domesticity, it concludes by quoting Holly, a 20-something member of a London-based Women's Institute who claimed:

> [W]hat makes this modern domesticity very different to the old-fashioned kind is that it is done out of choice, not out of duty or an attempt to impress men. In fact, some of these women clearly see this as a chance to carve out their own space away from men, a place where they can gather to celebrate and enjoy traditionally female crafts. 'It's got nothing to do with being married,' says Holly. 'That's why it can be seen as quite subversive because you're doing it as a single woman. It's for yourself. I don't think men expect this stuff anymore at all – they are not involved in it. It's a very female-led thing. My boyfriend doesn't really understand. He says, 'What on earth do you do at the WI?' He has no idea. And I'd much rather keep it that way. (Groskop 2008, p. G2 16)

While these women might very well freely participate in such domestic tasks, the rhetoric of choice ignores the ways that such tasks have historically been feminized. Consequently, those such as feminist writer Natasha Walter commented that the domestic revival indicates 'something more serious going on here' (cited in Groskop 2008, p. 16). She continued by noting that their glamourization only increased the difficulty in getting men to participate in domestic work. Consequently, this rhetoric of choice actually represents a potential step backwards for women's progress by re-casting (or maintaining as many would argue) domestic work as a feminized activity.

Beauty, feminism and empowerment

Another common discourse found in several supportive articles is that beauty and feminism can be mixed.[12] This sentiment is part of a larger postfeminist 'girl power' discourse, which encourages girls and women to identify both as feminine objects *and* as powerful feminist agents (Zazlow 2009), refuting claims that feminism is anti-feminine and that femininity is always sexist and oppressive (Genz & Brabon 2009). Exemplifying this discourse, feminist fashion zine editor Phoebe Frangoul stated in a *Times* feature: 'I write about the rights of women to wear high heels and still call yourself a feminist. I don't feel they're mutually exclusive, and my friends don't either' (Soames 2008, pp. 18–19). As Walter (2010, p. 122) indicated, far from being 'empowering', this culture obsessed with fashion and appearances is 'claustrophobic and limiting', particularly for those who do not want to use beauty as their path towards success and status. In these articles, being a feminist is empowering, not necessarily because of what one believes or does, but because of how one appears. According to feminist blogger Catherine Redfern, the media's attempts to 're-brand' feminism as something associated with fashion and beauty is problematic because it fails to interrogate stereotypes of feminists as boring, scary and ugly or to question their existence in the first place (Personal Interview 2010). Instead, contemporary news articles such as the one below associate young women's embodiment of a feminist identity through the appropriate look and attitude:

> I wear mine [T-shirt saying, 'This is what a feminist looks like'] with a mini and lipstick, and I tell anyone who asks that I love men, but that I'm also very clear about the importance of women having equality. I've learnt from Mum that being flirty and feminine is perfectly compatible with being a feminist. (Neustatter 2008, p. 7)

As Negra (2009, p. 4) indicated, postfeminist sentiments 'attaches importance to the formulation of an expressive personal lifestyle and the ability to select the right commodities to attain it'. In this case, a mini-skirt, lipstick and a 'This is what a feminist looks like' T-shirt are essential commodities in constructing the speaker both as a (legitimate, non-radical) feminist *and* an empowered woman. This 'commodity feminism' (Gill 2008), also known as girl power culture (Zazlow 2009, p. 6), enables women to consume a feminist identity through purchasing 'powerful' clothing, buying CDs with pro-women lyrics, or talking about 'girl power', none of which requires an investment in social change (see McRobbie 2009). Commodification, then, 'neutralizes' feminist politics (Gillis et al. 2004, p. 173) by promoting consumption as the quickest path towards empowerment, thereby reinforcing patriarchal paradigms of (white, middle-class, heterosexual) beauty and femininity. As a result, the increased emphasis on commodification raises important questions about the shifting nature of feminism and feminist identities (Cole & Crossley 2009).

Empowerment and beauty pageants

The discussion about beauty, empowerment and feminism was a particularly hot topic in the UK press in December 2008, when students from top universities such as the London School of Economics (LSE), King's College London and the School of Oriental and African Studies (SOAS) competed against one another for the title of Miss University London. The beauty pageant sparked a range of views – from those purporting that such events were as 'necessary to modern women as campaigning for equal rights was when my mum was our age' (Allen et al. 2008, p. 3) to those who likened beauty contests to cattle markets (Knight 2008, p. 18). Others acknowledged the difficulty in critiquing beauty contests in our 'postfeminist' age, noting that 'to find the idea of the contest objectionable immediately marks you as some sad old feminist throw-back with dungarees and armpit hair' (Knight 2008, p. 18). In fact, the term 'postfeminist' is used in this article as an indication that feminism is considered redundant, unnecessary and even retro (see also McRobbie 2007; Negra 2009). Furthermore, considering that feminists have historically been constructed as 'deviants' through their (assumed) aversion of femininity and men (Douglas 1994; Freeman 2001; Scharff 2010), it is taken for granted that they will automatically resist or critique events that reward women for embodying such feminine virtues. Therefore, beauty pageant supporters focused on feminists' 'irrational' prejudices (and likely jealousy) rather than valid critiques of femininity, patriarchy and gender roles.

From a critical perspective, once seen as a sign of sexual objectification, beauty pageants are a modern example of sexual *subjectification* in society, where masculinity and femininity are no longer demonstrated by psychological characteristics such as aggressiveness or passivity, but through a sexualization of the body (Gill 2007). This, in turn, means that men and women are increasingly judged on their ability to conform to physical ideals of masculinity and femininity, judgements that can be formally measured through beauty pageants. Such views are increasingly normalized in society, as is evident by the *Daily Mail's* Jan Moir, who wrote in defence of beauty pageants: 'Beauty contests, once seen as a form of female oppression, are now regarded by right-on thinkers as celebrations of female aesthetics' (2008, p. 30). The article not only dismissed feminist critiques of beauty pageants but encouraged women to buy into patriarchal ideologies through 'celebrations' of these restrictive norms. In the meantime, anyone claiming that beauty contestants were exploited were dismissively labelled 'feminists'.

What is noteworthy about many of the articles discussed so far is that, similar to articles found in the Second Wave, they frequently endorsed liberal feminist views. That said, there was a noted increase in articles attacking patriarchy, capitalism or other interlocking forms of oppression.

Radical discourses

While only a limited number of articles focused explicitly on the role of patriarchy, capitalism or oppression in society (nine articles or 2 per cent of total), radical critiques were also visible in articles discussing sexism, discrimination, abortion, prostitution, sexual and physical abuse and violence. For example, one *Guardian* feature critiqued the male domination of party politics, explaining why only certain types of women managed to succeed in such systems:

> 'The sad fact,' Valenti continues, 'is that when it comes to the Republicans, the women who tend to get access to power are explicitly anti-feminist, and anti-women, because it's the only way that they're able to rise through the ranks. The party is strategically coughing up women who won't rock male structures of power.' (Cochrane 2008b, p. G2 4)

As a consequence, we end up with candidates such as Sarah Palin, who is a model of femininity 'that is recognizable to most women: she's the kind of broad who speaks on behalf of other broads but appears not to like them very much [...] It's like some kind of dystopian future [...] feminism without any feminists' (Valenti 2008a, p. 34). Valenti here laments the fact that having any woman in politics is viewed as a feminist victory, when she makes clear that being a woman does not mean that one will automatically support women's issues, as is the case with Palin.

In addition to critiques about the political party system, the increased sexualization of society was an important catalyst for radical critiques.

This included the 'adultification of young girls – and the youthification of older women', which has led women to become 'so busy self-modifying or improving that little time is left over for learning or doing. We have the power to change the world, but it's too often subjugated to the culturally constructed need to change ourselves' (Ream 2008, p. N36). While this article does not explicitly mention patriarchy or capitalism, it recognized that the postfeminist, capitalist insistence of 'maintenance of the body' (Negra 2009) prevented women from fully participating in social, political and economic spheres of life – a fear Wolf also addressed in *The Beauty Myth* (1991).

Similarly, in discussing beauty pageants, one agony aunt asked:

> [W]hat that postchauvenist would have to say if we told him that beauty competitions reinforce and promote misogyny, prevent women from ever being taken seriously as anything other than lust objects, and reinforce the entrenched male values which, for centuries, kept women economically and politically disenfranchised? (Ross 2008, p. 55).

While the article does not explicitly lay out the 'entrenched male values', it clearly poses a radical critique to events that systematically reward women on their ability to adhere to (white, heterosexual, middle-class) notions of beauty.

While articles were more likely to discuss patriarchy than capitalism, feminist Shelia Jeffreys attacked the latter in her analysis of the economics of prostitution. She concluded that, contrary to popular belief, sex workers actually made very little money, as most profit goes to pimps, traffickers, brothel owners and others involved in managing the women. In demonstrating her fury at such oversights, she asked: 'Where is the criticism from the left of this gross capitalist industry? We can slate the tobacco and nuclear industries, but not the sex industry, in which the poorest and most disenfranchised women are abused' (Bindel 2008, p. G2 14). As the sex industry continues to grow and become more mainstream, I would suspect such critiques will become even rarer.

Also through addressing the role that capitalism plays in oppressing women, one column defended feminism against claims that it created a double burden of women's work in and outside the home, responding that this was, in fact, the result of 'capitalism', though one could also add gender roles (and thus patriarchy) since domestic work is still largely considered to be a feminine activity (Carey 2008, p. 14). Finally, another article specifically critiqued the *Oprah Winfrey Show* for 'its relentless insistence that women need to remake themselves, often through new purchases' (Johnson 2008, p. L4). This was one of the only articles that explicitly attacked the capitalist, consumerist culture. Although still few and far between, the increased presence of radical critiques provides evidence that patriarchal and hegemonic ideologies continue to be challenged, perhaps suggesting that the general public's understanding of patriarchy and capitalist ideologies has grown since the Second Wave.

Opposing feminism

One surprising finding in this sample was that the percentage of articles opposing feminism decreased since the Second Wave (from 31 to 26 per cent of total). Examples of oppositional articles include: 'Feminists sore losers' (Editorial 2008a, p. A18), 'Feminism Gone Mad' (Editorial 2008b, p. 12); 'Ditch this destructive self-pity and then your luck will change' (Mooney 2008, p. 44) and 'Fault lines in feminism' (Ream 2008, p. P5). Interestingly, opposition to feminism was constructed through similar means in both periods. For example, feminism was said to lead women down 'the wrong-track' (15 articles or 3 per cent of total), create new problems for women (11 articles or 3 per cent of total) and comprise 'deviant' women (59 articles or 16 per cent of total). Other themes that were not quantified, but which emerged in more qualitative readings, included notions that feminism runs contrary to 'natural' gender roles and that a backlash was occurring. While oppositional frames were found in all eight publications, they were hegemonic only in the *Daily Mail* (19 articles or 37 per cent of the publication's total) and the *Washington Times* (18 articles or 51 per cent of the publication's total)[13] – papers that were both included for their conservative leanings and an assumed opposition to feminism. Conversely, in the left-leaning *New York Times*, *Guardian* and *Washington Post*, oppositional articles were almost entirely absent.[14] These figures therefore indicate that while oppositional discourses were certainly still in circulation, they were unevenly distributed among my publications.

Deviant feminists

One perpetual theme present in many oppositional articles was the construction of feminists as 'shrill, strident, angry, ranting, unattractive' women (Zernike 2008, p. WS1), who love to 'bash' men (Moir 2008, p. 30) and are 'killjoys' (Letter to the Editor 2008e, p. 95). Other articles used new tactics such as labelling feminists hypocrites for applauding women's right to work and raise children one day, then criticize working

mothers like Sarah Palin the next (Fields 2008a, p. A21). A similar sentiment was published in one *Washington Times* column:

> 'What we are witnessing is the historic hypocrisy of Second Wave
> feminists. Whether you agree with Governor Palin or not, she is fem-
> inism in its truest and purest form,' said Michelle Bernard, president
> of the Independent Women's Forum.
> 'She has found a way to balance work and family the way all women
> hope to – with the help of a loving family. Sarah Palin is everything
> the feminists fought for,' Ms. Bernard said.
> Feminists are having none of it, though. (Harper 2008, p. A05)

The point of contention in this and other articles is that some pundits
believe that having *any* woman in the White House should be viewed
as a feminist victory, rather than acknowledging the fact that sex alone
does not guarantee the candidate will support women's rights.

Feminism as anti-family

Despite having gained some new negative connotations, feminism's
association as anti-family have withstood the test of time. As one *Daily
Mail* column insisted, their campaign is not only 'against marriage' but
'in favour of abortion and for every other disastrous liberal and socialist
cause that ever existed' (Hitchens 2008, p. 31). Similarly, one letter to
the editor from the same paper noted:

> Feminism's only success was in destroying the belief of good, lov-
> ing, committed men's love for women and family, replacing it with
> a nihilistic, selfish, womancentered ideology which believes that the
> destruction of the family has no consequence whatsoever. (Mooney
> 2008, p. 44)

While diatribes such as this were most likely to come from 'ordinary'
readers or authors, a handful were disseminated by prominent or well-
known speakers. Rebecca Walker, daughter of American feminist and
author Alice Walker, became well known for speaking publicly about
her unhappy childhood and the breakup of her family, which she
blamed on the Second Wave:

> As the child of divorced parents, I know only too well the painful
> consequences of being brought up in those circumstances. Feminism
> has much to answer for denigrating men and encouraging women

to seek independence whatever the cost to their families. (Walker & Cunningham 2008, p. 24)

Not only are such sentiments anti (Second Wave) feminist, they can also be viewed as part of a backlash addressing the series of new 'problems' feminism created for women, men or society at large (Faludi 1992; McRobbie 2007). These range from violent youth to the loss of men's libidos, to 'failing pre-schoolers, rising divorce rates, and many dysfunctional families' (Carroll 2008; Ormerod 2008, p. 18). One particular theme that re-emerged in various publications was that feminism had created a 'crisis' for men – a theme also identified by British and American media scholars (Beynon 2002; Gill 2003). Here, feminists were seen to be responsible for 'emasculating' men, and when asked: 'who turned men into sissies? The answer to that is we women [did]' (Jones & Platell 2008, p. 32). The authors then went on to argue that feminists had deliberately 'feminised men to make them less masculine, less challenging to our ambitions, less competition for us'.

Inherent in this article is a reaction against the so-called 'new man' which emerged in the 1970s and 80s as a response to feminism and changing gender roles (Beynon 2004). These 'new men' were said to be supportive of their wife's/girlfriend's careers, more nurturing, and happy to take part in household tasks (p. 199). While perhaps the ideal for many, patriarchal culture resisted such moulds, and the 1990s witnessed the rise of the 'new lad' – the new man's antithesis – a throwback to an aggressive, phallic masculinity, which opened up space for 'fun, consumption and sexual freedom unfettered by adult male responsibilities' (Gill 2003, p. 47). Present within several articles, then, is an ideological battle between these new forms of masculinity, with the new lad almost always emerging the victor. Ironically, it often results in women who reject the new man, despising them for their 'feminine behaviours', while resenting the fact that they were increasingly the ones 'bringing home the bacon' (Jones & Platell 2008, p. 32). One *Guardian* feature, for example, noted how feminists had turned 'good blokes' into 'nervous wrecks, metrosexuals, knobs and tossbags' because of their sanitization of public culture (Cochrane 2008c, p. G2 10). Another began with the bold statement:

Men are in trouble, and it's feminism's fault. Decades of go-girl cheerleading have shorn our metaphorical whiskers and reduced the proud American patriarch to either a feckless manboy or a serial abuser. The ocean of gender equity has heaved toward women. On the other side, men flop, gasping like fish out of water on the exposed sand. (Zak 2008, p. BW08)

These passages are classic backlash texts and attempt to counter shifts in gender roles through re-establishing a gendered hierarchy where masculinity retains its power (Faludi 1992; Gerhard 2005). In order for these discourses to function, they draw upon notions of gender essentialism and biological distinctions between the sexes. As Jane Gerhard argued, in order for the backlash to function, feminism's gains must be taken into account in order for the discourse to reassert and re-naturalize 'what in the 19th century was framed as the separate spheres of gender. Separate spheres are not just divided into private/public, but through ideas about women's distinct psychological reality (2005, p. 41). Consequently, these so-called 'natural' differences were frequently reinforced throughout this sample.

For example, one column stated that women's undeniable attraction to retrosexual (as opposed to metrosexual) men was 'genetic for a start; men and women are biologically different and that's what makes them fit together' (Besley & Stephen 2008, p. 28). The column went on to discuss how, deep down, women could not help but be attracted to a man of the 1950s or 1960s – one who would not compete for the bathroom mirror. Instead, audiences were told that all women desire 'a proper man who stands by them, brings home the bacon, puts up the shelves and is nice to their mum' (p. 28). In other words, a return to a more openly patriarchal period, where masculinity reasserted its authority over femininity. The column closed by listing the benefits of such a shift:

> The family unit will become happier and stronger as we play our natural roles. There will be a return to the stable marriage of the Fifties and Sixties as the man feels free to do things he wants to do and to be himself. For me, this change can't come fast enough. (Besley & Stephen 2008, p. 28)

While the discussion here represents a selective range of de-legitimizing discourses found in the sample, overall it indicates that patriarchal and capitalist ideologies identified during the height of the women's movement have remained in circulation. While the specific details or rhetoric might have shifted with time, the overall message is clear – feminism and feminists are bad for society – either because of the new 'problems' they bring or because they deviate from the (white, heterosexual, middle-class) feminine ideal. While it is disheartening to see feminism still being blamed for these so-called crises, it is encouraging to know that these discourses have at least not gained prominence over time.

Contradictory and complex feminism

Although there were many cases where the view towards feminism was clear cut, the discourse was less clear in 104 articles (23 per cent of total). As with the previous chapters, a significant proportion of this sample constructed feminism as a complex ideology. Of particular interest within this sample was the genuine conflict over what feminism was, or who could be called a feminist (56 articles or 13 per cent of total). This issue became particularly popular after Sarah Palin – a Republican known for her firm stance against abortion, even in cases of rape or incest – identified herself as a feminist. This announcement incited a flurry of responses – from those hailing her as an 'incredibly potent feminist symbol' (cited in Cochrane 2008d, p. G2 4) to those insisting she represented 'a sign of perverse progress' (cited in Cochrane 2008e, p. G2 16). Others explored the complex nature of feminism while being less willing to take sides:

> Palin is everything liberals have always purported to want for women – freedom to choose, opportunities for both career and family, a shot at the top ranks of American political life. With five children and an impressive resume, Palin should be the Miss July in the go-girl calendar.
>
> There's just one hitch: She doesn't believe in abortion except to save a mother's life. That's hard-core, even for pro-life Republicans, most of whom allow for abortion in cases of rape or incest.
>
> Women who won't budge on abortion have hit fast-forward in their heads and, given McCain's age, consider the risk too great that a President Palin would load the Supreme Court with pro-lifers who would overturn Roe vs. Wade. Whether that is a realistic concern is debatable, but what's perfectly clear is that feminism today is not about advancing women, but only a certain kind of woman. (Parker 2008, 21)

What is noteworthy about these articles is their acknowledgement of the debate surrounding what feminism was and who had the right to call themselves a feminist. While it would be condescending to suggest that any one person has the right to prevent others from adopting the feminist label, I would argue that it is not only necessary but essential that scholars, journalists and members of society interrogate *all* versions of feminism. The purpose here is not to determine what 'true' feminism is but to critically evaluate its liberating potential in western culture. Just as an unwavering pro-life position limits women's control over their own bodies, notions that feminism is mainly concerned with moving women into higher echelons of political life is short-sighted as it ignores the range of everyday forms of oppression that subordinates women based on class, race and sexuality. Consequently, a critical lens should be applied to all discourses surrounding feminism, and debates over what it means should be encouraged. After all, one of the Third Wave's strengths is its ability to make room for 'the differences and conflicts *between* people as well as *within* them' (Reed 1997, p. 124) and a recognition that feminism exists in both the 'Yale Gender Studies' and 'How Do I Reload This Thang' models (Noonan 2008, p. N22).

Summary

When reviewing news of feminism in 2008, it appears as though many questions are still unanswered regarding its status, meaning and membership. From an historical perspective, it is clear that the ways in which feminism is presented have changed – for example, there has been a shift from traditional 'hard' news reporting to a variety of 'soft' formats such as features, columns and letters to the editor. While some might argue that news reports are absent because feminist activism has decreased, interviews with British and American feminists indicate that they are indeed very active in organizing events, and make frequent attempts to attract media attention (Fox 2010; MacKay 2010; Norris 2010; Redfern 2010). Consequently, while it would be disingenuous to state that the news media ignores feminism, it placed a disproportionate emphasis on issues of 'lifestyle'. Rather than evaluating feminisms role in eradicating various forms of oppression, the discourse focused on which popular culture characters were feminists, or on ways to demonstrate one's empowerment through the appropriate 'look', choice or activity, rather than through collective social or political activism (McRobbie 2009). Consequently, much of the feminism represented in 2008 disconnected political issues from questions of patriarchy, capitalism, racism and ageism (see also Macdonald 2004; Roberts 2007; Sheriden et al. 2007) – a serious problem for those interested in promoting systematic social change.

While critical of the overall lack of collective recognition and calls to action regarding women's oppression, I argue that the inclusion of news of feminism is facilitated by the increase in softer news formats prominent within this sample, which provided journalists the opportunity to bypass traditional masculine news conventions, such as objectivity and balance. Furthermore, such formats afforded writers the opportunity to address issues such as sexism, objectification and discrimination, which normally would be excluded unless associated with a high-profile event. Consequently, just as Tuchman (1978c) identified the women's pages as a possible resource for feminism, I argue that soft news formats such as columns, features and letters to the editor also provide a potential space for in-depth feminist analysis.

When taking an overall look at how feminism was reported in 2008, I argue that, despite limitations in coverage, the data provides something to be hopeful for. Although oppositional frames continued to circulate, their numbers appear to be dwindling. That said, it is clear from the analysis that oppressive ideologies such as patriarchy, racism and capitalism have maintained their hegemonic position. Therefore, while feminism is slowly shedding its negative connotations, we must remember to be wary of ideologies that pretend to benefit women, when they only act to oppress them more. Furthermore, it is clear from the analysis that feminism is a concept currently in flux, and interrogations of its meaning should be encouraged. Ideally, the development of Third Wave theories will continue to encourage debates about women's role in society after all, as times have changed, there has been a continued need to understand interlocking forms of oppression. And while many of the issues tackled by the Second Wave continue to persist, new problems have also emerged, such as the rise of neoliberal discourses, the emphasis on consumption, cultural obsession with youth, and the increased pressure for women to (cosmetically) alter their bodies. While many Third Wave feminists are addressing such concerns through various forms of (online) activism, mainstream critical discussion is also necessary – and is something that feminist writers such as Jessica Valenti, Catherine Redfern and Kira Cochrane have successfully managed to do. More of it, however, is needed.

Conclusion

> [T]he media may operate within a political-economy condi-
> tioned by capitalist ownership, industrial organization, and
> bureaucratic proclivity, but these influences alone do not
> determine the content of the news media. To be sure, these
> are constraining factors, but journalistic norms and practices
> remain an important site of struggle. (Strutt 1994, p. 60)

Women in society today

When examining the role of women today, it is clear that much progress
has been made in the past 40 years. On the one hand, western women
have never before had such great access to as many opportunities –
whether in education, the workforce, travel or sport. The possibility of
new opportunities was made evident in 2008, when two women made
a run for the White House. In Britain, a woman held the Deputy Leader
position until 2010 (she now is the Deputy Leader of the Opposition
Party). On the other hand, there is continued evidence that both patriarchal and capitalist structures still restrict women's lives in a number
of ways. For example, women working full-time in Britain earn 17.1 per
cent less than their male counterparts – a figure that jumps to 35 per
cent for part-time workers (Fawcett Society 2009). In the US, women
fare worse, earning 22.9 per cent less than men in full-time work
(Institute for Women's Policy Research 2010). For minority and disabled
women in both countries, the situation is even worse.

While equal pay, rights and opportunities are important feminist
issues, so too are more 'private' issues such as sexual freedom, sexual violence and abortion – issues that disproportionately affect women's lives.
Furthermore, while women are more likely than men to be victims of

sexual violence, the figures are even higher for women of colour (Home Office 2007; RAINN 2009). In Britain, while access to free and safe abortions was granted in the 1967 Abortion Act, bureaucratic procedures such as long wait times and the requirement of two doctors' signatures can slow the process down (Redfern & Aune 2010). In the US, things are worse. While the 1973 *Roe v. Wade* case brought in legal abortions, research indicates that 88 per cent of all US counties have no identifiable abortion provider (National Abortion Federation 2003). This means that women often have to travel long distances to access the procedure, which, while getting less expensive, can still cost anywhere between $400 and $1500 (USD) (Jones and Kooistra 2011). Consequently, while many aspects of women's lives have improved, feminism is still needed. Because the media play an important role in helping people to understand the lives in which they live (Ericson et al. 1987), how the news has, and continues to, represent feminism matters for those interested in social change.

Feminism in the news

The day when it is the norm for people to call themselves feminists is the day when feminism will lose its huge and frightening power. Women need feminists. But we can't all be feminists. Most of us just aren't that heroic. (Orr 2003, n.p.)

When embarking upon research into how feminism, feminists and their goals were represented in the press between 1968 and 2008, I expected to be overwhelmed by a barrage of oppositional news reports. This assumption was based not only on previous research on feminism in the news (see Ashley & Olson 1998; Bradley 2003; Cancian & Ross 1981; Creedon 1993b; Davis 1991; Douglas 1994; Goddu 1999; Hinds & Stacey 2001; Morris 1973a, 1973b; Refern & Aune 2010; Strutt 1994) but from my own experiences growing up in a 'postfeminist' society, where it seemed everyone around me rejected this label while subscribing to (some) feminist beliefs. While I anticipated the resounding rejection of feminism contemporarily, I was also curious to find out whether this had always been the case. As van Zoonen argued:

An acknowledgement of the historic specificity of current dominant beliefs about women and men opens up new ways of conceptualizing gender, not as universally given, but as socially constructed. The use then, is [...] to analyse how and why particular constructions of masculinity and femininity arise in historical contexts, and how and why certain constructions gain dominance over others and how dominant constructions relate to the lived realities of women and men. (1994 cited in Freeman 2001, p. 7)

Consequently, in analysing news of feminism, this research was also interested in exploring the socially constructed nature of gender, masculinity and femininity within and between British and American cultures. What did this tell us about the (universal) nature of patriarchy, racism, capitalism and heterosexism? Did these ideologies operate differently across time and space? How did they negotiate with oppositional discourses and seek to maintain hegemony?

Much to my surprise, the research demonstrates that feminism *was* frequently supported in most of my eight publications, although it rarely critiqued the oppressive ideologies responsible for women's inferior hierarchical ranking in society. Furthermore, it became apparent that (neo)liberal feminist perspectives were overwhelmingly supported at the expense of radical critiques. The prominence of the former is problematic because, rather than seeking to restructure society, liberal feminism attempted to find space for women within patriarchal, capitalist, racist and heterosexist frameworks. As time went on, then, feminism was constructed as an ideology that was concerned primarily with equal rights, opportunities and pay, while frequently ignoring other systemic issues such as reproductive health, domestic violence, sexual abuse and sexuality.

That said, there were some instances of radical discourses, particularly in the 2008 sample. These included analyses of marriage as an oppressive institution, the political economy of prostitution and the nuances of interlocking forms of oppression. While it is difficult to determine exactly why these radical counter-ideologies became more visible, it could be that as women have gained further social, legal and economic rights, feminists and journalists have turned their attention to other topics. Furthermore, there has also been the growth of anti-capitalist movements in both nations, which perhaps have made the public more attuned to such issues.

Another notable finding was the continued reproduction of a limited, but effective, range of oppositional discourses used to reject feminists, feminism and its goals. Particularly prominent was the backlash discourse, which first emerged in this sample in the mid-1970s as the Second Wave was still developing. That the backlash first emerged *during* the height of the movement, and not in its aftermath, as has previously been noted (Faludi1992) is significant and indicates that such discourses were not just a response to feminist achievements but acted as a pre-emptive tactic to oppose feminism in the first place. Furthermore, many of these discourses reappear throughout the sample – often as 'new' trends such as a rise in female criminals, increased incidents of sexual violence against women and women's general unhappiness (Faludi 1992). These findings suggest that patriarchal and capitalist discourses have long relied on a limited repertoire of retorts against feminism, and while it is difficult to 'prove' their effectiveness without interviewing members of the public, that they were repeated over and over again indicates they must have had at least some success. Consequently, I argue that if feminists pay attention to these patterns, and learn what arguments will be made against them, they can begin to develop counter-strategies and build up evidence to debunk these myths. While I am not suggesting that it will be an easy task, understanding anti-feminist tactics could be a useful first step in reclaiming feminism and its accomplishments.

A final trend worth discussing is the range of articles framing feminism and its goals in a complex manner. Feminists have never agreed on everything – and that is fine. As Redfern & Aune (2010) write, no progressive social movement is completely unanimous in its views, and it is therefore disingenuous to 'single out feminism for particular criticism' on this level (p. 219). Consequently, while I personally reject some versions of feminism, the news media are still an important space where feminism can be discussed, interrogated and reflected upon without the need to reach firm conclusions. On the other hand, just because someone identifies a belief as 'feminist' does not mean we should simply take their word for it. Critical interrogation is needed to determine whether certain values, beliefs or practices erode or uphold women's oppression, and if it is the latter, from an emancipatory position, such views merit close scrutiny. After that, people can continue to label such views as they wish. So, what does this all mean for the future of feminism?

What is the future of feminism in the news?

While it is one thing to discuss how feminism has been represented in the past, it is quite another to predict or create changes in how feminism could be reported in the future. Previous scholars have identified difficulties when academics try and prescribe 'improvements' in media production practices, particularly as many suggestions contravene journalistic norms (Freeman 2001, p. 248). That said, my research demonstrates that softer news genres opened up possibility for change, as they do not require journalists to follow (masculine) conventions of objectivity, balance or the need for a diverse range of sources, thus enabling journalists to voice their opinions and potentially explore issues in more depth. While this might enable feminist perspectives to be more easily incorporated into the mainstream media, I am also aware that it provides space for anti-feminist voices just the same.

Consequently, it will take more than just changes in format to critique patriarchal, capitalist structures, but changes in journalists' perspectives, too. Many journalism schools and newsrooms provide training for journalists that incorporates feminist practices and principles (for example, how to report issues such as rape sensitively, or understanding the various ways in which journalism is gendered). However, despite this education, most media are capitalist enterprises, organized on patriarchal principles. Consequently, the structures in which many journalists operate can prevent them from employing truly critical positions. However, as Strutt (1994) argues, such systems are 'constraining factors, but journalistic norms and practices remain an important site of struggle' (p. 60). Authors such as Kira Cochrane, Jessica Valenti, Katha Pollitt, Judy Klemsrud, Eileen Shanahan and Liz Jones stand out for their commitment to feminist values, regardless of the general stance of the publications by which they were employed. These authors not only continually defended feminism, but critiqued women's oppression, highlighting inconsistencies in anti-feminist rhetoric. While they represent only a fraction of all the articles published, bit by bit, these advocates are chipping away the old feminist stereotypes and encouraging the possibility for a feminist future.

Notes

Introduction

1. There is criticism of First Wave feminists, however, for comparing their experiences to those of slaves, ignoring the differing experiences that race produced. For example, many female slaves experienced (sexual) violence and abuse from their white masters in a way male slaves did not (Bryson 2003).
2. In 1918, single British women over the age of 30 were given suffrage, but it was not until 1928 that the right was extended to all women over the age of 21 – the same age as men.
3. It should be noted in Clare Hemmings' (2005) work that some Second Wave feminists did indeed recognize various interlocking forms of oppression, but that these have been collectively forgotten in the recounting of the Second Wave's history.
4. Dean (2010) defines this as the 'domestication' of feminism, which refers to the 'process of drawing distinctions between different manifestations of feminism, some of which are repudiated at the same time that others are afforded space and legitimated' (p. 392).

1 Contextualizing the Issues

1. Before Marx, ideology was thought to be a free-floating set of ideas, unaffected by society's productive practices.
2. It is important to recognise that characteristics for masculinity and femininity vary depending on factors such as race/ethnicity, class and age. For example, where white, middle-class women were seen to be asexual, black and middle-class women were often seen to be hyper-sexual. These differences demonstrate the extent to which various forms of oppression interlock with one another to produce different ideologies for different groups.
3. Anthropologists have played a major role in providing evidence of the socially constructed nature of gender. Margaret Mead's work *Sex Temperament in Three Primitive Societies* (1935) is of note because she found three societies with different gender patterns in Papua New Guinea. The Arapesh of both sexes exhibited maternal qualities; the Mundugumor were hostile, and neither sex showed maternal/paternal qualities and the Tchambuli's sexes showed opposite gender patterns from Western cultures, where assertive, business-minded women were complemented by 'gossipy' male housewives. Mead's study shows the cross-cultural fluidity of gender roles and thus highlights the importance of socialization in gender-forming identities – a factor that is often taken for granted in Western cultures, where gender is often considered homogenous and static.

4. See *Bust* and *Ms Magazine* in the US; *Chatelaine* in Canada, *Sanada* in Bengal, and countless feminist zines.
5. While publications such as *The New York Times* report news from other parts of the US, the only truly 'national' newspaper is *USA Today*.
6. Halloran et al. (1970) created a similar categorization but used the terms 'quality', 'popular', and 'tabloid.'
7. While size was once the main difference between UK tabloids and broadsheets, the latter have increasingly adopted 'tabloid' formats in order to increase circulation and revenue. *The Independent* underwent this change in 2003, while *The Times* switched formats in 2004. Others, such as *The Guardian*. opted for a 'Berliner' format in 2005.
8. In her earlier writing (1994), van Zoonen argued that there is no universal female perspective and that values among female journalists differ as much as they do among men. This does not contradict her later writings but simply means that women share some common problems and concerns that men do not.
9. It is worth noting that they did not specifically define what 'female' issues encompassed.
10. There has been debate in this field over whether one overarching paradigm is more useful, as Entman stated (1993), or whether having differing paradigms is the way forward, as D'Angelo (2002) argues.
11. However, there are several anecdotal accounts of news coverage of the British women's movement (See Bouchier 1983; Coote & Campbell 1982; Graham et al. 2003; Rowbotham 1989).
12. The difference is that women's rights encompasses a wide range of topics, including abortion, childcare and maternity leave, whereas 'equal rights' often refers to equal opportunities in work and life, such as equal pay.
13. While groups such as the National Organization for Women formed in 1966, and the New York Radical Women in 1967, 1968 was a key year for feminist activism. In Washington, a group of 5000 women, called the Jeanette Rankin Brigade, staged a peace protest, while in Atlantic City feminists protested at the Miss America Pageant. 1968 was also the year when feminist publications such as *Voice of the Women's Liberation Movement* began publishing and the first national women's liberation conference was held in Chicago (Davis 1991). In the UK, 1968 was the year a group of fishermen's wives organized themselves in Hull for equal rights and when female workers at the Dagenham Ford factory held a three-week strike over their pay grade (Bouchier 1983). While 1970 was the first official meeting of a women's liberation movement, women had been actively campaigning before this event. More events in both countries soon followed.
14. The base became known as the 'Greenham Common Peace Camp', and women continued to live and protest there until 2000, long after it was closed (1993), demanding that the land be returned to the public.
15. Had I had more time and resources, it would have been fruitful to dip into other randomly selected years between 1982 and 2008 to examine how news of feminism shifted over time. However, given my constraints on budget and time, I only had time to examine one year of coverage.
16. While I could have extended the time frame beyond 2008 to increase the number of articles in the sample, it was difficult to identify a suitable time

period. Additionally, adding a range of other publications gave me the opportunity to explore constructions of feminism in a variety of other spaces. For example, *The Guardian* was well known for supporting the Second Wave feminist movement and was excluded from the first sample for fear of skewing the results. Additionally, the *Washington Times* and the *Daily Mail* strongly promotes 'family values', which are commonly perceived as being incompatible with feminism and were included as a result.

17. Interestingly, many of my original search terms were present within these articles, and indicate a structural problem with some digital archives. For example, many stories found using the term 'women' actually contained the exact phrasing from my previous search terms, which produced few or no articles (e.g., 'feminist', 'women's libbers).

18. The abbreviation for Equal Employment Opportunity Commission.

19. The abbreviation stands for Equal Opportunities Commission.

20. Preliminary research indicated that using these specific issues as search terms was not the most effective way to collect data on feminism, because many groups aside from feminists are involved in such issues. For example, search terms regarding sexual violence brought forth many individual cases but made no mention of feminist groups or critiques of such practices. Consequently, I decided to focus instead on search terms for feminism or women's movement members rather than their goals for this time period.

2   Reporting the Women's Movement, 1968–82

1. It was unclear who wrote a further 23 per cent, or 129 articles, either because no byline was given or because the journalist's name was one used by both sexes (e.g., Jamie or Leslie).

2. Annual women's liberation conferences were held until 1977, yet none attracted media attention in either the Daily *Mirror* or *The Times*. While women's liberation conferences were absent, trade union meetings and conferences, which frequently discussed women's rights, did receive media attention. See, for example, Beecroft 1969; Jones 1970; Law 1974.

3. Even Hesford (2005) notes that the more radical Second Wave feminists, such as Kate Millett, were more likely to be ignored by the mainstream press in the 1980s and 90s, because their radical politics challenged the patriarchal hegemony in a way that those such as Gloria Steinem and Betty Friedan did not, and were thus less likely to be tolerated.

4. Forty per cent of both *The New York Times* and the *Chicago Tribune* articles discussed causes of women's oppression/inequality. The figure was 65 per cent in the *Times* and 55 per cent in the *Daily Mirror*. Regarding solutions, only 25 per cent of *The New York Times* articles provided solutions, while the figure was 33 per cent in *The Chicago Tribune* and the *Daily Mirror* and 50 per cent in *The Times*.

5. The number of black feminist voices was not quantified in the content analysis but was noted in several articles as I read through the data, as it was still common practice at the time to indicate when sources were not white.

6. For an overview of alternative American lesbian publications where lesbian voices were prioritized, see Whitt (2008).

7. My coding sheet allowed me to code for up to six sources within each publication. Sources were only coded if direct quotes were used. A source could be coded more than once within a publication if his or her quotes were interspersed by someone else's.

8. Note that while such discourse was clearly not yet hegemonic, my coding sheet allowed me to record only the dominant cause or solution, thus ignoring less prominent instances where these were mentioned.

3 Reporting Equal Rights, 1968–82

1. Although the Act was passed in 1970, employers were given a five-year period to implement changes.

2. In some cases, trade unions continued to promote the concept of the 'family wage', thus securing men's place as the family's breadwinner. In other cases, however, equal pay was rejected in favour of protective legislation that prevented women from working the same hours or jobs as men. Such protests were based on assumptions of biological differences, stipulating that women were unsuited for certain jobs. However, by the 1960s, nearly all British trade unions affirmed their support for equal pay (Davis, n.d.).

3. One of the most famous examples included airline stewardesses who, through trade union involvement, forced various American airlines to change unfair work rules such as firing women once they reached 32 years of age or upon marriage (see Davis 1991).

4. In 1963, after a report from the Presidential Commission on the Status of Women, the Equal Pay Act was passed, prohibiting differential pay rates between men and women. The following year, the Civil Rights Act was passed, banning a range of discriminatory practices directed towards black people, gay people and women regarding employment, education and access to public facilities.

5. Worth noting is that both articles include contrasting assumptions about women's potential. While not explicitly stating women have a role in the public sphere, the former argues that their potential is inhibited by current legislation, while the latter article insinuates that they are best placed in the home in 'caring' roles. This tension reflects a common debate at the time, between those who believed that women should be treated the same as men, and those arguing that women were equal but different and consequently needed different protections (Davis 1991).

6. The only reference I found regarding opposition to the Equal Pay Bill comes from a *Times* article noting how a second reading was successfully opposed by one Conservative MP (No Byline 1969b). However, most of the article was devoted to organizations supportive of this legislation, and it closed with demands for MPs to pass the legislation by the year's end. Similarly, a column by Marjorie Proops mentions the blockage of an Anti-Discrimination Bill in 1972, noting women's fury and their determination not to allow it to happen again.

7. It was unclear who authored a further 200 articles (27 per cent), either because there was no byline included or the journalist's first name was ambiguous.

8. I will, however, note that this does not always happen in practice, particularly if sub-editors who might have their own position or view on the matter run other sections. Additionally, while counter-arguments certainly get published, the editor has significant control as a gatekeeper and has a degree of influence over how journalists frame certain stories.

9. Modern-day examples can be found within the CanWest newspaper chains in Canada, owned by the pro-Israel Asper family, and the pro-Iraq war sentiments found within media owned by Rupert Murdoch.

10. Sexism and discrimination were identified in 19 *New York Times* articles, 46 *Chicago Tribune* articles, 26 *Times* articles, and 21 *Daily Mirror* articles. Legislative changes were discussed in 22 *New York Times* articles, 46 *Chicago Tribune* articles, 8 *Times* articles, and 11 *Daily Mirror* articles.

11. Such sentiments continue to circulate more recently. In their book *Superfreakonomics*, Levitt and Dubner (2009) quote a study conducted by economists Bertrand, Goldin and Katz to determine the wage gap between men and women with MBAs. They conclude that 'while gender discrimination may be a minor contributor to the male-female wage differential, it is desire – or lack thereof – that accounts for most of the wage gap' (p. 45).

12. In total, 109 articles carried some form of backlash discourse (14 per cent). The most prominent of these was that feminism and equal rights were bad for women (44 articles), bad for society (18 articles) and bad for the family (11 articles). These figures only represent articles where backlash discourses were the dominant frame, and they do not take into account articles where these themes were secondary.

13. Over half of all 151 Daily Mirror articles on feminism and equal rights employed de-legitimizing frames. The most common ones included feminists as deviants (25 articles), as a movement in conflict (35 articles), as bad for women (13 articles) or pursuing 'frivolous' goals (12 articles).

14. Columnists Marjorie Proops and Christopher Ward are two particular examples of this. Both frequently began their columns with statements of broad support for feminism but swiftly proceeded to document the ways in which feminism harmed society.

15. Economist John Kenneth Galbraith offered an economic explanation for labelling homemaking as a 'higher calling'. He argued that such views had 'been forced on us by popular sociology, by magazines, and by fiction to disguise the fact that woman in her role of consumer has been essential to the development of our industrial society [...] Behaviour that is essential for economic reasons is transformed into a social virtue' (cited in Wolf 1991, p. 18).

16. Union leaders often earn high salaries, and their positions are those of authority. Therefore, while the workforce as such is represented through the union leaders, there still remains an absence of working-class voices.

17. The *Daily Mirror,* for example, had its own Industrial Correspondent and Editor during this sample period.

18. For example, the *New York Times* carried 22 articles, the *Chicago Tribune* 78 articles, the *Times* 5 articles and the *Daily Mirror* 9 articles.

4   Reporting Feminism in 2008

1. All articles gathered using digital archives were included in the sample, though care was taken in ensuring that the England editions were used in the case of the *Daily Mail*.

2. Some have argued that feminist activism is perhaps most vibrant and visible through online feminist blogs and websites (Cochrane 2006; Henry 2004; Redfern & Aune 2010; Valenti 2007). Popular examples include Feministing. com and Bitch Media in the US, and The F-Word and Carnival of Feminists in the UK.

3. In conducting my search, I limited findings using LexisNexis's digital database to only those articles where feminism was a 'major mention', in order to ensure that it was a significant part of the story and not part of the periphery. Consequently, my results cannot be read as representative of all news on feminism, just those where feminism was a major part of the story.

4. According to Curran and Seaton (2003), the increase in length was caused by the 1986–89 technological revolution, when it became easier and cheaper to produce copy, and when newspapers really began to recognize the potential of consumer lifestyle sections as a means of attracting advertisers (p. 97, 103).

5. The editor of the UK broadsheet *The Independent* also stated he now considered it to be a 'viewpaper', as it frequently includes a column and photo on the front page rather than a hard news story (cited in Franklin 2008, p. 637).

6. While all newspapers carried stories about popular culture, the proportion of articles per publication was not necessarily evenly spread out. For example, popular culture–inspired articles were particularly prominent within the *Daily Mirror* (13 articles or 57 per cent of total), which, as discussed, has increasingly become feature-driven (Brooks 2007). Twenty-two per cent of *The Guardian*'s stories were sparked by popular culture, while the figure rested at 24 per cent for *The New York Times* – a more surprising find given their broadsheet status. The *Chicago Tribune* and the *Washington Times*, on the other hand, both contained the smaller proportion of popular culture articles (4 articles or 7 per cent of total for the former, and two articles or 6 per cent of total for the latter). That these broadsheet newspapers carried few popular culture articles fits more closely with traditional broadsheet characteristics (Sparks 2000), however, most stories in these publications overall still comprised features and columns, even as they reported on current topics such as the US election.

7. Furthermore, this quote raises one of the study's limitations, in that it only included articles that specifically mention feminism rather than feminist groups, which might not have one of these keywords in the article.

8. Furthermore, as early as 1986, Gallup polls have shown that anywhere from half to two-thirds of American women identify as feminists. See Feminist Majority website http://feminist.org/welcome/index.html (accessed 20 May 2010). That said, recent research by Scharff (2010) of 40 British and German women found that 75 per cent rejected the feminist label.

9. *The Guardian* has been noted for its practise of asking many of its celebrities whether they are feminists are not – a testament to the paper's general support for feminism (Redfern 2010).
10. Similarly, during the Second Wave women's movement, certain journalists such as *The New York Times'* Judy Klemsrud were identified as playing a key part in producing supportive coverage of the movement (Bradley 2003; Tuchman 1978c).
11. While these issues were dominant in only 38 articles, they were present in many more.
12. Thirty-two articles (8 per cent of the total) specifically linked feminism to issues of appearances (and also frequently utilized discourses of freedom and choice).
13. Interestingly, the *Daily Mirror,* my one publication to consistently delegitimize feminism during the Second Wave, had an even number of 'positive' and 'negative' articles (eight articles each or 35 per cent of the publication's total). This shift could have resulted from the *Mirror's* move from a predominantly male to a predominantly female audience (Niblock 2008), who the paper might have felt would be more supportive of feminism.
14. Each publication carried only five such articles, constituting anywhere from 6 to 12 per cent of each publications' total.

Bibliography

Akass, K. and McCabe, J. (2004) *Reading Sex and the City* (London: IB Taurus).

Alexander, S. (1999) 'Messages to Women on Love and Marriage from Women's Magazines' in M. Meyers (ed.) *Mediated Women: Representations in Popular Culture* (Cresskill, NJ: Hampton Press).

Allan, S. (2005) *Journalism: Critical Issues* (Maidenhead: Open University Press).

Allen, V. Borland, S. and Porter, R. (2008) 'The frilly feminists; University students who'd rather fight to be crowned the campus beauty than battle for women's rights', *Daily Mail*, 4 December, p. 3.

Althusser, L. (1971) *Lenin and Philosophy, and Other Essays* (London: NLB).

Anderson, D. (1991) *The Unfinished Revolution: Status of Women in Twelve Countries* (Toronto: Doubleday Canada Ltd).

Anderson, L.M. (1997) *Mammies No More: The Changing Image of Black Women on Stage and Screen* (Lanham, MD: Rowman and Littlefield).

Anderson, S. (1999) 'Reader's Digest on Women: Antifeminist Articulations of *The Second Sex*' in M. Meyers (ed.) *Mediated Women: Representations in Popular Culture* (Cresskill, NJ: Hampton Press).

Ang, I. (1985) *Watching Dallas: Soap Opera and the Melodramatic Imagination* (New York: Routledge).

Appiah, P. (1969) 'Principal roles for women', *The Times*, 22 October, VII.

Appleyard, D. and Smith-Squire, A. (2008) 'The one-night stand generation', *Daily Mail*, 18 December, p. 42.

Arthurs, J. (2004) *Television and Sexuality: Regulation and the Politics of Taste* (Maidenhead: Open University Press).

Ashley, L. and Olson, B. (1998) 'Constructing Reality: Print Media's Framing of the Women's Movement, 1966–1986', *Journal of Mass Communication Quarterly* 75(2), 263–77.

Atton, C. and Wickenden, E. (2005) 'Sourcing Routines and Representation in Alternative Journalism: A Case Study Approach', *Journalism Studies*, 6(3), 347–59.

Baehr, H. and Dyer, G. (eds.) (1987) *Boxed In: Women and Television* (London: Pandora).

Ballaster, R., Beetham, M., Frazer, E., and Hebron, S. (1991) *Women's Worlds: Ideology, Femininity, and Women's Magazines* (London: Palgrave MacMillan).

Barakso, M. and Schaffner, B.F. (2006) 'Winning Coverage: News Media Portrayals of the Women's Movement, 1969–2004', *The Harvard International Journal of Press/Politics*, 11(4), 22–44.

Baker, R. (1978) 'Aunt Ms. needs you', *New York Times*, 24 June, p. 19.

Barker-Plummer, B. (2000) 'News as a Feminist Resource? A Case study of the Media Strategies and Media Representation of the National Organization for Women, 1966–1980', in A. Sreberny and L. van Zoonen (eds.) *Gender, Politics and Communication* (Cresskill, NJ: Hampton Press Inc).

Barker-Plummer, B. (2010) 'News and Feminism: A Historic Dialogue', *Journalism & Communication Monographs*. 12(3 & 4), 145–203.

Barnett, B. (2005) 'Feminists Shaping News: A Framing Analysis of News Releases From the National Organization for Women', *Journal of Public Relations Research,* 17(4), 341–62.

Barrett, M. (1997) 'Capitalism and Women's Liberation', in L. Nicholson (ed.) *The Second Wave: A Reader in Feminist Theory* (London and New York: Routledge).

Barrett, M. and McIntosh, M. (2005 [1985]) 'Ethnocentrism and Socialist-Feminist Theory', *Feminist Review,* 80, 64–80.

✓Baumgardner, J. and Richards, A. (2000) *Manifesta: Young Women, Feminism and the Future* (New York: Douglas & McIntyre Ltd.).

Baylor, T. (1996) 'Media Framing of Movement Protest: The Case of American Indian Protest', *The Social Science Journal,* 33(3), 241–55.

de Beauvoir, S. (1989) *The Second Sex.* Translated by H.M. Parshley (New York: Vintage Books).

Beck, D.B. (1998) 'The 'F' Word; How the Media Frame Feminism', *National Women's Studies Association Journal,* 10(1), 139–53.

Becker, H.S. (1967) 'Whose Side Are We On?' *Social Problems,* 14(3), 239–47.

Bedford, R. (1971a) 'An egg with a soft centre', *Daily Mirror,* 30 June, p. 9.

Bedford, Robert. (1971b). 'Baldness can send wives right off their heads', *Daily Mirror,* 2 June, p. 3.

Beecroft, J. (1969) ' "Equal rights for women", demand to TUC' *Daily Mirror,* 4 September, p. 4.

Belkaoui, A. and Belkaoui, J.M. (1976) 'A Comparative Analysis of the Roles Portrayed by Women in Print Advertisements: 1958, 1970, 1972', *Journal of Marketing Research,* 13(2), 168–72.

Bender, M. (1970) 'Women's Lib Bearish in Wall St'. *New York Times,* 11 October, p. 147.

Benedict, H. (1992) *Virgin or Vamp: How the Press Covers Sex Crimes* (New York: Oxford University Press).

Benford, R.D. and Snow, D.A. (2000) 'Framing Processes and Social Movements: An Overview and Assessment', *Annual Review of Sociology,* 26, 611–39.

Bennetts, L. (1978) 'Feminist drive is likely to persist even if rights amendment fails', *New York Times,* 31 May, p. 25.

Bennetts, L. (1980) 'Feminists dismayed by the election and unsure of what future holds', *New York Times,* November 7, 16.

Berger, J. (1972) *Ways of Seeing* (London: BBC/Penguin Books).

Bernstein, P. (1975) 'Old Westbury names the first woman mayor in Nassau', *New York Times,* 16 November, p. 128.

Besley, D. and Stephen, J. (2008) 'Who are you calling a metrosexual?' *Daily Mail,* 20 August, p. 28.

Betts, H. (2008) 'G2: Are we just mascohists?' *The Guardian,* 28 October, p. G2 10.

Beynon, J. (2002) *Masculinities and Culture* (Buckingham and Philadelphia: Open University Press).

Beynon, J. (2004) 'The Commercialisation of Masculinities: From the "new man" to the "new lad" ' in C. Carter, and L. Steiner (eds.) *Critical Readings: Media and Gender* (Maidenhead: McGraw Hill).

Bindel, J. (2008) 'G2: "Marriage is a form of prostitution", *The Guardian,* 12 November, p. G2 14.

Binyon, M. (1978) 'Soviet women given day off from "liberation"', *The Times*, 8 March, p. 8.

Bird, E.S. (1992) *For Enquiring Minds: A cultural study of supermarket tabloids* (Knoxville, TN: University of Tennessee Press).

Bleske, G.L. (1997) 'Ms. Gates Takes Over: An Updated Version of a 1949 Case Study' in D. Berkowitx (ed.) *Social Meaning of News: A Text-Reader* (Thousand Oaks, CA: Sage Publications).

Bordo, S. (1993) *Unbearable Weight: Feminism, Western Culture and the Body* (Berkeley, CA: University of California Press).

Bouchier, D. (1983) *The Feminist Challenge: The Movement for Women's Liberation in Britain and the United States* (London: Macmillan Press).

Bourke, J. (2008) 'Mini skirt or burka, that's my right', *The Times*, 8 March, p. 23.

Boycott, R. (2008a) 'The queen feminist thinking twice about employing young women' *The Times*, 18 May, p. 3.

Boycott, R. (2008b) 'As a feminist, I fought for greater maternity rights. As the boss of a small firm, I dread the consequences', *Daily Mail*, 15 July, p. 14.

Bradley, P. (2003) *Mass Media and the Shaping of American Feminism, 1963–1975* (Jackson, MS: University Press of Mississippi).

Bridge, M. (1993) 'The News: Looking Like America? Not Yet...' in *Women, Men and the Media* (Los Angeles, CA: Centre for Women, Men and the Media).

Brittain, V. (1971) 'A conspiracy to belittle women's liberation', *The Times*, 12 January, p. 12.

Brown, M.E. (1997) 'Feminist Cultural Television Criticism – Culture, Theory and Practice' in O. Boyd-Barrett, and C. Newbold (eds.) *Approaches to Media: A Reader* (London: Arnold).

Brozan, N. (1980) 'White House conference on the family: a schism develops', *New York Times*, 7 January, p. D8.

de Bruin, M. (2000) 'Gender, Organisational and Professional Identities in Journalism', *Journalism*, 1(2), 239–60.

Brunsdon, C. (1997) *Screen Tastes: Soap Opera to Satellite Dishes* (London: Routledge).

Brunsdon, C. (2000) *The Feminist, the Housewife and the Soap Opera* (Oxford: Oxford University Press).

Bryson, V. (2003) *Feminist Political Theory: An Introduction*, 2nd edn. (New York: Palgrave Macmillan).

Buchan, A., Rimmer, B, Price, A., Crowther, S., and Duncan, S. (1979) 'Who needs marriage?' *Daily Mirror*, 19 February, pp. 16–17.

Buchanan, P. (1975) 'The ERA: "We was robbed"', *Chicago Tribune*, 13 November, p. A4.

Budgeon, S. and Currie, D.H. (1995) 'From Feminism to Postfeminism: Women's Liberation in Fashion Magazines', *Women's Studies International Forum*, 18(2), 174–86.

Bulbeck, C. and Harris, A. (2007)'Feminism, Youth Politics and Generational Change' in A. Harris (ed.) *Next Wave Cultures: Feminism, Subcultures, Activism* (New York: Routledge).

Burton, P. (1975) 'The wise woman's guide to equality', *Daily Mirror*, 20 June, p. 5.

Bush, G. (2002) 'Foreword' in L. Edwards (ed.) *Our Times: The Washington Times 1982–2002* (Washington, D.C.: Regnery Publishing).

Butler, M. and Paisley, W. (1978) 'Magazine Coverage of Women's Rights', *Journal of Communication,* 28(1), 183–86.

Byerly, C. and Ross, K. (2006) *Women and Media: A Critical Introduction* (Malden, MA: Blackwell).

Byerly, C. and Warren, C.A. (1996) 'At the Margins of Centre: Organized Protest in the Newsroom', *Critical Studies in Mass Communication,* 13(1), 1–23.

Bywater, M. (1974) 'Belgium: A Woman's Party Goes into Battle," *The Times,* 6 March, 9.

Cancian, F.M. (1992) 'Feminist Science: Methodologies that Challenge Inequality', *Gender and Society,* 6(4), 623–42.

Cancian, F.M. and Ross, B.C. (1981) 'Mass Media and the Women's Movement: 1900–1977', *The Journal of Applied Behavioural Science,* 17(1), 9–26.

Carey, S. (2008) 'Crank up the statistics and let the blame game commence', *The Times,* 31 August, p. 14.

Carroll, S. (2008) 'Feminists Carrie the can for sexless men', *Daily Mirror,* 7 May, p. 17.

Carter, C.L. (1998) *News of Sexual Violence Against Women and Girls in the British Daily National Press.* Unpublished PhD Thesis, University of Wales, Cardiff.

Carter, C. and L. Steiner (eds.) (2004) *Critical Readings: Media and Gender* (Maidenhead: McGraw Hill).

Carter, C., Branston, G. and Allan, S. (1998) *News, Gender and Power* (New York: Routledge).

Chambers, D., Steiner, L. and Flemming, C. (2004) *Women and Journalism* (London: Routledge).

Charles, S. (1972) 'A chance to compare notes on discrimination against women', *The Times,* 22 November, p. 14.

Charlton, L. (1977) 'Sisterhood is Powerful But Not Omnipotent', *New York Times,* 17 July, 132.

Cirksena, K. and Cuklanz, L. (1992) 'Male is to Female As ___ Is to ___: A Guided Tour of Five Feminist Frameworks for Communication Studies' in L.F. Rakow (ed.) *Women Making Meaning* (New York: Routledge).

Cochrane, K (2006) 'The third wave – at a computer near you', *The Guardian,* 31 March. http://www.guardian.co.uk/world/2006/mar/31/gender.uk (date accessed 1 January 2010).

Cochrane, K. (2008a) 'Sidelines', *The Guardian,* 26 March, p. G2 17.

Cochrane, Kira (2008b) 'Why we love to hate Heather', *The Guardian,* 20 March, p. G2 4.

Cochrane, K (2008c) 'G2: The ugly face of Oz', *The Guardian,* 20 August, p. G2 10.

Cochrane, K. (2008d) 'G2: Secret weapon?', *The Guardian,* 2 September, p. G2 4.

Cochrane, K. (2008e) 'G2: Fair Game? She's the subject of a porn film and a sex doll has been made in her image. Shy why hasn't there been a bigger backlash against the misogyny aimed at Sarah Palin, asks Kira Cochrane', *The Guardian,* 24 October, p. G2 16.

Cochrane, K. (2010) Personal Interview. 10 May.

Code, L. (1997) 'Feminist Theory' in S. Burt, L. Code and L. Dorney (eds.) *Changing Patterns: Women in Canada*, 2nd edn. (Toronto: McClelland and Stewart).

Cole, N.L. and Crossley, A.D. (2009) 'On Feminism in the Age of Consumption', *Consumers, Commodities & Consumption: A newsletter of the Consumer Studies Research Network*, 11(1). [Online] http://csrn.camden.rutgers.edu/newsletters/11-1/cole_crossley.htm (date accessed 24 November 2010).

Coleman, J. (1970) 'Women's liberation in 50 MORE years', *Chicago Tribune*, 23 August, p. F9.

Collective, F.B. (ed.) (1981) *No Turning Back* (London: Women's Press).

Conboy, M. (2006) *Tabloid Britain: Constructing a Community Through Language.* (Abingdon: Routledge).

Connew, P. (1976) 'Bus Girls Demand A Fare Wage', *Daily Mirror*, 15 March, p. 13.

Cook, J. (1980) 'Barnard Class Told to Battle Bias', *New York Times*, 15 May, p. B3.

Coote, A. and Campbell, B. (1982) *Sweet Freedom: The Struggle for Women's Liberation* (London: Pan Books Ltd).

Costain, A.N., Braunstein, R., and Berggren, H. (1997) 'Framing the Women's Movement' in P. Norris (ed.) *Women, Media and Politics* (New York: Oxford University Press).

Cottle, S. (1993) *TV News, Urban Conflict and the Inner City* (Leicester: University of Leicester Press).

Cottle, S. (ed.) (2003) *Media Organisation and Production* (London, Thousand Oaks, and New Delhi: Sage Publications).

Couldry, N. (1999) 'Disrupting the Media Frame at Greenham Common: A New Chapter in the History of Mediations?' *Media, Culture and Society*, 21(3), 337–58.

Creed, B. (1993) *The Monstrous Feminine: Film, Feminism and Psychoanalysis* (London: Routledge).

Creedon, P.J. (1993a) 'The Challenge of Re-visioning Gender Values' in P.J. Creedon (ed.) *Women in Mass Communication: Second Edition* (Newbury Park, London, and New Delhi: Sage Publications).

Creedon, P.J. (1993b) 'Framing Feminism – A Feminist Primer for the Mass Media', *Media Studies Journal*, 7(1/2), 69–80.

Cresswell, T. (2006) 'Putting Women in Their Place: The Carnival at Greenham Common', *Antipode*, 26(1), 35–58.

Curran, J. and Seaton, J. (2003) *Power Without Responsibility.* 6th edn. (London: Routledge).

Currie, D.H. (1999) *Girl Talk: Adolescent Magazines and Their Readers* (Toronto: University of Toronto Press).

D'Acci, J. (1994) *Defining Women: Television and the Case of Cagney & Lacey* (Chapel Hill, NC: University of North Carolina Press).

D'Angelo, P. (2002) 'News Framing as a Multiparadigmatic Research Program: A Response to Entman', *Journal of Communication*, 52(4), 870–88.

Daniels, W. (1976) 'Battling blonde calls the law in fight for equal pay', *Daily Mirror*, 9 January, p. 7.

Davies, M. (1976) 'Waitress clear up pay dodge', *Daily Mirror*, 13 October, p. 5.

Davies, N. (1973) 'Menace of the gympslip bullies', *Daily Mirror*, 13 December, p. 11.

Davis, A. (1990) *Women, Culture and Politics* (London: Women's Press).
Davis, F. (1991) *Moving the Mountain: The Women's Movement in America since 1960* (New York: Simon & Schuster).
Davis, M. (n.d.) 'In Historical Introduction to the History of Equal Pay', *Winning Equal Pay: The Value of Women's Work* [Online] http://www.unionhistory.info/ equalpay/roaddisplay.php?irn=820 (date accessed 20 November 2010).
Deacon, D., Pickering, M., Golding, P., and Murdock, G. (1999) *Researching Communications: A Practical Guide to Methods in Media and Cultural Analysis,* (London: Arnold).
Dean, J. (2009) 'Who's Afraid of Third Wave Feminism?' *International Feminist Journal of Politics,* 11(3), 334–52.
Dean, J. (2010) 'Feminism in the Papers', *Feminist Media Studies,* 10(4), 391–407.
Decter, M (2002) 'A Nation Turning in a New Direction' in L. Edwards (ed.) *Our Times: The Washington Times 1982–2002* (Washington, D.C.: Regnery Publishing).
Delano, A. (2003). 'Women Journalists: What's the Difference?', *Journalism Studies,* 4(2), 273–86.
DeWitt, K. (1978) '100,000 Join March for Extension of Rights Amendment Deadline', *New York Times,* 10 July, p. 11.
Di Leonardo, M. and Lancaster, R. (2002) 'Gender, Sexuality, Political Economy' in N. Holmstrom (ed.) *The Socialist Feminist Project: A Contemporary Reader in Theory and Politics* (New York: Monthly Review Press).
Donovan, J. 1985. *Feminist Theory: The Intellectual Traditions of American Feminism.* (New York: Frederick Ungar).
Doughty, S. (2008) 'Equality laws at work "are unfair on men"' *Daily Mail,* 8 November, p. 47.
Douglas, S. (1994) *Where the Girls Are: Growing up Female with the Mass Media* (New York: Three Rivers Press).
Driscol, M. (1981) 'The dream that turned sour...' *Daily Mirror,* 11 December, p. 7.
Driscoll, M. (2008) 'The day a feminist icon resigned as my mother' *The Times,* 4 May, p. 3.
Durham, G. (1996) 'The Taming of the Shrew: Women's Magazines and the Regulation of Desire', *Journal of Communication Inquiry,* 20(1), 19–31.
Durham, G.M. (2003) 'The Girling of America: critical reflections on gender and popular communication', *Popular Communication,* 1(1), 23–31.
Dyer, G. (1987) 'Women and Television: An Overview' in H. Baehr and G. Dyer (eds.) *Boxed In: Women and Television* (London: Pandora).
Eason, Y. (1973a) 'Problems unite black feminists', *Chicago Tribune,* 3 December, p. C15.
Eason, Y. (1973b) 'Black feminists form battle line against racism, sexism', *Chicago Tribune,* 2 December, p. 32.
Editorial (1974) 'The push for ERA', *Chicago Tribune,* 19 April, p. 14.
Editorial (1975) 'Time to ratify ERA', *Chicago Tribune,* 4 March, p. A2.
Editorial (1982) 'Fasting for the ERA', *Chicago Tribune,* 6 June, p. A4.
Editorial (2008a) 'Feminists sore losers', *The Washington Times,* 12 August, p. A18.
Editorial (2008b) 'Feminism gone mad', *Daily Mail,* 29 July, p. 12.

Edley, N. and Wetherell, M. (2001) 'Jekyll and Hyde: Men's Constructions of Feminism and Feminists', *Feminism and Psychology*, 11(4), 439–57.

Edwards, L. (2002) 'The Millennium of the Media' in L. Edwards (ed.) *Our Times: The Washington Times 1982–2002* (Washington, D.C.: Regnery Publishing).

Eisenstein, Z. (1981) *The Radical Future of Liberal Feminism* (New York: Longman).

El-Calamawy (1969) 'Women win their way to higher public posts', *The Times*, 24 July, p. VII.

Elshtain, J.B. (1981) *Public Man, Private Woman* (New Haven, CT: Yale University Press).

Engel Manga, J. (2003). *Talking Trash: The Cultural Politics of Daytime TV Talk Shows* (New York and London: New York University Press).

Entman, R.M. (1993) 'Framing: Toward Clarification Of a Fractured Paradigm', *Journal of Communication*, 43(4), 51–58.

Erickson, C.L. and Mitchell, D.J.B. (1996) 'Information on Strikes and Union Settlements: Patterns of Coverage in a "Newspaper of Record"', *Industrial and Labor Relations Review*, 49(3), 395–407.

Ericson, R.V., Baranek, P.M., and Chan, J.B.L. (1987) *Visualising Deviance: A Study of News Organization* (Milton Keynes: Open University Press).

Ericson, R.V., Baranek, P.M., and Chan, J.B.L (1991) *Representing Order: Crime, Law, and Justice in the Media* (Toronto: University of Toronto Press).

Evans, J. (1970) 'It's Wrong to be Equal', *Daily Mirror*, 1 September, p. 12.

Faludi, S. (1992) *Backlash: The Undeclared War against Women* (London: Chatto & Windus).

Fairbairns, Z. (2003) 'Saying What We Want: Women's Liberation and the Seven Demands' in H. Graham, A. Kaloski, A. Neilson and E. Robertson (eds.) *The Feminist Seventies* (York: Raw Nerve Books).

Fairclough, N., Cortese, G., and Ardizzone, P. (eds.) (2007). *Discourse and Contemporary Social Change,* (Oxford: Peter Lang).

Falk, E. (2010) *Women for President: Media Bias in Nine Campaigns*, 2nd edn. (Chicago, IL: University of Chicago Press).

Fawcett Society (2009) 'Closing the gap: Does transparency hold the key to unlocking pay equality?' http://www.fawcettsociety.org.uk/?PageID=1022 (date accessed 12 November 2009).

Feminist Majority (2010) [Online] http://feminist.org/welcome/index.html (date accessed 20 May 2010).

Ferguson, M. (1983) *Forever Feminine: Women's Magazines and the Cult of Femininity* (London: Heinemann).

Ferree, M.M. (1987) 'Equality and Autonomy: The Women's Movements of the United States and West Germany' in C. Mueller and M. Katzenstein (eds.) *The Women's Movements of the United States and Western Europe* (Philadelphia, PA: Temple University Press).

Fields, S. (2008a) 'Putting the squeeze on Palin: Mid-game rule changes smack of hypocrisy', *Washington Times*, 11 September, p. A21.

Fields, S. (2008b) 'Fear and loathing of Palin: feminists can't stand too much of a good thing', *The Washington Times*, 30 October, p. A21.

Fine, C. (2010) *Delusions of Gender: The Real Science Behind Sex Differences* (London: Icon Books).

Finn, R. (2008) 'A Knack for putting feminism in film', *The New York Times*, 30 May, B4.

Fordham, A. (2008) 'Is Carrie Bradshaw a feminist? More importantly, am I?' *The Times*, 27 May, p. T2 7.

Fox, M. (2010) Personal Interview. 12 November.

Franklin, B. (1997) *Newszak and News Media* (London: Arnold).

Franklin, B. (2008) 'The Future of Newspapers', *Journalism Studies*, 9(5): 630–41.

Fraser, S. (1997). *A Woman's Place: Seventy Years in the lives of Canadian Women* (Toronto: Key Porter Books).

Freeman, B. (2001) *The Satellite Sex: The Media and Women's Issues in English Canada, 1966–1971* (Waterloo: Wilfred Laurier Press).

Freeman, J. (1975) *The Politics of Women's Liberation: A Case Study of an Emerging Social Movement and its Relations to the Policy Process* (New York: David McKay Company Inc).

Frenchman, M. (1972) 'In A Way Egypt Has Been the Cradle of Women's Lib', *The Times*, 18 May, p. II.

Freydberg, E.H. (2004) 'Sapphires, Spitfires, Sluts and Superbitches: Aframericans and Latinas in Contemporary American Film' in C. Carter and L. Steiner (eds.) *Critical Readings: Media and Gender* (Maidenhead: McGraw Hill).

Fritsch, J. (1976) '6,000 march on Capitol for ERA', *Chicago Tribune*, 17 May, p. 3.

Frohlich, R. (2007) 'Three Steps Forward and Two Back? Women Journalists in the Western World between Progress, Standstill, and Retreat' in P.J. Creedon and J. Cramer (eds.) *Women in Mass communication*, 3rd edn. (Thousand Oaks, CA: Sage Publications).

Friedan, B. (1963) *The Feminine Mystique* (New York and London: W.W. Norton & Company).

Gallagher, M. (1981) *Unequal Opportunities: The Case of Women in the Media* (Paris: United Nations Educational, Scientific and Cultural Organization).

Gallagher, M. (2001) *Gender Setting: News Agendas for Media Monitoring and Advocacy* (London: Palgrave).

Galtung, J. and Ruge, M.H. (1965) 'The Structure of Foreign News', *Journal of Peace Research*, 2(1), 64–90.

Gamson, W.A. and Wolfsfeld, G. (1993) 'Movements and Media as Interacting Systems', *Annals of the American Academy of Political and Social Science*, 528, 114–25.

Gauntlett, D. (2002) *Media, Gender and Identity: An Introduction* (London: Routledge).

Geertsema, M. (2009) 'Women and News: Making Connections between the Global and Local', *Feminist Media Studies*, 9(2), 149–72.

Genz, S. and Brabon, B.A. (2009) *Postfeminism: Cultural Texts and Theories* (Edinburgh: Edinburgh University Press).

Geraghty, C. (1991) *Women and Soap Opera: A Study of Prime Time Soaps* (Oxford: Polity).

Gerhard, J. (2005) '*Sex and the City*: Carrie Bradshaw's queer postfeminism', *Feminist Media Studies*, 5(1), 37–49.

Gibb, F. (1981) 'Women at work: the five wasted years', *The Times*, 11 June, p. 11.

Gill, R. (2003) 'Power and Production of Subjects: a Genealogy of the New Man and New Lad' in B. Benwell (ed.) *Masculinity and Men's Lifestyle Magazines* (Oxford: Blackwell).

Gill, R. (2007) *Gender and the Media* (Cambridge: Polity Press).

Gill, R. (2008) 'Commodity Feminism' in W. Donsbach (ed.) *International Encyclopaedia of Communication*. (Malden, MA: Blackwell).

Gillespie, C.R. (1999) 'Mammy Goes to Las Vegas: *Showgirls* and the Constancy of African-American Female Stereotypes' in M. Meyers (ed.) *Mediated Women: Representations in Popular Culture* (Cresskill, NJ: Hampton Press).

Gillis, S., Howie, G. and Munford, R. (2004) *Third Wave Feminism: A Critical Exploration* (Basingstoke: Palgrave MacMillan).

Gitlin, T. (2003) *The Whole World is Watching: Mass Media and the Making and Unmaking of the New Left* (London: University of California Press).

Glazer, N. (1980) 'Overworking the Working Woman: the Double Day in a Mass Magazine', *Women's Studies International Quarterly*, 3(1), 79–93.

Global Media Monitoring Project (2000) 'Who Makes the News?' *World Association for Christian Communication*. http://www.whomakesthenews.org/images/stories/website/gmmp_reports/2000/gmmp_2000.pdf (date accessed 30 January 2010).

Global Media Monitoring Project (2005) 'Who Makes the News?' *World Association for Christian Communication* http://www.whomakesthenews.org/images/stories/website/gmmp_reports/2005/gmmp-report-en-2005.pdf (date accessed 30 January 2010).

Global Media Monitoring Project (2010) 'Who Makes the News?' *World Association for Christian Communication*. http://www.whomakesthenews.org/images/stories/restricted/global/global_en.pdf (date accessed 30 January 2010).

Glynn, P. (1981) 'Marathon woman, outpacing the old style libber', *The Times*, 2 April, p. 9.

Goddu, J. (1999) ' "Powerless, Public-Spirited Women", "Angry Feminists", and "The Muffin Lobby": Newspaper and Magazine Coverage of Three National Women's Groups from 1980–1995', *Canadian Journal of Communication*, 24(2), 105–26.

Goffman, E. (1974) *Frame Analysis: An Essay on the Organization of Experience. New York: Harper and Row* (New York: Harper and Row).

Goffman, E. (1979) *Gender and Advertisements* (New York: Harper).

Goldenberg, S. (2008) 'Race for the White House: Leading ladies – Feminist claim Clinton and Palin paved the way for a new generation', *The Guardian*, 4 November, p. GH7.

Gomery, D. (1970) 'Let's face it. A housewife's job is bloody awful', *Daily Mirror*, 26 August, p. 13.

Gough-Yates, A. (2003) *Understanding Women's Magazines: Publishing, Markets and Readerships*. (London: Routledge).

Graber, D.A. (1978) 'Agenda-Setting: Are There Women's Perspectives?' in L.K. Epsetein (ed.) *Women and the News* (New York: Hastings House).

H. Graham, A. Kaloski, A. Neilson and E. Robertson (eds.) (2003) *The Feminist Seventies* (York: Raw Nerve Books).

Gramsci, A. (1971) *Selections from the Prison Notebooks* (London: Lawrence and Wishart Limited).

Gray, H. (1995) *Watching Race: Television and the Struggle for Blackness* (Minneapolis, MN: University of Minnesota Press).

Greer, G. (2008) 'Why do so many female artists put themselves in their work – often with no clothes on' *The Guardian*, 28 January, p. 28.

Griffiths, D. (2006) *Fleet Street: Five Hundred Years of the Press* (London, The British Library).

Grindstaff, L. (2002) *The Money Shot: Trash, Class and the Making of TV Talk Shows* (Chicago: University of Chicago Press).

Groskop, V. (2008) 'G2: Dancing Queens', *The Guardian*, 14 November, p. G2 16.

Haberman, C. and Herron, C.R. (1977) 'Woman Power in Houston', *New York Times*, 20 November, p. E3.

Hagerty, B. (1975) 'Helen's really a woman of today', *Daily Mirror*, 17 April, p. 9.

Hagerty, B. (1976a) 'I'm a pig and proud of it!' *Daily Mirror*, 5 October, p. 7.

Hagerty, B. (2003) *Read All About It! 100 Sensational Years of the Daily Mirror* (Lydney: First Stone Publishing).

Hagerty, L. (1976b) 'How I survive being married to HIM', *Daily Mirror*, 5 October, p. 7.

Hall, M. (1970) 'Men to baby-sit while wives talk', *Daily Mirror*, 28 February, p. 3.

Hall, M. (1978) 'Year of the burning y-front', *Daily Mirror*, 28 December, p. 13.

Hanson, H. (2007) Women in *Film Noir and the Female Gothic Film* (London: IB Taurus).

Hall, S. (ed.) (1980) *Culture, Media, Language: Working Papers in Cultural Studies, 1972–79* (London: Hutchinson for the Centre of Contemporary Cultural Studies, University of Birmingham).

Hall, S. (1982) 'The Rediscovery of 'Ideology': Return to the Repressed in Media Studies' in M. Gurevitch, T. Bennett, J. Curran, and J. Woolacott (eds.) *Culture, Society and the Media* (New York: Methuen & Co. Ltd).

Hall, S. (1997) *Representations: Cultural Representations and Signifying Practices.* (London: Sage Publications).

Hall, S., Critcher, C., Jefferson, T., Clarke, J.N., and Roberts, B. (1978) *Policing the Crisis: Mugging, the State and Law and Order* (Basingstoke: Palgrave Macmillan).

Halloran, J.D., Elliott, P., and Murdock, G. (1970) *Demonstrations and Communication: A Case Study* (Harmondsworth, England: Penguin Books).

Harcup, T. and O'Neill, D. (2001) 'What Is News?: Galtung and Ruge Revisited', *Journalism Studies*, 2(2), 261–80.

Harper, J. (2008) 'Palin triggers feminism reversal: "mommy wards" evolves in race', *Washington Times*, 17 September, p. A05.

Hartmann, H. (1997) 'The Unhappy Marriage of Marxism and Feminism' in L. Nicholson (ed.) *The Second Wave: A Reader in Feminist Theory* (New York, London: Routledge).

Hartocollis, A. (2008) 'Women weight use of clout in primary', *The New York Times*, 1 February, p. B1.

Hasinoff, A.A. (2009) 'It's sociobiology, hon!: Genetic gender determinism in *Cosmopolitan magazine*', *Feminist Media Studies*, 9(3), 267–84.

Hebron, S. (1983) *Jackie and Woman's Own: Ideological Work and the Social Construction of Gender Identity.* Unpublished BA Dissertation, Sheffield City Polytechnic.

Hemmings, C. (2005) 'Telling Feminist Stories', *Feminist Theory*, 6(2), 115–39.

Henningham, J. and Delano, A. (1998) 'The British Journalist' in D. Weaver (ed.) *The Global Journalist: News People Around the World* (Cresskill, NJ: Hampton Press).

Henry, A. (2004) *Not My Mother's Sister: Generational Conflict and Third-Wave Feminism* (Bloomington and Indianapolis: Indiana University Press).

Hermes, J. (1995) *Reading Women's Magazines: An analysis of everyday media use* (Cambridge: Polity Press).

Hesford, V. (2005) 'Feminism and its Ghosts: The Spectre of the Feminist-as-Lesbian', *Feminist Theory*, 6(3), 227–50.

Hinds, H. and Stacey, J. (2001) 'Imaging Feminism, Imaging Femininity: The Bra-Burner, Diana, and the Woman Who Kills', *Feminist Media Studies*, 1(2), 153–77.

Hissey, L. and Strutt, S. (1992) 'Feminism and Balance', *Canadian Journal of Communication*, 17, 61–74.

Hitchen, B. (1971) 'Punch-Up At the Women's Peace Rally', *Daily Mirror*, 13 April 13, p. 5.

Hitchens, P. (2008) 'Why the sisters will be gunning for Palin', *Daily Mail*, 31 August, p. 31.

HM Government (2010) 'The equality strategy – building a fairer Britain' http:// www.equalities.gov.uk/pdf/GEO%20Equality%20Strategy%20tagged%20version.pdf (date accessed 1 January).

Hole, J. and Levine, E. (1971) *The Rebirth of Feminism* (New York: Quadrangle).

Hollows, J. (2006) 'Can I go home yet? Feminism, Post-feminism and domesticity' in J. Hollows and R. Moseley (eds) *Feminism in Popular Culture* (New York: Berg Publishers) 97–118.

Holmstrom, N. (2002) *The Socialist Feminist Project: A Contemporary Reader in Theory and Politics* (New York: Monthly Review Press).

Home Office (2007) 'HM Government, Cross Government Action Plan on Sexual Violence and Abuse', April.

Hooks, B. (1982) *Ain't I a woman: black women and feminism* (London: Pluto).

Hooks, B. (2000). 'The oppositional gaze: Black female spectators' in J. Thomas (ed.) *Reading Images* (Basingstoke: Palgrave).

Huddy, L. (1996). 'Feminists and Feminism in the News' in P. Norris (ed.) *Women, Media and Politics* (New York: Oxford University Press).

Hudson, P. (2008) 'Polly Hudson has an urgent message for Mrs. Cole', *Daily Mirror*, 29 January, p. 10.

Institute for Women's Policy Research (2010) 'The Gender Wage Gap', *Fact Sheet*. [Online] http://www.iwpr.org/pdf/C350.pdf (date accessed 17 December 2010).

Jackson, S. (2006). 'Street Girl: "New" Sexual Subjectivities in a NZ Soap Drama?' *Feminist Media Studies*, 6(4), 469–86.

Jacoby, R.M. (1976) 'Feminism and Class Consciousness in the British and American Women's Trade Union Leagues, 1890–1925' in B.A. Carroll (ed.) *Liberating Women's History: Theoretical and Critical Essays* (Urbana, Chicago and London: University of Illinois Press).

Jaggar, A.M. (1983) *Feminist Politics and Human Nature* (New Jersey: Rowman & Allanheld).

Jamal, A. (2004) 'Feminist media discourse in Palestine and the predicament of politics', *Feminist Media Studies*, 4(2), 129–46.

James, P. (1970) 'She Wants to Ban the Bra!' *Daily Mirror*, 1 April, p. 12.

James, P. (1973) 'We are just slaves, says Mr. Men's Lib', *Daily Mirror*, 20 May, p. 7.

Jancovich, M. (ed.) (2002) *The Horror Film Reader* (New York: Routledge).

Jansen, S.C. (2002) *Critical Communication Theory: Power, Media, Gender, and Technology* (Lanham: Rowman & Littlefield Publishers).

Jenkins, R. (1985) 'The voice of the Thunderer', *The Times: Past, present, future* (London: Times Newspaper).

Jensen, K.B. (2002) 'The Qualitative Research Process' in K.B. Jensen and N.W. Jankowski (eds.) *A Handbook for Media and Communication Research* (London: Routledge).

Jhally, S. (1987) *The Codes of Advertising: Fetishism and the Political Economy of Meaning in the Consumer Society* (London: Pinter).

Johnson, S. (2008) 'Living la vida Oprah', *The Chicago Tribune*, 8 October, p. L4.

Johnston, L. (1972) '3,000 Heed Call to "Join Us, Sisters" in March and Rally Here for Equality', *New York Times*, 26 August, p. 54.

Jones, B. (1970) 'Equal Pay: Battle is only half won, unions warned', *Daily Mirror*, 12 December, p. 4.

Jones, D. and Platell, A. (2008) 'R.I.P. man', *Daily Mirror*, 17 December, p. 32.

Jones, L. (2008a) 'She's thrown in the wet wipe...and turned the clock back 30 years', *Daily Mail*, 28 September, p. 28.

Jones, L. (2008b) 'The wittering beauty queen is so wrong – we DO still need feminists', *Daily Mail*, 7 December, p. 26.

Jones R.K. and Kooistra, K. (2011) Abortion Incidence and Access to Services in the United States, 2008', *Perspectives on Sexual and Reproductive Health*, 43(1), 41–50.

Jowett, M. (2004) 'I don't see feminists as you see feminists': Young women negotiating feminism in contemporary Britain' in A. Harris (eds.) *All About the Girl: Culture, Power and Identity* (New York: Routledge).

Kahn, K.F. and Goldenberg, E.N. (1991a) 'The Media: Obstacle or Ally of Feminists?' *Annals of the American Academy of Political and Social Science*, 515, 104–13.

Kahn, K.F. and Goldenberg, E.N. (1991b) 'Women Candidates in the News: An Examination of Gender Differences in US Senate Campaigns', *The Public Opinion Quarterly*, 55(2), 180–99.

Kaplan, E.A. (1983) *Women and Film: Both Sides of the Camera* (New York: Metheur).

Kerner, O. (1968) *Report of the National Advisory Commission on Civil Disorders: Kerner Commission* (New York).

Kifner, J. (1976) 'Statewide ERA Faces Key Test in Massachusetts', *New York Times*, 1 November, p. 69.

King, H. (1977) 'Men's Lib Champ Tony Gets the Boot', *Daily Mirror*, 12 November, p. 5.

Kitzinger, J. (2004) 'Media Coverage of Sexual Violence Against Women and Children' in K. Ross and C. Byerly (eds.) *Women and Media, International Perspectives* (London: Blackwell).

Kitzinger, J. (2007) 'Framing and Frame Analysis' in E. Devereux (ed.) *Media Studies: Key Issues and Debates* (Los Angeles, London, New Delhi, and Singapore: Sage Publications).

Kleiman, C. (1972) 'This Campaign Strictly Feminist', *Chicago Tribune*, 3 February, p. W3.

Kleiman, C. (1974) 'Where the women's movement is today', *Chicago Tribune*, 6 October, p. D1.

Klemsrud, J. (1970) 'It Was A Great Day For Women on the March', *New York Times*, 30 August, p. 4.

Klemsrud, J. (1976) 'Equal right plan and abortion and opposed by 15,000 at rally', *New York Times*, 20 November, p. 32.

Klemsrud, J. (1977) 'Women's Movement at age 11: Larger, More Diffuse, Still Battling', *New York Times*, 15 November, p. 63.

Knickmeyer, E. (2008) 'In Turkey, Students Test a New Policy on Head Scarves', *The Washington Post*, 26 February, p. A10.

Knight, I. (2008) 'Come off it, girls – beauty contests are a man's game', *The Times*, p. 18.

Koenig, T. (2004) 'Reframing Frame Analysis: Systematizing the empirical identification of frames using qualitative data analysis software', Paper presented at the annual meeting of the American Sociological Association, San Francisco, CA, August 14. http://www.allacademic.com/meta/p110319_index.html (date accessed 19 July 2008).

Kolbe, P. (1970) 'Women: freedom but no power', *The Times*, 13 May, p. IV.

Krippendorff, K.(2004) *Content Analysis: An Introduction to Its Methodology* (Thousand Oaks, California: Sage Publications).

Kuumba, M.B. (2002) '"You've Struck a Rock': Comparing Gender, Social Movements and Transformation in the United States and South Africa', *Gender and Society*, 16(4), 504–23.

Lachover, E. (2005) 'The gendered sexualised relationship between Israeli women journalists and their male news sources', *Journalism*, 6(3), 291–311.

Lachover, E. and Brandes, S.B. (2009) 'A beautiful campaign?: Analysis of public discourses in Israel surrounding the Dove Campaign for Real Beauty', *Feminist Media Studies*, 9(3), 301–16.

Landis, L.L. (1974) 'The lady is a closet feminist', *Chicago Tribune*, 24 March, D1.

La Rocco, C. (2008) 'Here's looking at you and you, babe: taking a whack at female stereotypes', *New York Times*, 19 April, p. B9.

LaVelle, M. (1972) 'About equal Rights for women', *Chicago Tribune*, 13 March, 12.

Lavie, A. and Lehman-Wilzig, S. (2003) 'Whose News?: Does Gender Determine the Editorial Product?' *European Journal of Communication*, 18(1), 5–29.

Law, A. (1974) 'Unions warn on equal pay for women', *Daily Mirror*, 26 June, p. 11.

Law, A. (1977) 'How mean bosses give girls a raw deal' *Daily Mirror*, 29 October, 5.

Lazar, M.M. (ed.) (2005) *Feminist Critical Discourse Analysis* (Basingstoke: Palgrave MacMillan).

Lazier, L. and Kendrick, A.G. (1993) 'Women in Advertisements: Sizing Up the Images, Roles, and Functions' in P.J. Creedon (ed.) *Women In Mass Communication*. 2nd edn. (Newbury Park, London, and New Delhi: Sage Publications).

Lear, M.W. (1968) 'What do these women want? The Second Feminist Wave', *New York Times*, 10 March, pp. SM24–33.

Lears, T.J. (1985) 'The Concept of Cultural Hegemony: Problems and Possibilities', *The American Historical Review*, 90(3), 567–93.

LeGates, M. (2001) *In Their Time: A History of Feminism in Western society* (New York and London: Routledge).

Lemon, J. (1978) 'Dominant or Dominated? Women on Prime-Time Television' in G. Tuchman, A.K. Daniels, and J. Benet (eds.) *Hearth and Home: Images of Women in the Mass Media* (New York: Oxford University Press).

Lester, J. (1981) 'Where women provide their own discrimination', *The Times*, 8 December, p. 9.

Lester, M. (1980) 'Generating Newsworthiness: The Interpretive Construction of Public Events', *American Sociological Review*, 45, 984–94.

Letter to the Editor (1973) 'Phyllis Schlafly', *Chicago Tribune*, 8 July, p. 110.

Letter to the Editor (1974) 'ERA destroys choices' *Chicago Tribune*, 18 June, p. 10.

Letter to the Editor (1975) 'ERA foes "smeared"', *Chicago Tribune*, 10 June, p. A2.

Letter to the Editor (1980) 'Contrasting views on what ERA would accomplish', *Chicago Tribune*, 27 May, p. A2.

Letter to the Editor (2008a) 'Feminist contempt for prostitutes', *The Guardian*, 17 November, p. 33.

Letter to the Editor (2008b) 'When a woman runs for President', *New York Times*, 15 February, p. A22.

Letter to the Editor (2008c) 'Feminism as a force in US Politics', *The Guardian*, 13 September, p. 37.

Letter to the Editor (2008d) 'Don't blame feminism for male predicament', *The Times*, 10 August, p. 18.

Letter to the Editor (2008e) 'A rights killjoy', *Daily Mail*, 12 December, p. 95.

Letter to the Editor (2008f) 'Should she or shouldn't she run?', *Chicago Tribune*, 4 September, p. 23.

Levack, S. (2009) 'Stink Bombing the Beauty Pageant', *The F-Word*. [Online] http://www.thefword.org.uk/features/2009/04/stink_bombing_t (date accessed 30 November 2010).

Levine, E. (2008) 'Remaking *Charlie's Angels:* The construction of post-feminist hegemony', *Feminist Media Studies*, 8(4), 375–89.

Levitt, S.D., and Dubner, S.J. (2009) *Superfreakonomics* (London, New York, Toronto: Penguin Books).

Levy, A. (2005) *Female Chauvinist Pigs: Women and the Rise of Raunch Culture* (New York: Free Press).

Lewis, J. (1992) *Women in Britain since 1945* (Oxford: Blackwell Publishers).

Lind, R.A. and Salo, C. (2002) 'The Framing of Feminists and Feminism in News and Public Affairs Programs in U.S. Electronic Media', *Journal of Communication*, 52(1), 211–27.

Luce, A. (2010) Personal Interview. 10 July.

Macdonald, M. (1995) *Representing Women: Myths of Femininity in the Popular Media* (London, New York: Edward Arnold).

Macdonald, M. (2000) 'Rethinking Personalization in Current Affairs Journalism' in C. Sparks and J. Tulloch (eds.) *Tabloid Tales: Global Debates Over Media Standards* (Lanham, MD: Rowman & Littlefield Publishers Inc).

Macdonald, M. (2004) 'From Mrs. Happyman to Kissing Chaps Goodbye: Advertising reconstructs femininity' in C. Carter and L. Steiner (ed.) *Critical Readings: Media and Gender* (Maidenhead: McGraw Hill).

Machin, D. and Thornborrow, J. (2003) 'Branding and Discourse: The case of *Cosmopolitan*', *Discourse and Society*, 14(4), 453–71.

MacKay, F. (2010) Personal Interview. 28 February.

Mann, S.A. and Huffman, D.J. (2005) 'The Decentering of Second Wave Feminism and the Rise of the Third Wave', *Science & Society,* 69(1), 56–91.

Manning, P. (2001) *News and News Sources: A Critical Introduction* (London, Thousand Oaks, and New Delhi: Sage Publications).

Marciniak, K. (2008) 'Foreign women and toilets', *Feminist Media Studies,* 8(4), 337–56.

Marcus, R. (2008) 'Palin hits the Motherload', *The Washington Post,* 10 September, p. A15.

Margolick, D. (1982) 'Women Turn to Courts to Gain Rights', *New York Times,* 29 July, p. A21.

Margolis, D.R. (1993) 'Women's Movements Around the World: Cross-Cultural Comparisons', *Gender and Society,* 7(3), 379–99.

Margolis, J. (1977a) 'Factions square off at women's meet', *Chicago Tribune,* 18 November, p. 6.

Margolis, J. (1977b) 'Feminist movement suffers from problems of bad image', *Chicago Tribune,* 23 November, p. 2.

Margolis, J. and O'Connor, M. (1977) 'Women's Conference Foes Agree: It Must be Peaceful', *Chicago Tribune,* 13 November, p. 4.

Martindale, C. (1989) 'Select newspaper coverage of causes of black protest', *Journalism Quarterly,* 66, 920–23.

Marzolf, M.T. (1993) 'Deciding what's 'women's news', *Media Studies Journal,* 7(1/2), 33–47.

Marx, K. (1976) *Collected Works of Karl Marx and Frederick Engels* (London: Lawrence and Wishart).

Matthews, S. (1969) 'France's feminine feminist', *The Times,* 14 May, p. 11.

McCabe, J. & Akass, K. (eds). (2006) *Reading Desperate Housewives: Beyond the White Picket Fence* (London: IB Taurus).

McCarthy, J.D., McPhail, C., and Smith, J. (1996) 'Images of Protest: Dimensions of Selection Bias in Media Coverage of Washington Demonstrations, 1982 and 1991', *American Sociological Review,* 61, 478–99.

McCormack, P. (1973) 'What daughters think when mom's a drum-beating feminist', *Chicago Tribune,* p. B7.

McCracken, E. (1993) *Decoding Women's Magazines: From Mademoiselle to Ms.* (London: Macmillan).

McLaughlin, L. (1993) 'Feminism, the Public Sphere, Media and Democracy', *Media, Culture, and Society,* 15(4), 599–620.

McNair, B. (2008) 'I, Columnist in B, Franklin (ed.). *Pulling Newspapers Apart: Analysing Print Journalism* (London and New York: Routledge).

McNair, B. (2009) 'Journalism and Democracy' in K. Wahl-Jorgensen and T. Hanitzch (eds.) *The Handbook of Journalism Studies* (Abingdon: Routledge).

Mooney, B. (2008) 'Ditch this destructive self-pity and your luck will change', *Daily Mail,* 17 May, p. 44.

McRobbie, A. (1989) '*Jackie*: An Ideology of Adolescent Femininity' in B. Waites, T. Bennett, and G. Martin (eds.) *Popular Culture: Past and Present* (London: Croom Helm in association with the Open University Press).

McRobbie, A. (1991) *Feminism and Youth Culture* (Basingstoke: MacMillan).

McRobbie, A. (1996) '*More!*: new sexualities in girls' and women's magazines' in J. Curran, D. Morley, and V. Walkerdine (eds.) *Cultural studies and communications* (London: Arnold).

McRobbie, A. (2007) 'Post-feminism and Popular Culture: Bridget Jones and the New Gender Regime' in Y. Tasker and D. Negra (eds.) *Interrogating Post-Feminism* (Durham, NC: Duke University Press).

McRobbie, A. (2009) *The Aftermath of Feminism* (London: Sage).

Mead, M. (1935) *Sex Temperament in Three Primitive Societies.* 3rd edn. (New York: W. Morrow and Co.).

Meyerowitz, J. (1993) 'Beyond the Feminine Mystique: A Reassessment of Postwar Mass Culture, 1946–1958', *Journal of American History,* 79(4), 1455–82.

Meyers, M. (ed.) (1999) *Mediated Women: Representations in Popular Culture* (Cresskill, NJ: Hampton Press).

Millett, K. (1971) *Sexual Politics* (London: Hart-Davis).

Mills, K. (1990) *A Place in the News: From the Women's Pages to the Front Page* (New York: Columbia University Press).

Mills, K. (1997) 'What Difference Do Women Journalists Make?' in P. Norris (ed.) *Women, Media and Politics* (New York: Oxford University Press).

Mitchell, J. (1971) *Woman's Estate* (Harmondsworth: Penguin Books Ltd).

Moir, J. (2008) 'Ignore the po-faced feminists. Why shouldn't brains celebrate beauty?' *Daily Mail,* 5 December, p. 30.

Molotch, H.L. (1978) 'The News of Women and the Works of Men' in G. Tuchman, A.K. Daniels, and J. Bennett (eds.) *Hearth and Home: Images of Women in the Mass Media* (New York: Oxford University Press).

Morris, M.B. (1973a) 'Newspapers and the New Feminists: Black-Out as Social Control?' *Journalism and Mass Communication Quarterly,* 50(1), 37–42.

Morris, M.B. (1973b) 'The public definition of a social movement: Women's liberation', *Sociology and Social Research,* 57(4), 526–43.

Moseley, R. and Read, J. (2002) 'Having it Ally: popular television and (post) feminism', *Feminist Media Studies,* 2(2), 231–49.

Mukherji, A. (1973) 'Women: equality in cities but not in rural areas', *The Times,* 19 February, XI.

Mulvey, L. (1975) 'Visual Pleasure and narrative cinema', *Screen,* 16(3), 6–18.

Murray-Smith, J. (2008) 'Shackles and grenades', *The Guardian,* 21 July, p. G2 28.

Nagourney, E. (2008) 'Feminists more open-minded on weight', *The New York Times,* 25 March, p. F6.

National Abortion Federation (2003) [Online] http://www.prochoice.org/pubs_research/publications/downloads/about_abortion/access_abortion.pdf (date accessed 13 January 2010).

National Organization for Women (NOW) (2010) [Online] www.now.org (date accessed 31 October).

Negra, D. (2008) 'Structural Integrity, Historical Reversion, And The Post-9/11 Chick Flick', *Feminist Media Studies,* 8(1), 51–68.

Negra, D. (2009) *What a Girl Wants? Fantasizing the Reclamation of Self in Postfeminism* (Abingdon: Routledge).

Neustatter, A. (2008) 'The courage of their convictions', *The Times,* 10 August, p. 7.

Niblock, S. (2008) 'Features' in B. Franklin (ed.). *Pulling Newspapers Apart: Analysing Print Journalism* (London and New York: Routledge).

No Byline (1969a) '1,000 women march for equal pay', *The Times,* 19 May, p. 2.

No Byline (1969b) 'Firm stand on equal pay for women', *The Times*, 3 September, p. 8.

No Byline (1970) 'Bra-less', *Daily Mirror*, 17 November, 13.

No Byline (1971a) 'Drive to lure more women on to the labour market', *The Times*, 30 March, p. 4.

No Byline (1971b) 'Judge Gives A Boost to Women's Lib', *Daily Mirror*, 28 October, p. 16.

No Byline (1972a) 'So where have all the ladies gone?' *Daily Mirror*, 30 June, p. 11.

No Byline (1972b) 'Lunatic fringe', *Daily Mirror*, 10 April, p. 12.

No Byline (1973a) 'Drinks danger in women's lib', *Daily Mirror*, 2 April, p. 7.

No Byline (1973b) 'Down on the farm, a wife's life isn't the drudgery it used to be', *New York Times*, 28 May, p. 16.

No Byline (1974a) 'Chicago Jaycees urge end to sex discrimination; back ERA', *Chicago Tribune*, 25 April, p. 15.

No Byline (1974b) 'Feminist Movement Gains Growing Support', *The Times*, 24 May, p. 3.

No Byline (1974c) 'Equal rights approved by Maine; seven to go', *Chicago Tribune*, 19 January, p. S9.

No Byline (1974d) 'New suit planned on ERA ruling' *Chicago Tribune*, 24 May, p. C13.

No Byline (1976) 'Bank Girls in Pay Battle', *Daily Mirror*, 20 August, p. 4.

No Byline (1977a) 'Feminism Then and NOW', *New York Times*, 3 May, p. 40.

No Byline (1977b) 'Early Suffragette Exhorts Feminists to Fight Harder', *New York Times*, 26 August, p. 41.

No Byline (1978) 'ERA: keystone to other rights', *New York Times*, 5 April, p. A28.

No Byline (2008a) 'Fat Princess "disgraceful"' *The Daily Mirror*, 7 October, p. 24.

No Byline (2008b) 'Harman: no takeover bid', *The Daily Mirror*, 10 July, p. 8.

No Byline (2008c) 'Deaths; Schwartzman, Ruth', *New York Times*, 22 June, p. 29.

No Byline (2008d) 'Misreading "Twilight"', *The Washington Post*, 27 August, p. A12.

No Byline (2008e) 'Football: Predator – exciting news', *Daily Mirror*, 12 January, p. 8.

Noonan, P. (2008) 'What others are saying', *The Chicago Tribune*, 4 September, p. N22.

Norris, S. (2010) Personal Interview. 9 March.

North, L. (2009) *The Gendered Newsroom* (Cresskill, NJ: Hampton Press).

Object (2010) http://www.object.org.uk/ (date accessed 10 November).

Ogersby, B. (2001) '"So You're the famous Simon Templar" *The Saint*, masculinity and consumption in the early 1960s!' in B. Ogersby and A. Gough-Yates (eds.) (2001) *Action TV: Tough Guys, Smooth Operators and Foxy Chicks* (London: Routledge).

Oliver, P.E. and Maney, G.M. (2000) 'Political Processes and Local Newspaper Coverage of Protest Events: Selection Bias to Triadic Interactions', *American Journal of Sociology*, 106(2), 463–505.

O'Reilly, J. (1982) 'Every Woman has become a feminist in her own way', *Chicago Tribune*, 27 June, p. A1.

Ormerod, J. (2008) 'Don't blame feminism for male predicament', *The Times*, 10 August, p. 18.

Orr, D. (2003) 'Who Would Want to Call Herself a Feminist?' *Independent*, 4 July, p. 15.

Oscarsson, M. (2008) 'A victory for the Topless Front', *Daily Mail*, 29 March, p. 19.

O'Sullivan, Sue. (n.d.) 'Passion, bitterness and feminism' *Feminists and Flourbombs*. http://www.channel4.com/history/microsites/F/flourbombs/essay.html (date accessed 23 June 2010).

Paglia, C. (2008) 'Sarah Palin: a feminist triumph or the most underqualified vice president ever?' *Washington Times*, 14 September, p. 6.

Palmer, J. (1976a) 'Girl Thugs', *Daily Mirror*, 13 September, p. 1.

Palmer, J. (1976b) 'Why Adrienne Doesn't Want to be a Man', *Daily Mirror*, 5 October, p. 7.

Parker, K. (2008) 'Who needs feminists?' *The Chicago Tribune*, 3 September, 21.

Parr, J. (1995). 'Introduction' in J. Parr (ed.) *A Diversity of Women: Ontario, 1945– 1980* (Toronto: University of Toronto Press).

Parsons, C. (2008) 'For women voters, age gap matters', *The Chicago Tribune*, 2 February, p. 1.

Phillips, A. (2008) 'Advice Columnists' in B. Franklin (ed.). *Pulling Newspapers Apart: Analysing Print Journalism* (London and New York: Routledge).

Philo, G. (2007) 'Can Discourse Analysis Successfully Explain the Content of Media and Journalistic Practice?' *Journalism Studies*, 8(2), 175–96.

Pingree, S. and Hawkins, R.P. (1978) 'News Definitions and Their Effects on Women' in L.K. Epstein (ed.) *Woman and the News* (New York: Hasting House).

Pizzey, E. (2008) 'A sinister sisterhood', *Daily Mail*, 29 July, p. 12.

Pollitt, K. (2008) 'We owe Hillary', *The Chicago Tribune*, 9 June, p. 19.

Poussaint, A. (1971) 'No!' *Chicago Tribune*, 6 June, p. E12.

Pratt, S. (1974) 'Men join women on equal rights', *Chicago Tribune*, 16 April, p. 3.

Projansky, S. (2007) 'Mass magazine cover girls' In Yvonne Tasker and Diane Negra (Eds). *Interrogating Post-Feminism*. pp. 40–72.

Proops, M. (1971) 'Lib and Let Lib', *Daily Mirror*, 25 March, p. 11.

Proops, M. (1973) 'Why can't a woman be more like a man?' *Daily Mirror*, 1 February, p. 9.

Proops, M. (1977) 'Look Out Girls, the Sex Symbol is Back', *Daily Mirror*, 5 July, p. 9.

Proston, M. (1975) 'Tomorrow's Woman: Defining female in the year 2000, *Chicago Tribune*, 1 January, p. C1.

Puddlefoot, S. (1973) 'Women of the world unite – in song, laughter, work and protest', *The Times*, 2 July, p. 8.

Rape, Abuse & Incest National Network (RAINN) (2009) 'Who are the victims?' [Online] http://www.rainn.org/get-information/statistics/sexual-assault-victims (date accessed 13 January 2010).

Rakow, L.F. and Kranich, K. (1991) 'Women as Sign in Television News', *Journal of Communication*, 41(1), 8–34.

Rakow, L.F. (ed.) (1992) *Women Making Meaning* (New York: Routledge).

Rasberry, B. (1982) 'ERA is rising again', *Chicago Tribune*, 26 July, p. A13.

Ream, A.K. (2008) 'Fault Lines in Feminism', *Chicago Tribune*, 21 September, p. P5.

Redfern, C. (2010) Personal Interview, 24 May.

Redfern, C. and Aune, K. (2010) *Reclaiming the F-Word* (London: Zed Books).

Reeds, R. (1975) 'In the South, Road to Equal Rights Is Rocky and Full of Detours', *New York Times*, 20 March, p. 51.

Reed, J. (1997) 'Roseanne: A 'killer bitch' for Generation X' in L. Heywood and J. Drake (eds.) *Third Wave Agenda: Being Feminist, Doing Feminism* (Minneapolis and London: University of Minnesota Press).

Reese, S.D. (2001) 'Prologue – Framing Public Life: A Bridging Model for Media Research' in S.D. Reese, O.H. Gandy, and A.E. Grant (eds.) *Framing Public Life: Perspectives on Media and our Understanding of the Social World* (Mahwah, NJ: Lawrence Erlbaum Associates).

Reid, I. and Stratta, E. (eds.) (1989) *Sex Differences in Britain. 2nd edn.* (Aldershot: Gower Publishing Company).

Reinharz, S. (1992) *Feminist Methods in Social Research* (New York and Oxford: Oxford University Press).

Rhode, D.L. (1995) 'Media images, feminist issues', *Signs: A Journal of Women, Culture and Society*, 20(3), 685–711.

Rhode, J. (2001) 'Journalism in the New Millennium: What's a Feminist to Do?' *Feminist Media Studies*, 1(1), 49–53.

Richardson, J.E. (2007) *Analysing Newspapers: An Approach from Critical Discourse Analysis* (Basingstoke and New York: Palgrave Macmillan).

Richardson, N. (2006) 'As camp as Bree: The politics of camp reconsidered by *Desperate Housewives*', *Feminist Media Studies*, 6(2), 157–74.

Rifkind, R. (2008) 'Rod Liddle', *The Times*, 13 March, 13.

Roberts, M. (2007) 'The Fashion Police: Governing the self in What Not to Wear' in Y. Tasker and D. Negra (eds.) *Interrogating Postfeminism* (Durham, NC: Duke University Press).

Roberts, S.V. (1979) 'The Women Talk and the Candidates Listen Hard', *New York Times*, 16 December, E4.

Robinson, G.J. (2005) *Gender, Journalism and Equity: Canadian, US, and European Perspectives* (Cresskill, NJ: Hampton Press Inc).

Rohlinger, D. (2002) 'Framing the Abortion Debate: Organizational Resources, Media Strategies, and Movement-Counter Movement Dynamics', *The Sociological Quarterly*, 43 (4), 479–507.

Rohter, L. (2008) 'Ruth Cardoso, 77; Ex-first lady of Brazil', *The New York Times*, 2 July, B7.

Ronan, T. (1978) 'Battle Begins for Women's Votes', *New York Times*, July 9, p. WC16.

Roseneil, S. (1995) *Disarming Patriarchy: Feminism and Political Action at Greenham* (Buckingham, PA: Open University).

Ross, D. (2008) 'Feminism rules! Now, where's my swimsuit?' *Daily Mail*, 6 December, p. 55.

Ross, K. (2001) 'Women at Work: journalism as an en-gendered practice', *Journalism Studies*, 2(4), 531–44.

Ross, K. (2005) 'Women in the boyzone: gender, news and *her* story', in S. Allan (ed.) *Journalism: Critical Issues* (Maidenhead: Open University Press).

Ross, K. (2007) 'The journalist, the housewife, the citizen and the press: Women and men as sources in local news', *Journalism*, 8(4), 449–73.

Ross, K. (2010) *Gendered Media and Politics: Women, Men and Identity Politics* (Lanham, MD: Rowman & Littlefield).

Rowbotham, S. (1972) *Resistance and Revolution* (New York: Vintage Books).

Rowbotham, S. (1989) *The Past is Before Us: Feminism in Action since the 1960s* (London: Pandora).

Rubin, G. (1997) 'The Traffic in Women' in L. Nicholson (ed.) *The Second Wave: A Reader in Feminist Theory* (New York and London: Routledge).

Sanders, V. (2006) 'First Wave Feminism', in S. Gamble (ed.) *The Routledge Companion to Feminism and Postfeminism* (London: Routledge).

Sax, L. (2008) 'Twilight sinks its teeth into feminism', *The Washington Post*, 17 August, p. B07.

Schaffer, K. (1998) 'Scare words: "Feminism," postmodern consumer culture and the media', *Continuum: Journal of Media and Cultural Studies*, 12(3), 321–34.

Scharff, C. (2010) "Young women's negotiations of heterosexual conventions", *Sociology*, 44(5), 827–42.

Shipler, D.K. (1976) 'Life for the Soviet Woman Is All Hard Work and Little Status', *New York Times*, 9 August, p. 8.

Schudson, M. (1989) 'The Sociology of News Production' *Media, Culture and Society*, 11(1), 263–82.

Schudson, M. (2003) *The Sociology of News* (New York: W.W. Norton & Company).

Sebba, A. (1994) *Battling for News: The Rise of the Woman Reporter* (London: Hodder & Stoughton).

Sheridan, S, Magarey, S, and Lilburn, S. (2007) 'Feminism in the news' in J. Hollows and R. Moseley (eds) *Feminism in Popular Culture* (New York: Berg Publishers), pp. 25–40.

Shoemaker, P.M. (1975) 'A Father's Lament', *New York Times*, 15 June, p. E17.

Shoemaker, P.J. and Reese, S.D. (1991) *Mediating the Message: Theories of Influences on Media Content* (New York: Longman).

Short, R. (1975) 'Women can take the lead in making Parliament more efficient', *The Times*, 2 April, p. 7.

Shuttac, J.M. (1997) *The Talking Cure: TV Talk Shows and Women* (New York: Routledge).

Sigal, L.V. (1973) *Reporters and Officials* (Lexington, MA: Lexington Books).

Smith, A. (1976) 'The violent sex', *Daily Mirror*, 29 April, p. 7.

Smith, J. (2003) 'I'm a feminist so I must be dead', *The Independent*, 6 July [Online] http://www.independent.co.uk/opinion/commentators/joan-smith/im-a-feminist-so-i-suppose-i-must-be-dead-585886.html (date accessed July 5, 2010).

Smith, J. (2008) 'Feminism isn't a four-lettered word', *The Times*, 14 August, p. 7.

Soames, G. (2008) 'Funky, fun and feminist', *The Times*, 21 December, 18–19.

Sparks, C. (2000) 'Introduction: The Panic Over Tabloid News' in C. Sparks and J. Tulloch (eds.) *Tabloid Tales: Global Debates Over Media Standards* (Lanham, MD: Rowman & Littlefield Publishers Inc).

Sparks, C. and Tulloch, J. (eds.) (2000) *Tabloid Tales: Global Debates Over Media Standards* (Lanham, MD: Rowman & Littlefield Publishers Inc).

Springer, K. (2007) 'Divas, Evil Black Bitches and Bitter Black Women: African-American women in postfeminist and post-civil-rights popular culture' in

Y. Tasker and D. Negra (eds) *Interrogating Post-Feminism* (Durham, NC: Duke University Press).

Stacey, J. (1986) 'Are Feminists Afraid to Leave Home? The challenge of Conservative Pro-Family feminism' in A. Oakley and J. Mitchell (eds.) *What is Feminism?* (Oxford: Blackwell).

Stacey, J. (2002) 'The family is dead: Long live the family' in N. Holmstrom (ed.) *The Socialist Feminist Project: A Contemporary Reader in Theory and Politics* (New York: Monthly Review Press).

Steeves, H.L. (1993) 'Gender and Mass Communication in a Global Context' in P.J. Creedon (ed.) *Women in Mass Communication*. 2nd edn. (Newbury Park, London, and New Delhi: Sage Publications).

Steeves, H.L. (1997) *Gender Violence and the Press: The St. Kizito Story* (Athens, OH: Ohio University Centre for International Studies).

Steiner, L. (2005) 'The feminist cable collective as public sphere activity', *Journalism*, 6(3), 313–34.

Strutt, S.M. (1994) *Framing Feminisms: Feminist Critiques of Patriarchal News Media* (MA Dissertation. Simon Fraser University).

Sutter, D. (2001) 'Can the Media Be So Liberal? The economics of media bias', *Cato Journal*, 3(Winter), 431–48.

Symon, P.H. (1971) 'Advertising: setting the standards – encouraging women', *The Times*, 28 June, p. 8.

Taft, J. (2004) 'Girl Power Politics: Pop-Culture Barriers and Organisational Resistance' in A. Harris (eds.) *All About the Girl: Culture, Power and Identity* (New York: Routledge).

Talbot, M. (2000) 'Strange Bedfellows: Feminism in Advertising', in M. Andrews and M. Talbot (eds.) *All the World and her Husband: Women in Twentieth-Century Consumer Culture* (London: Cassell).

Y. Tasker and D. Negra (eds.) (2007) *Interrogating Postfeminism* (Durham, NC: Duke University Press).

Taylor, G. (1993) *Changing Faces: A History of The Guardian, 1956–88* (London: Fourth Estate).

Taylor, G. (1993) *Changing Faces: A History of The Guardian, 1956–88* (London: Fourth Estate).

Taylor, V. (1989) 'Social Movement Continuity: The Women's Movement in Abeyance', *American Sociological Review*, 54(5), 761–75.

Thimmesch, N. (1978) 'One Big ERA Problem: NOW's Manners Turn People Off', *Chicago Tribune*, 5 June, p. C2.

Thom, M. (1993) 'The Personal is Political, Publishable Too', *Media Studies Journal* 7, 223–30.

Thoma, P. (2009) 'Buying up baby: Modern feminine subjectivity, assertions of 'choice', and the repudiation of reproductive justice in postfeminist unwanted pregnancy films', *Feminist Media Studies*, 9(4), 409–25.

Thomson, A. and Sylvester, R. (2008) 'Harman struggles to shine a positive light as Labour fights economic gloom', *The Times*, 6 September, p. 33.

Thomas, D. (1970) 'At last – it's men who are feeling the pinch', *Daily Mirror*, 7 April, p. 17.

Thomas, D. (1971) 'Purely in the name of women's liberation, our girl Deborah acts like a man for the day', *Daily Mirror*, 31 March, p. 11.

Thornham, S. and Pengpeng, F. (2010) 'Just a slogan:' Individualism, post-feminism, and female subjectivity in consumerist China', *Feminist Media Studies*, 10(2), 195–211.

Thussu, D.K. (2007) *News as Entertainment: the Rise of Global Infotainment* (London: Sage Publications).

Tickner, L. (1988) *The Spectacle of Women* (Chicago: University of Chicago Press).

Todd, R. (1975) 'Women rap toothless watchdog', *Daily Mirror*, 30 December, p. 1.

Todd, R. (1977) 'Equal pay a "con"', *Daily Mirror*, 25 July, p. 14.

Tuchman, G. (1972) 'Objectivity as Strategic Ritual: An Examination of Newsmen's Notions of Objectivity', *American Journal of Sociology*, 77 (January), 660–79.

Tuchman, G. (1976) 'Telling Stories', *Journal of Communication*, 26, 93–97.

Tuchman, G., Daniels, A.K., and Bennett, J. (eds.) (1978). *Hearth and Home: Images of Women in the Mass Media*. New York: Oxford University Press.

Tuchman, G. (1978a) *Making News: A Study of the Construction of Reality* (New York: The Free Press).

Tuchman, G. (1978b) 'The Symbolic Annihilation of Women by the Mass Media' in G. Tuchman, A.K. Daniels, and J. Bennett (eds.) *Hearth and Home: Images of Women in the Mass Media* (New York: Oxford University Press).

Tuchman, G. (1978c). 'The Newspaper as a Social Movement's Resource' in G. Tuchman, A.K. Daniels, and J. Bennett (eds.) *Hearth and Home: Images of Women in the Mass Media* (New York: Oxford University Press).

Valenti, J. (2007) *Full Frontal Feminism: A Young Woman's Guide to Why Feminism Matters* (Emeryville, CA: Seal Press).

Valenti, Jessica (2008a) 'The F-card won't wash: Sarah Palin is disastrous for women's rights, no matter how Republicans frame her as a feminist, *The Guardian*, 12 September, p. 34.

Valenti, J. (2008b) 'G2: Sense and humour: Female comedians are rare – feminist ones even rarer', *The Guardian*, 19 November, p. G2 14.

van Dijk, T. (1991) *Racism in the Press* (London: Routledge).

van Zoonen, L. (1992) 'The Women's Movement and the media: Constructing a public identity', *European Journal of Communication*, 7(4), 453–76.

Varvus, M.D. (2002). *Postfeminist News: Political Women in Media Culture* (Albany: State University of New York Press).

Varvus, M.D. (2007) 'Opting Out Moms in the News', *Feminist Media Studies*, 7(1), 47–63.

Walker, R. and Cunningham, T. (2008) 'Mum, how could you disown me in the name of feminism?' *Daily Mail*, 23 May, p. 24.

Wahl-Jorgensen, K. (2002) 'The construction of the public in letters to the editor: Deliberative democracy and the idiom of insanity', *Journalism*, 3(2), 183–204.

Walter, N. (2010) *Living Dolls: The return of sexism* (London: Virago).

Ward, C. (1970) 'Christopher Ward', *Daily Mirror*, 28 October, p. 7.

Ward, C. (1971) 'Christopher Ward', *Daily Mirror*, 26 May, p. 10.

Ward, C. (1972) 'Christopher Ward', *Daily Mirror*, 7 June, p. 6.

Ward (2008) 'Gingrich calls Palin threat to feminists, slams media' *Washington Times*, 13 September, p. A03.

Wardle, C. (2004) *Monsters and Angels: A Comparison of Broadsheet and Tabloid Press Coverage of Child Murders from the US and UK, 1930–2000* (Unpublished PhD Dissertation, Penn State University).

Weaver, K. and Carter, C. (2003) *Critical Readings: Violence and the media* (Maidenhead: Open University Press).

Weaver, D. and Wilhoit, G. (1996) *The American Journalist in the 1990s: US News People at the End of an Era* (Mahwah, NJ: Lawrence Erlbaum Associates).

Weinberg, S. (2008) 'Bond girls are feminist icons!' *Daily Mail,* 6 November, p. 49.

Weinraub, B. (1970) 'British Women's Rights Groups Hold Spirited Meeting at Oxford', *New York Times,* 2 March, p. 3.

Wendt, L. (1979) *Chicago Tribune: The Rise of a Great American Newspaper* (Chicago: Rand McNally).

Whelehan, I. (2000) *Overloaded: Popular Culture and the Future of Feminism* (London: The Women's Press).

Whelehan, I. (2005) *The Feminist Bestseller: From Sex and the Single Girl to Sex and the City* (Basingstoke: Palgrave MacMillan).

Whitt, J. (2008) *Women in American Journalism: A New History* (Urbana and Chicago: University of Illinois Press).

Wigham, E. (1969) 'Firm stand on equal pay for women', *The Times,* 3 September, p. 8.

Wignall, A. (2008) 'Can a feminist really love *Sex and the City?'* *The Guardian,* 16 April, p. 18.

Williams, K. (2003) *Understanding Media Theory* (London: Hodder).

Williams, Z. (2008) 'Old lady Madonna: Even veteran pop icons can't avoid the usual stereotypes and slurs against ageing women', *The Guardian,* 23 October, p. 35.

Wilson, P. (1972) 'You can't have it all your own way, girls', *Daily Mirror,* 12 April, p. 25.

Wilson, S. (2003) *Oprah, Celebrity, and Formations of the Self* (Basingstoke: Palgrave).

Winship, J. (1987) *Inside Women's Magazines* (London and New York: Pandora).

Winter, C. (1974) 'Feminists vs. the working-class women', *Chicago Tribune,* 26 May, p. D3.

Winton, M. (1970) 'Women's lib, Maoists, Trotskyists and Mothers in Action', *The Times,* 19 October, p. 9.

Wittner, D. (1973) 'All Women's Liberationists Hate Men and Children', *Chicago Tribune,* 20 May, p. H12.

Wolf, N. (1991) *The Beauty Myth* (London: Vintage Publishers).

Wolfe, S. (1973). 'Only 24 words in Equal Rights, but millions of words about it', *Chicago Tribune,* 1 April, p. 33.

Wollenstonecraft, M. (1792) *A Vindication of the Rights of Woman* (Boston: Peter Edes).

Women in Journalism (1998) *The Cheaper Sex: How Women Lose Out in Journalism* (London: Women in Journalism).

Wood, E.M. (2002) 'Capitalism and Human Emancipation: Race, Gender and Democracy' in N. Holmstrom (ed.) *The Socialist Feminist Project: A Contemporary Reader in Theory and Politics* (New York: Monthly Review Press).

Wood, H. (2009). *Talking with Television: Women, Talk Shows and Modern Self-Reflexivity* (Chicago: University of Illinois Press).

Worthington, N. (2008) 'Progress and Persistent Problems. Local TV News Framing of Acquaintance Rape on Campus', *Feminist Media Studies*, 8(1), 1–16.

Wright, D. (1973) 'No Love Lost as Billy Meets Bobby', *Daily Mirror*, 20 September, pp. 20–1.

Young, A. (1990) *Femininity in Dissent* (London and New York: Routledge).

Younge, G. (2008) 'Ranking race against gender is the first step towards fundamentalism', *The Guardian*, 17 March, p. 31.

Zahour, F. (1971) 'Women Seeking Political Posts, Long-Time Strongholds of Men', *Chicago Tribune*, 15 April, p. S1.

Zak, D. (2008) 'Enough to make a grown man cry', *The Washington Post*, 14 September, p. BW08.

Zald, M.N. and Ash, R. (1966) 'Social Movement Organizations: Growth, Decay, and Change', *Social Forces*, 44(March), 327–40.

Zazlow, E. (2009) *Feminism, Inc.: Coming of Age in a Girl Power Media Culture* (New York: Palgrave).

Zernike, K. (2008) 'Postfeminism and other fairy tales', *The New York Times*, 16 March, W1.

Zoch, L.M. and Turk, J.V. 1998. Women Making News: Gender as a Variable in Source Selection and Use. *Journalism and Mass Communication Quarterly* 75(4), 762–75.

van Zoonen, L. (1994) *Feminist Media Studies* (London: Sage Publications).

van Zoonen, L. (1995) 'Gender, Representation and the Media' in J. Downy et al. (eds.) *Questioning the Media: A Critical Introduction*. 2nd edn. (Thousand Oaks, London, and New Delhi: Sage Publications).

van Zoonen, L. (1998) 'One of the Girls? The Changing Gender of Journalism' in C. Carter, G. Branston, and S. Allan (eds.) *News, Gender and Power* (London, New York: Routledge).

Index

abortion, 4, 6, 19, 37, 51, 68, 76, 94,
    100, 114, 122, 141, 152, 155, 158,
    161–2, 167

backlash against women's rights, 6,
    19, 75, 80, 109, 113–14, 129, 144,
    154, 156–7, 163, 170
beauty pageant, Miss University
    London, 136, 151–3
bra-burning, 35–6, 39, 70, 86, 117,
Bristol Feminist Network, 139, see
    Norris, Sian
broadsheet newspaper, 24–5, 96, 120,
    135, 167, 171

capitalism, 2, 14–15, 22, 24, 28, 42,
    49, 63, 64, 67, 88, 126, 130, 145,
    148, 152–3, 159–60, 163
Castle, Barbara, 91
Chicago Tribune, The, 2, 9–10, 25,
    43–4, 49–51, 57, 59, 61–2, 64, 69,
    76–7, 85, 88, 90, 92, 99, 100, 103,
    111–12, 114, 118, 120–3, 128, 131,
    133, 168, 170–1
Clinton, Hillary, 42, 135,
    137, 141–3
Cochrane, Kira, 94, 139, 142, 147–8,
    152, 156, 158, 160, 165, 171
commodity feminism, 150, see also
    girl power feminism
content analysis, 9, 45–6, 168
critical discourse analysis, 2, 9, 12,
    45–7, 49, 87, 127

Daily Mail, The, 2, 10, 25, 43, 131–3,
    144, 148, 152, 154–5, 168, 171
Daily Mirror, The, 2, 9–10, 24, 43–4,
    49–51, 57, 61–2, 69, 72–4, 76,
    78–80, 83, 85, 90, 92–6, 100–1,
    103, 113–14, 116–21, 123, 127–8,
    131, 133–5, 143, 168, 170–2
discourse analysis, see critical
    discourse analysis

discrimination, 11, 27, 45, 54, 61–2,
    67, 70, 76, 78–9, 90–1, 94, 101–2,
    111–12, 126, 141, 143–4, 152, 160,
    169–70

Equal Employment Opportunity
    Commission, 45, 168
Equal Opportunities Commission, 45,
    91, 168
Equal Pay Act, 45, 54, 79, 90, 95, 103,
    169
Equal Rights Amendment (ERA), 4,
    38–9, 41–2, 44, 51, 54, 59–60,
    76, 91–4, 99, 100, 102–3, 107–10,
    113–15, 118, 120–1, 123, 127, 129

Faludi, Susan, 6, 37, 75–6, 80, 113–14,
    116, 129, 144, 146, 156–7, 163–4
Fawcett Society, 45, 88, 101, 132,
    139–40, 161
Feminine Mystique, The, 4, 14, 16, 36,
    48, 73–4, 168, see also Friedan,
    Betty
femininity, 2, 5, 7, 13–14, 16–19,
    21–2, 24, 27, 35, 41, 48, 59–61,
    63, 70, 77–8, 80, 89, 94, 96, 111,
    118–19, 126, 146, 148–52, 157–8,
    162, 163, 166
First Wave Feminism, 3, 132, see suffrage
Fox, Muriel, 6, 33–4, 36, 132, 147, 159
frame analysis, 30–3, 35, 40–1, 47,
    50, 56–7, 59, 69–71, 73–4, 83–6,
    88, 98–9, 103, 110–12, 119–20,
    122–3, 127–9, 132, 138, 144–5,
    154, 157, 160, 167, 170
Friedan, Betty, 4, 14, 16, 36, 48, 73–4,
    168, see Feminine Mystique, The

gender roles, 4, 9–10, 13–15, 33–6, 41,
    48, 62, 70–1, 77–8, 80, 82–6, 88,
    101–3, 108, 111, 115, 119, 126–7,
    129, 137, 140–1, 151, 153–4,
    156–7, 166

Gill, Rosalind, 11, 16–18, 21–2, 34, 37, 75, 77, 148, 150–1, 156
girl power feminism, 19, 150–1, *see also* commodity feminism
Gramsci, Antonio, *see* hegemony
Greenham Common, 34, 42, 133, 167
Guardian, The, 2, 10, 25, 43, 115, 126, 131, 133, 135–6, 139, 146–7, 152, 154, 156, 167–8, 171–2

hard news, 24–7, 30, 52–4, 98, 159, 171
hegemony, 8, 10, 12–13, 16, 18, 35–6, 39, 49, 69–71, 75, 78–9, 88, 128–9, 163, 168

Labour Party, British, 69, 91, 103, 128, 138
lesbian, 10, 18, 22, 35, 40, 45, 63, 70–2, 108, 120, 146, 168
liberal feminism, 4–5, 9–10, 37, 39–40, 66–7, 78, 88, 98, 100, 152, 163

MacKay, Finn, 139, 159
masculinity, 5, 13–14, 22, 24, 27, 29, 35, 40, 48, 52, 78, 86, 89, 97, 119, 151, 156–7, 160, 162–3, 165–6
McRobbie, Angela, 6, 16–19, 34, 37, 75, 77, 79, 139, 146, 148, 151, 156, 159
mid-market newspaper, 24–5
Millett, Kate, 5, 40, 55, 168
minority women, 4, 19–20, 22, 29, 38, 57, 64–6, 71, 86–7, 93, 101, 108, 120, 122, 161, 166, 168–9

National Black Feminist Organization (NBFO), 65–6, 87
National Organization for Women (NOW), 30, 33–4, 36, 39, 45, 50, 60–1, 66–8, 87, 91, 102, 114, 132, 140, 167
National Women's Political Caucus (NWPC), 50, 87, 91
Neo-liberal ideology, 10, 22, 37, 132, 145, 148, 160, 163
New York Times, The, 2, 9–10, 25, 36, 38, 43–4, 49–51, 57–8, 61–2, 65–6, 69, 76, 90, 92, 99–100, 113, 115, 120–1, 131, 133, 136, 154, 167–8, 170–2
Norris, Sian, 139, 159, *see* Bristol Feminist Network

oppression, 5, 7, 13, 17–19, 22, 24, 28, 31, 41–2, 46, 52, 56, 61–6, 70, 79, 87, 89, 91, 101–2, 111, 122, 130, 137, 140–3, 145, 148, 150, 152–3, 159–60, 163–4, 165–6, 168

Palin, Sarah, 42, 135–6, 138, 141–2, 144, 152, 155, 158
patriarchy, 2, 5, 13–14, 22, 24, 28, 42, 49, 62–4, 67, 78–9, 88, 126, 130, 136, 141, 145, 149, 151–4, 159–60, 163
postfeminism, 8, 10–11, 17, 19, 22, 37, 75–80, 89, 117, 144, 148, 150–1, 153, 162
private sphere, 13–14, 26, 35, 40–1, 48, 52, 89, 124
public sphere, 13–14, 32–4, 48, 52, 54, 83–5, 88–9, 98, 108, 118, 169

racism, 2, 22, 24, 42, 56–7, 64–5, 79, 88, 102, 111, 130, 132, 145, 159–60, 163
radical feminism, 5, 9, 40–1, 68, 71, 78, 88, 150
Redfern, Catherine, 2, 34, 45, 132, 135, 138, 139–40, 150, 159–60, 162, 164, 171–2
Roe v. Wade, 158, 162

Schlafly, Phyllis, 44, 103, 107–10, 113, 120
Second Wave Feminism, 1–2, 4–9, 13–14, 19, 28, 34, 37, 42, 44–5, 48–9, 52–3, 57, 61, 66, 68, 72–3, 75–6, 79, 86–7, 89–92, 94, 96, 98, 113, 127, 131–2, 134–5, 139–40, 144, 146–7, 152, 154–6, 160, 163, 166, 168, 172, *see also* Women's Liberation Movement
Sex Discrimination Act, 45, 76, 78, 90, 94

sexism, 4, 57, 61–2, 65, 79, 101–2, 111, 141–3, 150, 152, 160, 170
socialist feminism, 2, 5, 13, 39, 41–2
soft news, 26–7, 30, 52–5, 97–8, 135, 159–60, 164
Steinem, Gloria, 38, 142, 147, 168
suffrage, 4, 99, 132, 166, *see* First Wave Feminism,

tabloid newspaper, 24–6, 44, 96, 135, 167
Third Wave Feminism, 2, 6–8, 18, 34, 37–8, 42, 131–2, 135, 139, 159–60, *see also* postfeminism
Times, The, 2, 9–10, 25, 43–4, 49–51, 57, 61–2, 69, 73, 88, 90, 92–6, 100, 110, 111–12, 120, 124–5, 127–8, 131, 133, 138, 150, 167–70
trade union, 4, 55, 59, 70, 91–2, 94–5, 103, 120–1, 128, 168–70

Valenti, Jessica, 37, 45, 135–6, 138–9, 146–7, 152, 160, 165, 171
van Zoonen, Liesbet, 2, 15, 17, 27–8, 32–3, 35–6, 40, 46, 52, 56, 61, 100, 162, 167

Washington Post, The, 2, 10, 25, 30, 43, 131, 133, 154
Washington Times, The, 2, 10, 43, 131–4, 154–5, 168, 171
Wollenstonecraft, Mary, 3
Women's Liberation Movement, 3, 44, 60, 74, 79–80, 117, 167
working class women, 12, 14, 31, 60, 69, 74, 85, 99, 101, 103, 110–11, 116, 120–2, *see also* trade union